Endorsements

"*Strategic Planning: as Simple as A, B, C* is a must read for leaders concerned about the future. Dave McClean provides a gift of knowledge, tools, and ideas that work regardless of the size of your company or organization. His considerable experience rings through in clear prose and his timeless ideas offer a steady guide in this dynamic and unpredictable time. This is a must read for all leaders."
Brian Layer, CEO, N2growth, Brigadier General, US Army, Retired

"In many organizations, strategic planning is just a myth. You hear a lot about, but never see it. Dave McClean takes a very complex activity, oversimplify the steps to do strategic planning, and more importantly creates a step by step process for you to execute it!! I resoundingly suggest you read and put into action the process Dave outlines in his book. You must get this book and start your strategic path to sustained success."
Michael Diamond, CEO LEADERSnMotion, Major General, US Army, Retired

A "must-read" addition to the libraries of all C-Suite members and their staffs. David McClean de-mystifies a very complex subject and by expertly simplifying, explaining, and blending military and corporate approaches to strategic planning; and providing plenty of practical, common sense, and easy-to-use tools to make strategic planning as *"Simple as A, B, C"*. His model of strategic planning can help any organization develop a process to ensure organizational relevance, public worth, profitability, and success in both the organization's day-to-day and long-term life. If carefully followed, David's tips and techniques can empower your organization to deliver a strategic plan that can profitably shape its future for a decade to come, or more.
Kathy Gainey, Senior VP, Logistics; Cypress International, LTG (Ret), US Army

David has done a masterful job in defining what strategic planning is, why it is critical to success, how to actually develop a strategic plan and how to measure execution progress – all in terms, context and easily understood rationale. He has covered all the bases and do so in a manner which will materially benefit any individual, team or organization that decides to follow his guidance. WELL DONE!!

David A. Whaley, President, Archigos, Major General, US Army Retired

A brilliant concept finally put to paper! His book brings together the very best of executive level training with his vast entrepreneurial experience producing a logical step by step guide to strategic planning. A must read for any executive finding themselves in a complex organization struggling with it vision and more importantly its path to achieve that vision.

Jim Hickey, Vice President, Aetna Health Plans

In *Strategic Planning: Simple as A, B, C*, David McClean has provided the blueprint for any organization to design a focused, usable strategic plan. It combines knowledge, theory, and experience into one logically presented reference that tells how to build a comprehensive plan and guides you through every step. Procedures laid out in this book impart an immediate return on investment by decreasing plan development time, and leading your organization to success through opportunity identification and effectively focusing resources to achieve objectives. *Strategic Planning: Simple as A, B, C* should be kept on your desk, not your shelf.

R. L. Etter, President, Practical Concepts Consulting, LLC

As the Commanding General, my lead strategic planner, Dave McClean, cut through the fog of strategic planning and delivered a logical, eminently workable process. Dave's approach showed us how to translate priority issues into specific actions, accompanied by appropriate diagnostics and measures – the plan consistently yields desired results and more.

James Hodge, President, Institute for Defense and Business, Major General, US Army, Retired

Dave McClean's book *Strategic Planning: as Simple as A, B, C* is a brilliantly succinct book that brings strategy planning and implementation down from the vaporous conceptual heights of theory and makes it concrete, practical, and accessible. Each year management teams are formed to refine their organization's current strategy or design a new one, and the first action these teams should do this year is start by reading *Strategic Planning: as Simple as A, B, C*. Dave speaks directly to the reader in easy to understand language, with sound advice on planning preparation, process designing, and thinking strategically.

Larry J. Lust, Associate Professor, USA Command and General Staff College, Major General, USA, Retired

Must read for growth oriented organizations. This is a masterful guide to developing a relevant business strategy, a process critical to business success but too often misunderstood and inadequately formulated. Dave provides a comprehensive, understandable, and implementable approach to creating your winning business strategy. He is an acknowledged "big thinker" who possesses the rare ability to simply the complex without sacrificing the key elements needed for success. He brings years of practical experience as a strategist, planner, analyst, operator, and teacher to create this valuable work. This is an invaluable tool for novice and expert alike, I give it my highest endorsement.

Charlie Fletcher, President, McLane Advanced Technologies, Major General, USA, Retired

STRATEGIC PLANNING
As Simple as A,B,C

David R. McClean

ISBN: 978-1-4834-2244-2 (sc)
ISBN: 978-1-4834-2243-5 (e)

Library of Congress Control Number: 2014922002

Lulu Publishing Services rev. date: 1/9/2015

Contents

Illustrations

Tables

Exercise

Task

Activities

Preface

I think most people would agree that three decades of experience in planning and strategy development

> *"Failing to plan is planning to fail."* (Benjamin Franklin)

qualifies one to propose a "grand theory" of strategic planning. In assuming that, most people would be right—and wrong. Right, because experience does count. Wrong, because grand theories are just that—theories. And overhyped theories, at that. In fact, if my thirty-plus years in the profession mean anything, they are as a testament to the value of a simple strategic methodology. As a businessman and former military strategic planner, I don't want to be bogged down in a strategic swamp, mired in wasted time and resources, and neither do you. Expensive consultants? A waste; get rid of 'em. If you, like just about everyone else in business, want to get the most out of the debit side of your ledger, this book is all you need to become an expert strategic planner.

I've written *Strategic Planning: As Simple as A, B, C* to lift the curtain on strategic planning. Yes, strategic planning is a must for every entity, from the corner sandwich shop to Wall Street megabanks to the most bloated of government bureaucracies, but I'm here to tell you it is not rocket science—or science of any kind. In simplifying the strategic planning process, I have demystified and rendered understandable and accessible that which has all too often been made out to be unnecessarily complex. Understanding the planning process can be as simple as learning the alphabet. That's right: as *simple as A, B, C.*

The idea behind *Strategic Planning: As Simple as A, B, C* is to break planning into discrete, manageable tasks, thus making the process easier to grasp and implement. In helping carry out that idea, I will be your personal strategic planning consultant, explaining every step you take, from your first meeting to delivering and implementing your final plan. In addition, I will provide all the supporting documents and briefings you will need, in an editable format, for every step of your journey.

As both a CEO and a manager in the strategic planning field, I have hired contractors at various times to guide me through a formal strategic planning process. In doing so, I have also, unfortunately:

- ✓ Paid a fee of over $300,000 to a firm that didn't know what it was doing.
- ✓ Endured many missed deadlines on the part of the planners I hired.
- ✓ Been forced to expend valuable time I should otherwise have been devoting to my organization to giving directions to the contracted planners. In one particularly egregious case, I became so frustrated that I ended up writing the plan myself.
- ✓ Belatedly realized in most cases that I was extremely dissatisfied with the "brainpower" in which I had unwittingly invested.

I've also seen the planning process from the other side and found myself scratching my head there, too. I recall working with organizations, guiding them through the planning process, and not being able to fathom that I was actually being paid, and paid handsomely, for *applying common sense to a simple process*. There I was, charging money to tell clients something as simple as learning the alphabet: *A, B, C*.

In a world where all eyes are on the bottom line, this book aims to get you through the strategic planning process at not much more than the price of what you're holding in your hands. My book will also save you time (which is even more valuable than money) and the squandering of other significant resources, primarily the expenditure of effort and concern on your part and that of your fellow employees.

While my strategic plan approach will prove fruitful to private-sector organizations (such as athletic and academic organizations) and businesses, it will be even more well suited to public-sector organizations, at every level (federal, state, and local), especially given my personal and professional experience working with such organizations. So to frugal public-funded entities of every stripe, I say: we're all for saving taxpayer dollars, and using this book as your foundation for strategic planning will do just that. I truly believe that every government organization must have a strategic plan.

Okay, I'm hooked. But what exactly is strategic planning?

Strategic planning is a deliberate, disciplined effort to produce a strategy that results in actions that shape what an organization is, what it does, why it does it, and what it will do in the future. My strategic plan approach provides a methodology to help ensure the long-term relevance and survival of your organization or business and the community in which it operates. Kenneth Andrews, in *The Concept of Corporate Strategy,* notes:

> Strategy is the pattern of decisions in a company that determines and reveals its objectives, purposes, or goals, produces the principal policies and plans for achieving those goals, and defines the range of business the company is to pursue, the kind of economic and human organization it intends to be, and the nature of the economic and noneconomic contribution it intends to make to its shareholders, employees, customers, and communities.

This is a great definition of strategy because it highlights many of the key elements that make up sound strategic planning. It looks at the mission of the organization (*purpose, goals, objectives*); it discusses the *policies and plans* of the organization for achieving its goals; it identifies the *scope* of the organization (the range of opportunities to be pursued); and it outlines the *values* of the organization (the contributions to employees, shareholders, customers, and community). My book has been written to simplify this definition and propel your organization to success within its competitive environment.

In their 1986 book *Applied Strategic Planning: How to Develop a Plan That Really Works,* Pfeiffer, Goodstein, and Nolan define strategic planning as "the process by which members of the organization envision its future and develop the necessary procedures in operations and other functional areas of the organization to achieve that future." Envisioning is more than an attempt to anticipate the future and prepare accordingly. It involves a belief that aspects of the future can influence change in what we do now. To put it another way, it's the belief that how we currently plan and execute can influence or, even better, control the future to increase effectiveness and enhance the return on an organization's accumulation of capital assets, time, knowledge, and relevance.

At its best, strategic planning is visionary and proactive rather than reactive. Moreover, strategic planning is not one thing but rather a set of concepts, procedures, methodologies, tools and techniques, and actions that can help businesses, organizations, and communities become more successful in defining and achieving their mission, vision, and guiding principles for creating significant and enduring public value and worth. Such should be no different for families and other household units. Think about it. Every household should have a strategy for the future: What's your vision and how

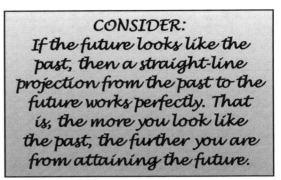

CONSIDER:
If the future looks like the past, then a straight-line projection from the past to the future works perfectly. That is, the more you look like the past, the further you are from attaining the future.

are you going to get there? Take, for example, retirement: What is your vision for retirement and given your current resources, how are you going to get there?

A strategic plan

A strategic plan is a document that provides a formal roadmap for describing how an organization executes a deliberate strategy; that is, where the organization is positioning itself to be over the next few years, and how it will get there. Again, and not meaning to simplify, developing a strategic plan is *as simple as A, B, C.* There are three stages in the overall concept of strategic planning.

Stage *A* involves determining your current state, the "as-is" condition of the organization (what I call the baseline). Stage *B* involves determining your future state, the "to-be" state of the organization. For example, how do you envision your organization in the next five to ten years? What will it look like? Will it still be here? Will it be relevant? Finally, Stage *C* represents the "how" state: how you are going to get from the as-is state to the to-be state. Stage *C* includes the concepts, procedures, methodologies, tools and techniques, and actions the organization will carry out to move from its current state to its presumed future state. Stages *A*, *B*, and *C*, then, answer the following questions:

- ✓ *A*: What are you now?
- ✓ *B*: Where are you going?
- ✓ *C*: How are you going get there?

I submit that answering these questions is truly *as simple as A, B, C* if you follow the steps outlined in this book. The steps can also be put in the form of a formula, where *A* = analysis, *B* = planning, and *C* = implementation. Thus, *A+B+C* = strategic plan success. It's as simple as that! Consider this approach as a way to bridge the gap between where you are and where you want to be. The strategic bridge graphic shown in Figure 1, Strategic bridge, illustrates this concept.

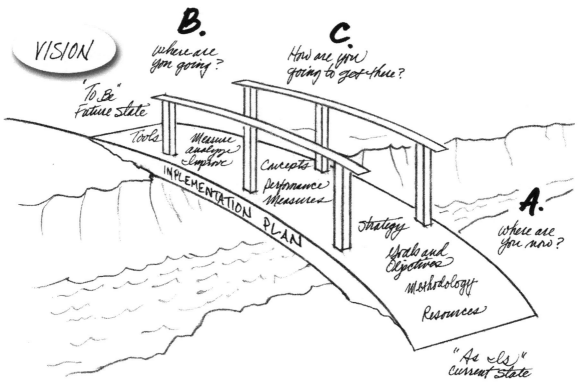

Figure 1. Strategic bridge

As you look at the figure, you (or your organization) are at the right of the bridge (the as-is state), and the bridge (implementation plans, goals, objectives, concepts, procedures, methodologies, tools and techniques, and actions) is the path to the other side (the to-be state). See? *It's as simple as A, B, C!*

Asking and answering our *A, B, C* questions (see figure 1) requires an ongoing, deliberative conversation among dedicated strategic planning team members and key stakeholders in your organization.

Strategic Planning: As Simple as A, B, C provides a model of strategic planning that will help your organization develop a process that can ensure organizational relevance, public worth, profitability, and success in both the organization's day-to-day and long-term life. If carefully followed, the *A, B, C* process will empower your organization to deliver a strategic plan that can profitably shape its future for a decade to come, or more.

As a planning professional, I never cease to be amazed at how so many organizations, both public and private, question, or are at best unaware of, the benefits of strategic planning. From what I have seen, their thinking goes something like this: Why should I put my organization through changes and, possibly, a time-consuming transformation that has the potential to bring conflict and disruption to the organization and its stakeholders? I acknowledge as a given that whenever people are asked to focus in a serious way on what is expendable in their organization and to consider doing things differently, their culture, conditions, values, structures, processes, and interaction patterns can be threatened. So why should they put themselves through such a demanding process? The simple answer is that if they don't, their organization will stagnate and possibly even fail.

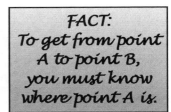

FACT:
To get from point A to point B, you must know where point A is.

Consider the examples of "lifetime" brands and organizations that remained stagnant and eventually failed. Kodak is one of the more infamous examples that comes to mind. Here was an iconic company that was stuck in the present, if you will, failing to implement change to keep up with, let alone overtake, the more technologically determined and visionary players with which it found itself competing, unsuccessfully, as it turned out. At one point, Kodak was the undisputed leader in photography, focusing as it did for most of the twentieth century on film, camera, and paper production. Then, when digital photography became the new future, Kodak failed to adapt and was eventually forced into bankruptcy. One can only assume the onetime "king of photography" believed it had achieved lasting perfection, and, thus, said to itself, why plan for the future? If, on the other hand, you or your organization doesn't believe you have reached perfection, continue reading. Organizations should *anticipate* change rather than adapt (or worse, fail to adapt) to it after the fact. As a business owner or a manager of a public entity, you should dedicate your tenure to developing a strategy that allows the organization you lead to navigate from the as-is to the to-be state—to anticipate the new environment before it's too late. Strategic planning is a tool for you to adapt—a tool with three winners: the owner/manager (the one who gets most of the credit for success), the customer (your organization's reason for existence), and the employee (without whom the organization cannot function).

Below are some of the benefits of creating and implementing a strategic plan:

- ✓ Increased effectiveness
- ✓ Increased efficiency
- ✓ Improved understanding of the organizational environment and growth
- ✓ Better decision making
- ✓ Enhanced organizational capabilities
- ✓ Improved communications and public relations effectiveness
- ✓ Increased political, community, and consumer support
- ✓ Improved relevancy of and within the organization
- ✓ Improved organizational and employee growth
- ✓ Improved organizational culture
- ✓ Increased compliance with environmental changes

In "Silly Love Songs," Paul McCartney sings, "Some people wanna fill the world with silly love songs. And what's wrong with that?" In the same vein, why write another book on strategic planning? The answer is simple: I want to save you time

> *"He who controls the past, controls the future. He who controls the present, controls the past." (George Orwell, 1984)*

and money—lots of money (remember my $300,000 mistake)—by developing a viable and solid strategic plan for your organization. In all the research I've done and the books I've read on strategic planning, not one puts the strategic plan together so that it can be executed without extensive and expensive external support. Again, picture us working through the process together with me as your (practically free) consultant. I am conveying my entire store of knowledge, tools, and techniques to you. I help you control the past and the present so you can control the future. And I say, what's wrong with that?

Those who develop a strategic plan will always be ready; those who do not will always be surprised. Don't be the one who's always surprised. *Don't be a Kodak. If you stick your head in the sand, you become easy prey.*

With the strategic plan approach and strategic planning model, you and your team will have the roadmap, tools, depth of knowledge, and experience to develop a strategic plan at minimal cost and on time. Plan now to start planning. It's *As Simple as A, B, C!*

Together, let's build your strategic bridge.

> **CAUTION:**
> *Don't just tweak the existing process —move beyond it.*

Grateful acknowledgment and thanks to:

The many strategic scholars (far too numerous to mention here) who provided their valuable knowledge via their books and other writings.

BG Brian Layer (USA Ret.), CEO N2Growth, for strategic guidance.

Theresa Cruz, for offering insight on conducting and analyzing surveys.

Richard Lowenstein, of AllWrite Writing Consultants, for laboriously proofing and correcting my verbiage.

David R. Zamudio, of Zamudios Art Studios, LLC, for creating and producing the outstanding graphics.

Gelu Ionas, Practical Concepts Consulting LLC, for website development.

Introduction

The Strategic Plan—Do You Really Need It?

Absolutely! Because, as Winston Churchill said, "He who fails to plan is planning to fail!" Whether you realize it or not, you plan at a conscious level in almost everything you do. When you make financial decisions, family

> CONSIDER:
> Strategy should be a map that allows you to steer into the future.

decisions, marriage decisions, decisions about which school to attend, and almost everything else, you are creating and executing a strategic plan. It is "strategic" in the sense that it is at the top of your hierarchy. To put it more accurately, you are creating a *vision* of where you want to be at some point in the future. Based on your current situation, you decide what you are going to do to make your plan a reality; you are creating a map or a plan to realize your vision.

In applying strategy, you are analyzing where you are (*A*), where you want to go (*B*), and how you are going to get there (*C*). The more highly developed the process you apply to arrive at your strategy, the greater your chance of success. Consider a complex organization such as the United States military and compare it with your organization as you read the following paragraphs.

The US military is structured at three levels of war: strategic, operational, and tactical. At the strategic level are the key policymakers such as the president and his administration, the Pentagon with its Joint Chiefs of Staff, and the branches of service—the army, navy, marines, air force, and coast guard. This level is where broad-based policies are laid out.

Introduction

At the operational level are the organizations within the services, such as the divisions (e.g., the 101st Airborne Division) within the army. Divisions are large organizations numbering as many as ten thousand people. The operational level occupies roughly the middle ground between the strategic and tactical levels and comprises a vital link between strategic objectives and the tactical employment of forces. Operations are where the strategic objectives are reached.

At the tactical level are the small units from brigades to squads (from about one thousand to nine people). These are the "heavy-spade-work" or "where the rubber meets the road" organizations where the focus is on the tactics of an engagement or operation. The tactical level is where the execution of the operation occurs.

This is how military power is developed from political objectives. More precisely, it is how the means and ends of war are tied together. Goals are reached by the men and women who execute the plans at the tactical level to achieve the operational results and thus carry out the national strategy or policy. Accordingly, it can be seen how the military implements its strategic plan. It does so as a hierarchical organization where the strategic units are at the top of the hierarchy and the organizational and tactical units are tiered below.

> *"Strategy without tactics is the slowest route to victory. Tactics without strategy is the noise before defeat." (Sun Tzu)*

Strategic versus operational planning

Most federal, state, and local organizations are structured in the same manner as the military: strategic, operational, and tactical (although the vast majority will not concede their similarity to the Department of Defense). In much the same way that these governmental organizations follow this structure, whether implied or actual, so too do large corporations, with the major difference, of course, being that the organizational/governmental sector is not profit driven, while the corporate sector is primarily focused on profit.

In strategic planning, you'll be concerned about doing the right things rather than doing things right. Doing things right occurs at the tactical level. To put it another way, strategic planning focuses on "what you do" while tactical planning focuses on "how you do it." Thus, strategic = doing the right things and tactical = doing things right. In Table 1, Differences between operational and strategic planning, consider the differences between strategic and operational planning.

> *Strategic planning: doing the right things rather than doing things right. Tactical planning: doing things right.*

Strategic Planning	Operational Planning
Is long term (usually 5-10 years)	Is short term (usually 1 year or less)
Focuses on future achievments and conditions	Focuses on annual achievments and "low-hanging fruit"
Weighs a series of alternatives before making choices	Choices already made; alternatives not considered
Usually integrates several functions	One functional area or related set of levels
Integrates strategies for resource allocation	Uses resources for implementation usually mobilized with activities (sustainability plans) already identified

Table 1. Differences between strategic and operational planning

Now consider your organization. Where are its strategic, operational, and tactical levels? Contrast it to the military structure. Who are your policymakers (strategic level)? Who translates those policies into goals and objectives (operational level)? Who develops the objectives into action (tactical level)? The answers to these questions are important to the development of your strategy and your strategic plan. Before charting the course for developing your plan, you must have a thorough understanding of your organization and its purpose. Every organization must have a primary purpose. Along with that purpose, you must understand the organization's structure, policies, vision, mission, guiding principles, and more. I'm always startled by the following statistics:

✓ About 95 percent of the typical workforce does not understand the organizational strategy.
✓ Nearly 90 percent of all organizations fail to execute their strategy.
✓ Some 86 percent of executive teams spend less than one hour per week discussing strategy.

   ✓ An estimated 60 percent of executive teams do not link strategy to budgeting.

I have worked with or observed many organizations in which a vast majority of the employees do not understand organizational strategy, hierarchy, or vision. Worse, they don't even know what these are. Strategy should be integrated into the organization as a whole. It must be understood from the bottom to the top of any organization; that is, from the tactical to the strategic. This understanding is a key factor for breeding success. *Strategic* means it's about management—the strategic level. Management benefits from the plan, but employees make it happen. (Perhaps it should be called a wage-earner plan, not a strategic plan.) Figure 2, Bottom-up/top-down approach, illustrates my point that in many organizations the bottom tier (employees) is not in sync with the top tier (management).

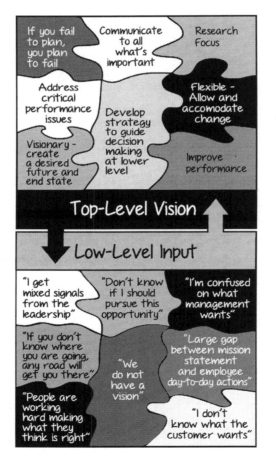

Figure 2. Bottom-up/top-down approach

Do not be too concerned if some of these organizational concepts are unknown to you or your organization. We will guide you through them and the process and work toward the development of your strategic plan.

Moving forward is critical

I'm often told by senior managers: "We don't need a strategic plan. We know what we have to do, and we just do it." These managers could not be more wrong! This is like sailing a boat without a chart or observable stars. Organizations without a strategy will not move forward; they *will* remain stagnant, stranded in still waters. Granted, you may know what you have to do in order to move forward, increase productivity, gain greater customer satisfaction, and increase return on investment. However, if you do not have a structured process to reach these goals, the results will be a confused and dysfunctional organization that will result in mission failure or worse: organizational collapse. Believe me, organizations are never too big or too strong to fail (our so-called too-big-to-fail banks and other institutions to the contrary notwithstanding). I've seen this happen with numerous organizations, small and large. You yourself saw this in the 2008 economic collapse. Lack of a coherent direction of management at lower levels encourages organizations to chase objectives that can differ disastrously from the organization's overall strategy. The result can be dysfunctional management and failure—a sharp pin moving toward a balloon.

The development, execution, and monitoring of a structured strategic plan is critical for any organization, regardless of size, to move forward. Celebrated basketball coach Bobby Knight said, "The will to practice to win must be greater than the will to win." The development of a strategic plan is the practice session. The desire to create and execute a strategic plan must be greater than the desire to succeed. Organizations that develop and execute strategy are winning organizations; they create and foster intellectual capital—strong value to the customer.

What is a strategic plan?

Recall Kenneth Andrews's definition of strategy from the Preface. Again, this is a great definition because it highlights many of the key elements that make up business strategy. It looks at the mission of the organization (objectives, purpose, goals); it discusses the policies and plans for achieving the goals; it identifies scope (the range of opportunities to pursue); and it lays out the value of the organization (what are the contributions it will make to its employees, shareholders, customers, and communities.) Forward-thinking organizations must develop a plan that captures the essence of this definition and at a minimum discusses all the following key questions:

- ✓ Where are we now?
- ✓ Where do we want to go in the future?
- ✓ How do we get there?
- ✓ How much will it cost?
- ✓ When do we get there?
- ✓ Who's responsible for getting us there?

Strategic Planning: As Simple as A, B, C will answer these questions. It will do so by taking you through each phase of my strategic planning approach and strategic planning model discussed in the approach. The approach and the model will provide you with a strategic plan that at a minimum will include the following:

- ✓ A vision for the future (vision statement)
- ✓ A mission statement
- ✓ A list of strategic relationships
- ✓ An organizational assessment
- ✓ Strategies the organization plans to achieve—that is, long-term goals and objectives
- ✓ A Plan of action and milestones (POAM) to implement goals and objectives.
- ✓ A list of strategic perspectives
- ✓ A communications-strategy plan

In my view, a strategic plan should be specific and detailed but simple; in other words, not something wordy and cumbersome that no one reads. As we mentioned before, the plan should be easy to understand so that the lowest-ranking member of your organization can read it and know where the organization is headed. My book focuses on developing a strategic plan that is simple in format, quickly completed, effortlessly communicated, easily measured, and readily adjusted.

Ensure that your plan makes "cents"

As stated the plan should be effective and comprehensive but not ponderous. A good strategic plan drives the organization so that every employee is moving in the same direction and seeking the same goal. An effective strategic plan is built on a foundation of:

- ✓ Accurate information
- ✓ Strong ideas
- ✓ Committed people
- ✓ People, particularly leadership, involved throughout the entire process
- ✓ Objective research
- ✓ Best ideas and practices
- ✓ A purpose-driven, mission-based approach
- ✓ The integration of elements
- ✓ Executable parts
- ✓ Dynamism
- ✓ A holistic organizational environment

- ✓ Simplicity
- ✓ Achievable goals and objectives

These foundational elements will be examined in detail throughout the book.

It's an unfortunate fact of business and organizational life that most strategic plans never get implemented. I can't tell you how many strategic plans I've seen that fill a two-inch binder that, other than the author, few people read. If it's not read, it's not implemented. As I have said, the key to successful planning and execution is simplicity. Does your organization have a simple plan? Don't wait. Begin, revisit, or rewrite your plan so that your organization can be successful and long lived!

Expertise is preferred but not required

Clients sometimes question my ability to guide their strategy and develop their strategic plan because I may lack expertise or a strong background in their market sector. I have limited experience, for example, in manufacturing, the auto industry, the sciences, and several other areas. Does this mean I cannot develop and execute a strategic plan for those clients? It most certainly does not. In fact, in some cases it may actually be beneficial to the process when the strategic planner is not familiar with or is foreign to that particular organization and its culture. This unfamiliarity eliminates bias and gives the planner a clear and clean look at the organization. What is important is the process. *Process is the simple solution*. Once you have a valid process, it can be applied to any organization or situation. Don't misread me; experts in their particular fields can add beneficial insight and a vast array of experience. So having an expert on your team can be extremely valuable. However, in the event you do not have the resources to engage such an individual, *Strategic Planning: As Simple as A, B, C* teaches you the process for developing and executing a strategic plan no matter what your organization's core interest may be. Once you understand the process, you can apply it to any situation.

> *"There is nothing worse than a sharp image of a fuzzy concept." (Ansel Adams)*

Resources and metrics are critical

If you don't measure it, you can't manage it. You must make a strong commitment to execute your plan and gauge its progress. In the event that you already know your organization will not commit the time and resources to develop and execute the plan, **STOP HERE!** This book is written to enable your organization's success, not to overcome its inflexibility. One of the book's key strategies is the development and execution of POAMs and the metrics to determine their success. If you or your organization do not intend to apply resources to execute goals and objectives, then the book's strategies will be futile. If you are willing to allocate resources to fulfill initiatives, then it is important to gauge their success. These success metrics are continually examined throughout the execution of the plan. The results will enable you to determine when to "flex and pivot" so that you maintain the integrity of your initiative, your objectives, and, ultimately, your goal. We will discuss, measure, and quantify how "good is good" and how "bad is bad" in chapter 5.

Plan failure

> An executive committee once informed me that they did not have the financial resources required to implement any of the strategic plan initiatives or action plans I had recommended. What they wanted, essentially, was a strategic plan simply to meet a policy requirement—said requirement being to develop an annual strategic plan! My recommendation to the executive committee was to simply change the dates on the current strategic plan and save the organization tens of thousands of dollars. The point? If you're not going to do it right, then don't do it at all. If you want planning for planning's sake ("check the box"), understand that there's no value in that course of (in) action.

Throughout my career, I've seen strategic plans fail. Most often the ones that fail begin with robust fervor and excitement, and then die a slow, (un) natural death. The number one recurring deficiency of failed plans is a lack of commitment by leadership to see them through. Plans fail because:

✓ *They lack a comprehensive commitment.* Strategic plans fail for many reasons, but the number one reason they fail is due to the absence of a comprehensive commitment by the organization. The organization as a whole (from the CEO to the lowest-ranking employee) must be committed to the planning process and the execution of goals within the plan. Yes, that is easier said than done, but that doesn't make it any less true. Why, specifically, do plans fail? Because the organization or plan lacks resources or is timid in allocating resources. A plan for whose execution the organization will not allocate resources is destined for failure.

✓ *They lack effective communication strategies*. Too few individuals or parts of the organization are aware of the vision, goals, and objectives of the plan.

✓ *They lack ownership*. There is no clear accountability for planning, executing, and monitoring the plan. If no one is accountable, and metrics are not analyzed on a regular basis, the plan will be overwhelmed by the organization's day-to-day operations. Responsibility and accountability are a must.

✓ *They lack simplicity*. What good is a plan with an impressive-looking list of fifteen goals that is incomprehensible and, thus, unimplementable? The plan should be achievable and manageable and written in a clear, concise manner so that every member of the organization can understand it. Complexity = catastrophe.

✓ *People don't care*. This reason is self-explanatory (and inexcusable).

✓ *They lack metrics*. You can't manage it if you can't measure it. You must implement metrics to determine "how good is good; how bad is bad."

FACT:
The strategic plan should be exciting and not feel like a burden.

Let this book be your field manual

I want you to use this book as an instructional or field manual (FM). Follow the five phases of my approach and the steps in the model. Each chapter discusses one phase of the approach—thus, five chapters for a five-phase approach. Follow the chapters in the book. They will serve as your guide or syllabus. You will find that the process begins with your first meeting with leadership and ends with the execution and monitoring of your strategic plan. Complete each task and exercise as you encounter it. Get your teams involved in these and brainstorm your way to success.

Use the worksheets, briefings, and resources (see below) provided on my company's website at *www.allonscg.com*. You will find tips, suggestions for step-by-step preparation and meetings, and much more. Use these documents, briefings, and charts as if they were your creations. Just tailor them to fit your organization, such as adding your organization's logo to all the briefings. Throughout the book, there are recommendations in the shaded text boxes. Most boxes will have a different prompt or preparatory command. For example, I will use preparatory commands such as "advice," "suggestion," "hint," "guidance," "opinion," and several others. These "call points" are important. While I'm not insisting that you follow them, neither do I want you to ignore them. At a minimum I want you to *read* them. Also throughout the book, you'll find a text box titled "Where Are We Now?" The intent of this box is to take a look at where you are (or where you should be) on your project plan. I recommend using this as a checklist to ensure that you've accomplished all the "major muscle movements" at a given juncture in the book. It's a point (once completed) from which to move forward.

Exercises, tasks, and activities

In several chapters and the appendices, I provide additional details and work assignments (exercises, tasks, and activities) that you should complete. I urge you not to skip them. Do the work; it will pay dividends.

The support website

All PowerPoint briefings for meetings, briefings, and other events in the planning process are available at my company's website. There are also graphics that you can use to tailor your presentations to meet your needs. At the website you will also find Microsoft Word documents that include meeting agendas, sample meeting minutes, and other planning forms. Most important, you'll find a six-month project-creation-and-implementation plan. With only minor deviations from the plan, you should be able to produce and begin implementing a strategic plan within those six months. Feel free to use some or all of these documents as you choose. There is no pride of ownership or authorship here. Rearrange the briefings and documents to fit your environment, your culture, your personality. That is the primary purpose of the website—to provide information that is editable and usable. After all, this is your plan, and you are the lead strategic planner who will deliver it. One important last note: Please don't hesitate to contact me during your adventure for assistance or advice on any matter in or related to this book. My website address is www.allonscg.com/book/download

As I have noted, *Strategic Planning: As Simple as A, B, C* is written so that you can follow the steps for developing and executing a strategic plan. At this point you've determined that a strategic plan is required for your organization, and you're ready to begin the process. But first I want you to read, or at least skim, the entire book before you begin the planning proper. Get a feel for what is required. Once you've completed the book, go back to the beginning, follow the process, and start using it as your FM.

GUIDANCE:
Do not just copy and paste portions of the book. In other words, go through the processes outlined in all the chapters and avoid the temptation to cut corners and use outdated documents you may have "on the shelf" at your organization. Remember, if it's comfortable, it's probably wrong. Do the work.

Ready? Let's build a plan!

The Approach

A Five Phase Plan

An important component of effective strategic planning is called down-board thinking. This concept is analogous to the way world-class chess players think. They must not only decide on their immediate moves, they must look "down board" and consider their opponent's possible responses to their moves and plan a number of moves ahead (L. D. Goldstein et al., 1993). So it is with strategic planning: the planning team must look down the board, consider the implications of its plan, and then base its decisions and actions on those implications. Try to predict down the board how you can influence your organization's future. The strategic planning approach discussed in this chapter applies down-board thinking to strategic planning to change or at a minimum influence your organization's future. I want you to use this approach as your roadmap for developing your strategic plan.

> *IDEA:*
> *The further you go into the future, the more likely it is to be different from the past. Go further.*

The strategic planning approach

My strategic planning approach is formulated in phases and nested in the Hoshin process and numerous other proven models. The approach is geared to ensure that your organization's strategic plan focuses on top-level vision while garnering input from the organization's lower levels as well as its external environment. This focus is critical to the ontological cohesiveness of the

> *I worked for an outstanding leader who gave us ten objectives. He said that whatever you're doing, if it doesn't link to these objectives, don't do it.*

organization. As shown earlier in Figure 2, I look at the signals and insights of the lower levels and compare their interpretation of the organizational strategy with that of the upper levels. In the majority of cases, there is a disconnect between these levels. This disconnect ultimately leads to flaws in the organizational strategic execution and reveals a lack of a unified strategy. Later in the book, I will discuss some techniques for learning about the signals and insights of the lower levels. For example, you will ask such questions as What are customers thinking? Are employees focused on the right things? Are stakeholders satisfied with our organizational outputs? And is the organization as a whole working toward realization of the organization's vision? My approach ensures that you will unite the lower and upper levels of the organization to get them focused on the same organizational vision.

Strategic planning success for your organization involves dealing with a unique set of circumstances that consists of numerous factors and constraints. My approach offers a roadmap or guide that can provide a general framework, useful methodologies, and helpful solutions to facilitate transformation, reduce variation, and minimize constraints on formulating your plan.

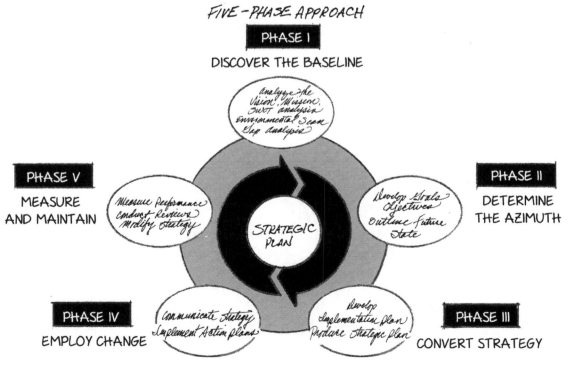

Figure 3. Strategic planning approach

In brief summary: I will outline the approach to strategic planning that will serve as the bedrock of this book and as your roadmap.

As you will see, my five-phase strategic planning approach operates at the macrolevel. (See Figure 3, Strategic planning approach.) The phases are:

Phase I—Discover the Baseline
Phase II—Determine the Azimuth
Phase III—Convert Strategy to Operations
Phase IV—Employ Change
Phase V—Measure and Maintain

Phase I (Discover the Baseline) consists of an extensive assessment of your internal and external environment. Using this assessment, you solidify the mission and vision as well as the strengths, weaknesses, and gaps within your organization. It is in this phase that you define the boundaries of your internal and external environment or landscape. The assessment commonly includes but is not limited to stakeholders, customers, and constituencies. The intent is to construct the organizational baseline's as-is state. Here, the organization's as-is (or current) culture, leadership, and level of in-house expertise can be leveraged to gather data during the assessment.

During **phase II** (Determine the Azimuth), a strategic planning model is designed and customized to your organizational vision. The approach shown in Figure 3 is one that I have found fits most organizations. Drilling into the approach, you have a clear yet deliberate methodical process to fit your organization. During this phase, the new strategic vision is developed or modifications are made to the existing vision. Here goals and objectives are also developed and prioritized so that the vision can be realized. These goals and objectives serve as your azimuth, a directional point that guides you into the future. In phase II, you will also develop and prioritize the strategic perspectives and link the goals and objectives to each strategic perspective so that you can attain the to-be—that is, future—state.

Phase III (Convert Strategy to Operations) involves the actual construction of the strategic plan. This phase takes the goals and objectives and converts them into action. Here you write the plan, obtain approval from leadership, and disseminate the plan throughout the organization and the external environment. Most important to phase III is the plan of action and milestones (POAM) implementation. POAM implementation is a critical foundation for realizing your strategic vision. The POAM dissects each objective to create an achievable project plan focused on realizing specific outcomes.

Phase IV involves employing change. This phase guides the execution of the strategic plan. Responsibilities are fixed so that the plan can be budgeted, resourced, and implemented. Phase IV also introduces the development of performance measures for tracking each POAM through a program-management process.

In summary, then, phase I assesses your environment, which yields goals and objectives (phase II), providing the foundation to build a POAM (phase III), which is executed in phase IV.

Phase V (Measure and Maintain) involves continuous measurement of the execution process to ensure adherence to the established and agreed-upon POAM. Via metrics and analytics, you will create dashboards for decisions that will guarantee successful prosecution of the strategic plan. It is in this phase that flex and pivot actions occur to mitigate the interference of external distracters. In this phase, your subject-matter expert in performance-based metrics with the capability to review and interpret data, develop a balanced scorecard, conduct analysis, and display performance dashboards can assist in providing clear and concise solutions when the dashboards indicate results are lagging. I will discuss the balanced scorecard (BSC) in chapter 5.

Strategic planning model (SPM)

Designing the strategic planning model is critical and must be specifically tailored to your organization. The purpose of the SPM is to walk you step by step through the strategic planning process. It answers the *A, B, C* questions (*A*: Where are you now? *B*: Where you going? *C*: How are you going to get there?) by allowing you to address and accomplish tasks outlined in each phase. I will guide you through each phase of the strategic planning approach in chapters 1 through 5, and each chapter will discuss all the topics annotated in the SPM. You must engage with your strategy team and collectively focus on the way forward to develop a sound strategic foundation in your particular market sector. The SPM helps you accomplish this. The SPM depicted in Figure 4, Strategic Planning Model, breaks down the five-phase approach into specific tasks. It details the "simplicity" of our *A, B, C* strategic planning approach.

A. Where are you now?	B. Where are you going?	C. How are you going to get there?		
What is your baseline?	What is your future state?	What is your plan to get there?	How will you employ change?	How will you measure results?
Environmental Scan Analyze current Vision, Mission and Guiding Principles (Internal Scan) Stakeholders Analysis Conduct SWOT Analysis (External Scan) Conduct Gap Analysis Develop Solution Sets/ Recommendations	Prepare and Conduct Focus Group Offsite Develop restated Vision, Mision, Guiding Principles Outline the Future State Develop Goals and Objectives Prioritize Goals and Objectives Link Goals and Objectives to Strategic Perspective	Produce the Strategic Plan Document Communicate Strategies and New Strategic Plan Develop Implementation Plan Develop Plan of Action and Milestones (POAM)	Develop Performance Measures Fix Responsibilites Apply Resources Execute POAM Develop Training	Conduct Implementation Review and Measure Performance Refine Goals, Strategies and Processes Align Organization to Support Strategy Measure, Improve, Analyze
Phase I (Chapter 1)	Phase II (Chapter 2)	Phase III (Chapter 3)	Phase IV (Chapter 4)	Phase V (Chapter 5)
Discover the Baseline	Determine the Azimuth	Convert Strategy to Operations	Employ Change	Measure and Maintain

Figure 4. Strategic planning model

The SPM is a vision- or goal-based planning model. This model is typically used by organizations that have not done much strategic planning or need to revisit a long-neglected strategic plan. The process might be implemented and then embellished in later years with more planning phases and activities to ensure a well-rounded direction for the organization. The SPM planning process includes answering basic strategic questions for each phase of the strategic planning approach, such as:

- ✓ Phase I (Discover the Baseline) questions: Where are you now? What is your baseline?
- ✓ Phase II (Determine the Azimuth) questions: Where are you going? What is your future state?
- ✓ Phase III (Convert Strategy to Operations) questions: How are you going to get there? What is your plan to get there?
- ✓ Phase IV (Employ Change) question: How will you employ change?

The Approach

    ✓ Phase V (Measure and Maintain) question: How will you measure success?

Again, use the strategic planning approach and the SPM as your roadmaps to chart your course through the strategic planning process. Let's face it: as the lead strategic planner, you have a daunting task. Although I have outlined a simple process, don't misunderstand—this may require a lot of work depending on your current organization's condition and your familiarity with strategic planning.

Revisit the bridge graphic outlined in the Preface and ensure that you understand the *A, B, C* concept. Once you're comfortable with the concept, the approach, and the planning model, move on to the next section of the book, "Let's Get Started."

Let's Get Started

What should you do first, what's next, and so on? At the outset I suggested you read or, at a minimum, skim, the book in its entirety before beginning to study and use it in earnest. That's

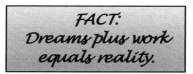

because I want you to get a feel for the task ahead so that you can internally assess your capabilities for executing the planning program. Have you read the book? Because from this point on, we're getting down to work.

Put your house in order: get organized

Be realistic about your ability to plan. Ensure that you have the resources, the time, and the energy to see the undertaking through. Again, go through the entire book before you begin the process. If you determine that you're unable to perform team-leader functions, ensure that you have the personnel resources that can assist. Your strategic plan champion (discussed later) can be a source of significant assistance in providing direction and leadership. The key to developing and executing a successful strategic plan is making sure that your organization is ready. Have the CEO send an "all-hands" letter to the entire organization indicating that you are beginning the strategic planning process and instructing employees to provide you support as needed. See appendix A for a sample CEO all-hands e-mail. Some additional "keys" that contribute to success include:

- ✓ Ensuring adequate participation by critical stakeholders.
- ✓ Making sure the process has a skillful champion or sponsor.
- ✓ Building your team to support wise strategic thinking, acting, coaching, and learning.
- ✓ Cultivating necessary political support.
- ✓ Fostering effective decision making and implementation.
- ✓ Having a process that will succeed. (I've already done that for you.)

✓ Managing the process effectively.
✓ Being confident. It's *as simple as A, B, C.*

Resourcing

It is critical to your success that you understand the financial challenges of the strategic planning and execution process. Implementing the process, in short, will cost time and money. The operative word is "implementing." The main expense of the planning process (as opposed to the

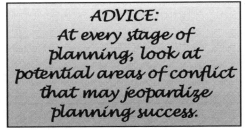

ADVICE:
At every stage of planning, look at potential areas of conflict that may jeopardize planning success.

implementation) is time, human resources, and a minimal cost for focus group sessions and standard office supplies. Implementing the plan and accomplishing the objectives and actions required to realize the vision are where higher costs of time and money are incurred. We will discuss resourcing requirements (financial, human, technological, and so forth.) in chapter 4. I strongly recommend approaching the way forward in the following sequence:

✓ Revise the strategic plan approach and the strategic planning model.
✓ Create a project plan.
✓ Brief leadership.
✓ Create and educate the planning teams.
✓ Execute the requirements outlined in each chapter of the book.

Revise the strategic planning approach and the strategic planning model (SPM)

Task #1: Solidify the Strategic Planning Approach and Strategic Planning Model (SPM)

I want you to either adopt the approach that I outlined in "The Approach" (Figure 3, Strategic planning approach) or adjust it to fit your needs. If you choose to make adjustments, I recommend they be minor since the approach serves as the guide for the remaining chapters in the book. After your vision has been completed, thoroughly review the SPM. Look at all the headings and the questions for each phase. Review the *A, B, C's* in Figure 4 and study the subheads below each heading. Are the questions in the headings applicable to your organization? Do you need to add more tasks or sculpt existing ones in some way? Is the sequencing of these tasks suited to your needs? Remember, the strategic planning approach (henceforth referred to as the approach) and the SPM are your global positioning system—use them to navigate and develop your strategic plan. It is critically important to make any changes in the SPM now, as the SPM is your guide to the end product. At this point, my recommendation is that you adopt the approach and the SPM as shown and proceed.

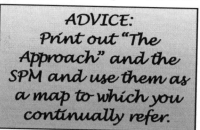

ADVICE:
Print out "The Approach" and the SPM and use them as a map to which you continually refer.

Create the project plan (planning to plan)

One of my favorite maxims is "Getting ready to get ready to start." In order to be productive and to assure that the planning process is on schedule, the lead strategic planner (you) must avoid the "getting ready to get ready to start" syndrome. Forget the waffling: parachute into the hot-drop zone and start the strategic planning process! As the lead planner, you must decide where to allocate time and resources. By "planning to plan," we are referring to the in-depth consideration of how the strategic plan will be carried out. For example, who will be involved? What will the timetable be? What are the likely consequences of the plan, both anticipated and unanticipated? What resources will be required to carry out the plan?

The first step in planning to plan is to create a project plan in macro form. The project plan will be used to develop a timeline and track task-completion progress. There are several methodologies for creating a project plan, including program-management software that provides numerous templates (such as Gantt and project-timeline charts) and that only requires the input of data. Such software provides graphically displayed project plans that can be used for presentations as well as for the tracking of day-to-day execution. Although more time consuming, a hand-drawn plan works as well. The project plan on my website was constructed using Microsoft Project 2010.

Creating the project plan requires you to:

- ✓ Determine the organizational readiness for strategic planning (i.e., when to begin the process)

✓ Identify resource requirements, including how requirements will be planned, tracked, and reported

✓ Develop your project team using tools and techniques such as interpersonal skills, training, teambuilding activities, establishment of ground rules, and so on

✓ Build your timeline (i.e., ascertain task duration)

✓ Determine the process for managing any change(s) to the project

✓ Manage information about the project's progress, such as when activities have started, how they are proceeding, and when they have been finished

✓ Monitor and control cost

✓ Perform quality assurance—the process of minimizing errors within the project

✓ Develop progress reports to indicate performance, status, and progress

Figure 5, Project plan (in appendix B), is an example of a project plan in a Gantt chart format. As you can see, time is allotted to modify the approach and creation of the plan. The plan extends over a six-month period. This translates into six months from the beginning of the strategic planning process to the end. The timeline stops at phase IV because this is the place where the plan implementation begins. For obvious reasons, I did not schedule phase V in the planning timeline. Phase V is the monitoring and tracking of the plan's execution. This is a lengthy process and depending on the scope of some objectives, can take up to several months or even years for completion. Note that the six-month timeline for the project plan is elastic and should be flexible to adjust to your resources or constraints. In other words, you may expand the process beyond the six months, or you may *reduce* the period to less than six months. Your choice is dependent solely on the state of your organization. If this constitutes the first strategic plan your organization has developed, it would be a mistake to reduce the time period and the tasks of the project plan. The plan should include some of the resources required throughout the process, including, for example, personnel, and any upfront financial, logistical, and operational costs.

Task #2: Develop the Project Plan

Review the proposed project plan (appendix B). Can you meet these timelines? If you're not sure, reread the book to gauge the complexity of the tasks. The six-month plan provides ample time to meet the time allocated for each task. Revise the plan as you desire, then finalize it with your core planning team (CPT) members and the strategic plan champion. (Team selection will be discussed later in this chapter). Each task depicted in the project plan will be examined in detail throughout the book. Remember to measure your resources and any financial requirements and note them on the project plan. It is also important to consider adding buffers to the timeline. For example, if your organization is slow to react and needs continual prodding, you may want to allocate more time to build your teams or conduct an exercise. The time frame I give for each task is based on a slight "tic" above a novice to strategic planning.

Selecting the strategic plan champion

The organization's leadership team or individual leader, such as the CEO, typically appoints the strategic plan champion. The champion's primary responsibility is to keep the CPT on track and ensure that the strategic plan is developed and executed in accordance with leadership's vision, organizational mission, values, and budgetary constraints. He or she must have enough status, power, and authority to commit the organization's resources to strategic planning and to hold people accountable for doing the planning well. This person must have a vested interest in achieving success and doing what he or she can to ensure that success. The champion is your "go-to" person when you're stuck. Nevertheless, it's best to use this asset sparingly, only for those times you just cannot move forward with your team, peers, supervisors, or other organizational resources. As a valued resource, the strategic champion should:

- ✓ Articulate the purpose and importance of the overall effort to the organization and its stakeholders
- ✓ Commit the necessary resources and emphasize throughout the process that the results are important to the organization's mission, mandates, and stakeholders
- ✓ Encourage and reward hard work, smart and creative thinking, and constructive dialogue
- ✓ Be cautious about the need for outside consultants
- ✓ Be willing to exercise power, funding, and authority to keep planning on track
- ✓ Serve as a link between the planning team and the CEO

Briefing leadership

Once you are satisfied with the proposed project plan, you should present it to the strategic plan champion and the CEO to gain their approval. Remember, however, that this is a fluid document. It can continually change. The presentation (in briefing format) must outline the strategic planning approach, resource requirements, and the way forward. In addition to presenting the project plan, you should present a synopsis of your process. Discuss the approach I discussed earlier as well as the tasks depicted in the SPM.

Task #3: Develop and Conduct an Initial Briefing to Leadership

Now is the time to articulate your requirements for developing the strategic plan. You may add to or sculpt from the sample briefing (see appendix C, First Brief to Leadership) to meet your organization's and leadership's requirements. While the purpose of the briefing is to provide a logical flow of how you intend to design, construct, execute, and monitor the organization's strategic plan, you should also use the briefing as a decision point to gain approval of the plan by your leadership,

IMPORTANT: Ensure that everything you present to the organization's senior leader or leaders is reviewed and approved by the strategic plan champion beforehand.

following which you will then communicate with executive decision makers to help management teams think more deeply about their enterprise than they had previously. Leadership must assist in winning internal and external support for the strategic plan. In addition to the briefing, you may also present a 250-word-or-so executive summary of the plan. This will provide leadership and upper management with all relevant information concerning the plan's development.

> ### Where are you now?
> ✓ You've solidified your strategic planning approach (reviewed and edited, as necessary).
> ✓ You've reviewed all the tasks in the strategic planning model.
> ✓ You've created your project plan.
> ✓ You've briefed and obtained approval from leadership for the process and the way forward.
> ✓ You've updated your project plan and annotated your completed tasks.

Creating and educating the planning teams

I will now embark on a discussion about creating teams and team building, an important topic. Getting the right people and having them available at the right time with the right skill sets is a critical factor in your strategic planning success. If you do not try from the beginning to get this right, you will experience frustration and setbacks throughout the process. Remember, you have a project plan with a timeline to which you must adhere. Your entire organization can be adversely affected by an unworkable or delayed strategic plan. While input from all facets of the organization is needed to create the plan, not everyone can or should be involved in the actual planning process—although everyone should be included (directly or indirectly) in the *execution* of the plan. When building a team, I always remind myself of Vilfredo Pareto and his principle of factor sparsity, more commonly known as the 80-20 rule (so named because, according to Pareto, roughly 80 percent of the output comes from 20 percent of the input). When selecting team members, you want individuals who will "input" more than their 20 percent numbers would predict. You want individuals giving *110 percent.* As you know, 110 percent is better than perfect.

Developing the planning team

Developing planning teams is a process of improving the competencies, team interactions, and overall team environment to enhance project performance. You, the team leader, should acquire skills to identify, build, maintain, motivate, and inspire your team to achieve the performance and tasks spelled out in your project plan. For a helpful resource, consider reading

William G. Dyer's *Team Building: Current Issues and New Alternatives*, a book that I think you will find extremely informative about the art and science of team building. The book emphasizes the importance of the commitment of the team leader and of team members' spending time to develop a cohesive and effective unit.

Teamwork is a critical factor in your project's success, and developing effective teams is one of the primary responsibilities of the team leader. It is he or she who creates the environment that promotes teamwork. The leader should continually motivate the team by providing challenges and opportunities, timely feedback and support, as needed, and recognition and rewards for good performance.

The team-selection process should be marketed as a prestigious opportunity to participate in the envisioning of the organization's future, not, as is often the case, as a chore of seemingly endless meetings that distract from other work assignments without producing any positive impact on how the overall planning process is progressing. Groups of five typically are the most effective for problem-solving tasks, while groups of more than ten provide so much "air time" for members to agree or disagree that it can be difficult for other members to make their contributions. Much of team members' resistance to any change effort comes from misunderstanding or, at least, from nonunderstanding. Therefore, it is important to devote significant time at the end of the team-selection phase to informing the planning team members as to how they were selected and what is expected of them. Materials should be distributed—such as this book, a letter from the CEO, and/or a brief orientation from the strategic plan champion—so that team members develop a sense of purpose and responsibility to the team as a whole. Typically, there are several other groups that are not formally members of the organization but that feel as though they have an investment in the organization. These groups are called stakeholders, and the only requirement for being a stakeholder is a sense of involvement, a purposefully very fluid criterion. We will discuss stakeholders in more detail in chapter 1.

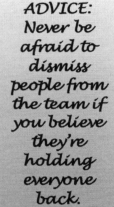

ADVICE: Never be afraid to dismiss people from the team if you believe they're holding everyone back.

Below are some tools and techniques that may prove beneficial in developing your planning teams. As the team leader, you can greatly reduce problems and increase cooperation by understanding the sentiments of team members, anticipating their actions, acknowledging their concerns, and following up on their issues. Look for team members who thrive on little supervision and possess:

- ✓ The fundamental skills to do the job
- ✓ Initiative (the drive that makes the difference)
- ✓ Knowledge and expertise, and the willingness to share them
- ✓ Respect for the opinions of others
- ✓ A willingness to listen
- ✓ Dependability (the follow-through to fulfill all tasks assigned)
- ✓ An orientation to action

The Tuckman Ladder of team development asserts that there are five stages of development that teams should go through. Usually these stages occur in order. However, it is not uncommon for teams to get stuck in a particular stage or slip back to an earlier stage. Also, if team members have worked together in the past, they might be inclined to skip some of the stages. Tuckman's key point is that each stage builds on the others and prepares for the performing stage and that skipping any stage will affect the performing stage. The five stages are:

Forming. This stage is where the team is formed and told about the project and what each member's formal roles and responsibilities will be. Team members tend to be independent and not as open to team building in this stage.

Storming. During this stage, the team begins to address the planning of work requirements, technical decisions, and project-management approaches. If team members are not collaborative and open to keeping different ideas in perspective, the environment can become destructive.

Norming. In the norming stage, team members begin to work together and adjust work habits and behaviors in support of the team. Team members begin to trust one another.

Performing. Teams that reach the performing stage function as a well-organized unit. They are independent and work through issues smoothly and effectively.

Adjourning. In the adjourning stage, the team completes its work and moves on from the project.

You, as the team leader, should be focused on these team dynamics:

- ✓ **Influencing the team.** This means you are aware of and influence when possible those human resource factors that may affect the planning process. Such factors include team environment, geographical locations of team members, communication among stakeholders, internal and external politics, cultural issues, organizational uniqueness, and other such "people factors" as may alter the project's performance. While you will encourage a variety of perspectives, you also will value balance.

ADVICE: Nothing is better than a good idea; however, not all ideas are good.

- ✓ **Promoting professional and ethical behavior**. The core team should be aware of, subscribe to, and ensure that all team members engage in ethical behavior.

You will develop two basic teams. The first is a core planning team (CPT); the second is a strategic planning committee (SPC). The CPT should consist of four to six people. Larger teams tend to get mired in debate and delay progress. This is not to encourage an authoritarian or dictatorial construct on your part. You must choose a team of experienced and dedicated members where ideas are free flowing and the "agree-to-disagree" concept prevails.

At a minimum, the CPT should include a strategic plan champion, a team leader, two strategic planners, and an administrative assistant. Once in place, the team serves as the nucleus of your organization's strategic planning process. The CPT is responsible for planning, guiding, developing, executing, and monitoring the full spectrum of the organization's strategic plan, from concept to execution to monitoring.

Developing the human resource plan

Developing the human resource plan involves identifying and documenting roles, responsibilities, and required skills; reporting relationships; and creating a staffing management plan. There are essentially two approaches for human resources in constructing the strategic plan. First, your organization already has a strategic planning section with personnel assigned to that unit or section. Or, second, your organization must build the team from other departments within the organization, a more challenging if more prevalent occurrence. In the latter circumstance, the human resource plan documents roles and responsibilities, project-organization charts, and the staffing management plan, as well as the timetable for staff acquisition and release. This means that resources you get from other departments are assigned to your teams for a fixed time, with a definite date of release (strongly recommended) back to their department(s) of origin so that they can continue with their normal job responsibilities. Those resources can come from within or outside the organization that is performing the strategic planning process, although it is recommended that they come from within. I will discuss the external facilitation requirement later in the book. In the event that you cannot get team members loaned to you, at least ensure that they are assigned to the team even if they spend the majority of their time carrying out their normal day-to-day duties and even though this will require more managerial input on your part. The key is to communicate continually, assign tasks as required, and enforce due-dates. Remember, you are responsible for your team's success.

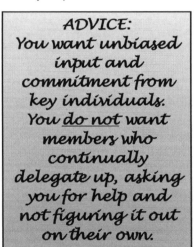

ADVICE:
You want unbiased input and commitment from key individuals. You <u>do not</u> want members who continually delegate up, asking you for help and not figuring it out on their own.

Staffing management plan

The staffing management plan is part of the human resources plan. It describes when and how human resources requirements will be met. The staffing management plan does not necessarily have to be a formal, highly detailed, or broadly framed plan. Rather, it can be created and tailored according to the structure of your organization and its strategic planning process. Remember, we recommended team-staffing requirements earlier in the chapter. The plan is updated continually during the planning process to direct ongoing team-member, acquisition-developmental actions.

A number of questions arise when planning the acquisition of team members. For example, will the team members need to work in a central location, or can they work remotely? What are the costs associated with the level of expertise needed for the planning process? How much assistance can the organization's human resource and functional managers provide to the strategic planning teams? And will human resources come from within the organization or from an external, contracted source, as, for example, when the organization lacks the in-house staff needed to complete the plan? Such outsourcing can involve hiring or contracting with individual consultants to fill resource gaps. I have served as a consultant on numerous occasions. Recall that the purpose of this book is to guide you through the process using internal, cost-effective resources, not external resources. However, as we will discuss in chapter 1, you may decide to contract a facilitator for your focus group offsite.

Choosing the project team involves confirming human resources availability and obtaining the team necessary to complete the planning process and all the tasks associated with it. You may or may not have direct control over team-member selection because of reporting relationships or for various other reasons. In some cases, you get what the functional departments give you. In addition, sometimes it is just not worth "falling on your sword" to fight for the results of your selections. After all, everyone has some value. Determine what that value is and get the most out of it. If adjudication is required, see your strategic plan champion. It is important that the following steps be carried out or taken into consideration during the process of putting together the strategic planning team:

You should effectively negotiate with and influence others who are in a position to provide the required human resources for the project.

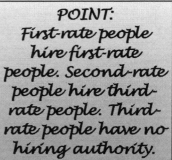

POINT: First-rate people hire first-rate people. Second-rate people hire third-rate people. Third-rate people have no hiring authority.

- ✓ You should realize that failure to select the necessary human resources for the project might affect project schedules, budgets, customer satisfaction, quality, and risk.
- ✓ If the necessary human resources are not available due to various constraints, economic factors, or previous assignments to other projects, you should be prepared to assign alternative resources, perhaps with lower competencies, or external support, if affordable.

At a minimum, you should determine the method and timing for releasing team members. This benefits both the planning team members and their originating departments. When team members are released, any costs associated with them are no longer charged for the planning, thus reducing expenditures. I estimated a six-month human resource requirement for your organization when I constructed the project plan. Therefore, the organizational staff should expect their personnel to be on loan for at least six months to produce the strategic plan. However, there is a human resource requirement to implement the goals and objectives within the plan. The actual personnel requirement is based on the scope and complexity of the objectives and thus is not a fixed obligation. Remember to ensure rewards for organizational members' contributions, for they help in producing the strategic plan and promote and reinforce positive behavior. To be effective, recognition and rewards should be based on activity and performance that are under your control.

Virtual teams

The use of virtual teams creates new possibilities when acquiring planning team members. If your organization is spread out geographically, the use of virtual team members to fill your resource requirements, given today's technology, should not be a burden. Virtual teams can be defined as groups of people whose shared goals fulfill

> **POINT:**
> Proactive team: gives customers what they want before they ask for it. Reactive team: always one step behind. You want proactive teams.

their roles with little or no time spent meeting face to face. The availability of electronic communication tools such as e-mail, audio conferencing, web-based meeting, and videoconferencing has made such teams feasible. The virtual team format makes it possible to:

- ✓ Form teams of people from the same organization who operate in widespread geographical areas
- ✓ Make available special expertise to offer the planning team even though the experts are not in the same geographic area
- ✓ Incorporate employees who work from home offices
- ✓ Form teams of people who work different days or hours
- ✓ Include people with mobility limitations or other challenges
- ✓ Move forward on projects that might otherwise have been ignored due to travel expense

As we discussed earlier, developing teams involves the process of organizing, managing, and leading the strategic planning team. The planning team is comprised of the people with assigned roles and responsibilities for completing the strategic plan. The type, number of team members, and structure of the team can change frequently as the planning process progresses. However, I highly recommend the organizational construct depicted in Figures 6 (Core planning team organizational diagram) and 7 (Strategic planning committee organizational diagram).

Core planning team (CPT)

The CPT is responsible for managing the entire planning and implementation process and conducting leadership activities such as initiating, planning, executing, monitoring, controlling, and closing the various phases of the planning process. It sets the rhythm for the planning and execution of the strategic plan. The CPT leader at a macrolevel will consider such matters as funding for the planning process, clarifying its scope, monitoring its progress, and influencing others in order to benefit the process.

Task #4: Select the Core Planning Team (CPT)

Work with the strategic plan champion to decide who should comprise the CPT. I highly recommend qualified, experienced PhD-level (or just a notch below) thinkers. The CPT planners should be well respected among both the organizational rank and file and the leadership. You want individuals to whom, when they speak, people listen. In some cases, the strategic plan champion will send an e-mail to the department heads of prospective team members asking for volunteers. I've used this approach several times with excellent results.

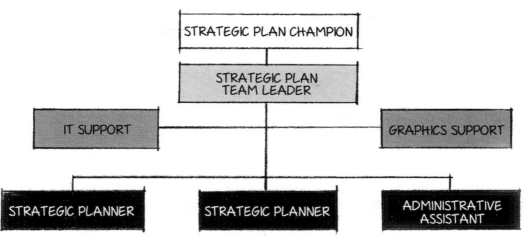

Figure 6. Core planning team organizational diagram

Figure 6 is a graphical representation of the CPT. The duties and responsibilities of the various CPT team members are listed below.

The strategic plan team leader

The strategic plan team leader must be motivated. He or she serves as the project manager responsible for all the decisions that affect the development, execution, and monitoring of the strategic plan. The team leader should have experience with project management, operational planning, and strategic development. The bottom line is that the team leader is responsible for everything that goes right (and everything that goes wrong) in developing the strategic plan and ensuring that all goals and objectives are met and met on time. This is a huge responsibility. However, it's *as simple as A, B, C.* As the team leader, you must possess the fundamental skills to do the job, but you do not necessarily have to be proficient at the job. That's why I wrote this book: to guide you along.

Understanding the "different hats" you need to wear and when you need to wear them will provide you with a sense of purpose—that you are in charge and that you know what you are doing. There is a "brainy quote" I like that goes, "Some of it, plus the rest of it, equals all of it." I want you to heed these words. They mean you are responsible for *some of it*, the members of your teams are responsible for *the rest of it,* and together you will get done *all of it.* Do not attempt the Herculean task of trying to do all of it yourself. Select team members upon whom you can rely to do the rest of it and do not micromanage them. I cannot make it any clearer than this. You, as the CPT leader, are the "easy button" on every aspect of the strategic plan from "cradle to cradle"—from birth to rebirth.

> *Note that I use the phrase "cradle to cradle." Normally, the phrase is "cradle to grave." That is not the case with strategic planning. It is a continuous cycle. While in execution, the plan is constantly being monitored and analyzed, with changes made accordingly. Thus, it is a living document that is nursed, nurtured, adjusted, and reborn.*

The strategic planner (assistant team leader)

This person is responsible for assisting the team leader with his or her responsibilities and acts as the team leader in the leader's absence. He or she must have a background in strategic planning. You do not necessarily need an expert. (If *you* are an expert, then perhaps you don't need this book!) I recommend at least two strategic planners because in phases I, II, and III the requirements tend to be more demanding—hence, the need for two planners rather than one. The strategic planner's primary responsibility is to keep the team and the organization on course, to keep track of progress, and to pay attention to all the details that pertain to the strategic planning process. This individual must also be skilled in the art of group dynamics and interpersonal relationships. It is extremely beneficial if one of the strategic planners has some expertise as a facilitator, for you will utilize this skill when conducting focus groups. Other recommended skills are in metrics and balanced scorecard (BSC). Both skills will be advantageous in phases IV and V as well. Some of the strategic planner's responsibilities include:

- ✓ Keeping strategic planning high on people's agendas
- ✓ Being committed to a successful process, not to predetermined solutions
- ✓ Thinking about what has to come together (people, information, resources, completed work)
- ✓ Rallying participants to push the process along
- ✓ Being sensitive to power differences and being able to engage all implementers in finding ways to share power in order to increase the chances of planning success

✓ Developing solutions to the exercises and tasks discussed in this book

The administrative assistant

This individual is responsible for performing all administrative tasks associated with the planning and execution of the plan. It is advantageous to ensure that the administrative assistant has skills in software such as Microsoft Office. Skills in other software such as Microsoft Project Manager and Adobe graphics are also advantageous. These are only recommendations for software requirements; use what best suits your requirements and the systems that are uniform within your organization. In addition to having software capabilities, the administrative assistant must be able to develop meeting agendas, take copious notes, maintain scheduling, document and archive materials, and carry out numerous administrative tasks associated with project-management protocols.

Strategic planning committee (SPC)

The SPC is subordinate to but larger than the CPT in that it includes representation from the various functional areas within the organization. The makeup of the SPC will vary and is dependent upon the configuration of your organization. Configuration aside, do not include in this group more than ten to twelve individuals. In any planning group, use the least-is-best approach whenever possible.

The committee should include personnel from functional areas of your organization such as personnel, finance, operations, marketing, logistics, and information technology—personnel, in other words, who have a direct influence on the course of

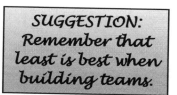

SUGGESTION: Remember that least is best when building teams.

the organization's day-to-day functioning. Depending on the size of these functional areas, more than one person may represent a given department's interests. For example, if the operations division has a complex structure and many employees (in excess, say, of three hundred) it may require more than one representative on the SPC. Remember, however, that as a rule, less is more (that is, least is best). Figure 7, Strategic planning committee organizational diagram, is a graphical representation of the SPC.

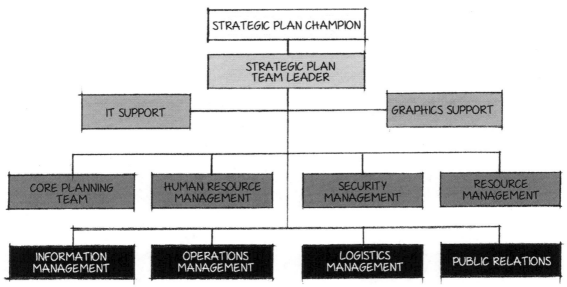

Figure 7. Strategic planning committee organizational diagram

It is extremely important that SPC team members be middle-to-senior-level management personnel who are knowledgeable about their organization or departments and who can make decisions that will affect the organization's future and move the planning process forward. For example, deputy directors, executive officers, branch managers, and similar personnel from middle-to-senior levels can be excellent choices to form the SPC. On the other hand, individuals who have to go back to their managers for answers to every question regardless of how simple will produce little more than wasted time and unnecessary delay.

> *INSTRUCTION:*
> *Develop a point of contact listing of all members of the CPT and the SPC. This listing should, at a minimum, include name, organization or office, e-mail address, phone number, and cellular number, and should be continually updated by the administrative assistant and distributed to all team members. Be sure to include an "as-of" date.*

Task #5: Select the Strategic Planning Committee (SPC)

Work with the CPT and the strategic plan champion to decide what functional areas should make up the SPC. As we discussed in the previous paragraph, the SPC essentially is a representative body of all the functional areas within the organization.

Task #6: Distribute Team-Welcoming E-mail

As soon as all team members are chosen and identified, send a welcoming e-mail to each in the form of a concise message that explains your mission: who you are, what you're doing, when you're going to do it, how you will do it, and why you're doing it. A sample team-welcoming e-mail can be found in appendix D, Sample Team-Welcoming E-mail.

> *Where are you now?*
> ✓ You have confidence that you have the right people on your teams.
> ✓ You have validated communications and commitments from each team member and have his or her contact information.
> ✓ You have updated your project plan and annotated your completed tasks.

First CPT meeting

Your first CPT meeting should focus on a brief introduction along with words on planning the way forward. What makes for an effective meeting? Having a purpose, preparing ahead of time, setting follow-on goals during the meeting, and making provisions for follow-through and assessment are critical. All too often meetings take place without a purpose, are too long, and conclude with little having been accomplished other than the wasting of valuable time. A clear understanding and articulation of objectives is essential to an effective meeting. Once a purpose is determined, questions as to who will attend and where and when to meet must be addressed.

You must devote time and effort to preparing for your meetings. As the lead strategic planner, you will conduct numerous meetings not only with your team but also with leadership and subordinates. Your conduct at these meetings can provide significant credibility to your mission and as a result can influence others to follow. Obviously, the opposite is also true. I urge you to conduct sharp, focused meetings so that participants can see issues with clarity and thus provide meaningful input.

Let's Get Started

It is important to lay out the strategy and get unanimous agreement on the strategic planning approach and the strategic planning model. If you revised the approach and/or strategic planning module in Task #1, use that version as the basis for your presentation. The next points of discussion and consensus among the team will be the project plan and the timeline. You must present the timeline so that everyone understands all the major muscle movements that have to be accomplished. Agreement will also be required on the topics for the first SPC meeting. A proposed project plan is found in appendix B.

Some of the areas that must be covered in the first CPT meeting are:

- ✓ Why we are here (purpose)?
- ✓ What are the CPT's responsibilities, as a team and as individuals?
- ✓ What is the project plan? Discuss and reach agreement on the CPT and SPC organization charts.
- ✓ Which individuals comprise the SPC?
- ✓ What are the team guidelines and rules (e.g., limit meeting time to a specific length, be on time, and be prepared)?
- ✓ What is the overall theme for the development of the strategic plan?

Once the CPT has met and you are comfortable that the team can move forward, the next step is to bring together the SPC.

> **TRUE STORY:**
> During a year spent as a consultant for a major US railroad, I once saw senior executives making notes on napkins prior to a key meeting they were holding. Needless to say, the meeting was disorganized and all but pointless. This event was extremely painful for me to watch as our government provides funding to offset some railroads' losses.

Task #7: Conduct First CPT Meeting

Using the techniques and recommendations you have learned thus far, bring the CPT together, and conduct your first meeting. Appendix E provides a sample CPT meeting agenda. Appendix F provides a sample CPT orientation briefing. Obviously, you will have to adjust these documents to meet your requirements.

First strategic planning committee meeting

The purpose of this meeting is to introduce the members of the SPC to the CPT and outline the way forward and tasks that must be accomplished to develop the strategic plan. This is a significant meeting, and you must be thoroughly prepared to respond to the challenge. Fear not, as I will guide you through this frightful endeavor! The meeting may be a challenge because, at least in my experience, conflict invariably arises at such inaugural sessions. For example, you may find individuals who are opposed to developing a strategic plan. I've heard it said at strategic planning meetings that "this is just a waste of time." Or, "We do this every two years, and nothing changes." Or, "I am way too busy for this," along with many other objections (some of which are too politically incorrect to include in this book). Be aware that some individuals may not want to be at such meetings if only because their attendance was mandated, finding such participation to be an interruption of their already busy schedules. Alternatively, you may find individuals who are disgruntled with the organization and believe that meetings such as these are just another burden. Even though such naysayers are in the minority, still, be prepared for them. Remember, you are doing this because you believe in it. Okay, also because leadership demands it. But they demand it because they believe in it. And that is the bottom line.

Meetings should start on time and end on time. They should be focused and relevant. This first meeting is not the place to pontificate on what could be or should be. The purpose is to provide an introduction and orientation. Some topics that should be covered include:

- ✓ The SPC's purpose
- ✓ The SPC's responsibilities, as a team and as individuals
- ✓ The project plan
- ✓ CTP and SPC organization charts
- ✓ Team guidelines and rules (e.g., a specific meeting length, promptness, preparation)
- ✓ The overall theme for the development of the strategic plan

> INSTRUCTION: Always have someone (a recorder) at the meeting taking notes on what was said and by whom it was said. You should review these notes and disseminate them to team members no more than twenty-four hours after the meeting. (See Sample Team Meeting Minutes in appendix G.)

Task #8: Conduct First SPC Meeting

This meeting should follow the same format as the CPT meeting. This is an introductory meeting. Have the recorder take notes, but do not get into prolonged discussions, which should be saved for another time. Keep in mind my planning rule that says "Show concern, but don't act on concern." After all, the purpose of both the CPT and the SPC meetings is essentially the same. You can and should use the same ["PowerPoint"?] slides with only slight modifications to ensure relevance to the instant audience. Appendix E provides a sample meeting agenda. Appendix F provides a sample orientation briefing. Modify them to fit the context of the SPC team members.

Now what?

For you as the strategic planning team leader, now is the time to "get your house in order," for the work to begin. I want you to make sure you have a good handle on the tasks to be accomplished in chapters 1 through 5. More immediately, you must focus on the tasks in chapters 1 and 2. I strongly believe those tasks involve the most intense and time demanding of all the work involved in developing your plan. Once you know what the tasks are and feel confident in their execution, you will have a mental map of how to proceed. Therefore, before going any further, I want you to reread chapters 1 and 2. They will help you focus on how and where you should allocate your time and resources. The purpose of rereading the chapters is for you to stay, and to keep you, one step ahead: even as you're executing one task, you should be thinking about executing the next (remember, down-board thinking). Synchronize the SPM with the project plan and update as necessary, and then discuss with the CPT what resources are required to accomplish the tasks in chapters 1 and 2.

> *TACTIC:*
> *Always develop your plan with the rest of*
> *the organization in mind.*

Chapter 1
Discover the Baseline

Where are you now? What is your baseline?

Plans are nothing; planning is everything. —Dwight Eisenhower

In this chapter, I will help you answer the following two questions: Where are you now? And what is your baseline? The main focus of the chapter is to discover your baseline; that is, the current state of the organization, and assess the gaps (phase I of the approach). I trust the approach section has given you a solid understanding of my five-phase approach to strategic planning. The "scheme of maneuver" (how to accomplish the intent) for this chapter involves discussing all the tasks in phase I of the strategic planning model. I will address each task and provide enough information so that you can develop and execute all aspects of each at the focus group offsite (FGOS). Heed GEN Eisenhower's quote. In our construct it means, *it is not the end product, it's the process that's important.* I strongly urge you to follow my process. It is at the offsite that you will tie all these phase I tasks together to create a baseline, or as-is, state of the organization. The chapter will conclude with solution sets and recommendations and a means to determine the to-be state of the organization. The to-be state is discussed in greater detail in phase II (chapter 2).

These phase I and II tasks will culminate at the offsite. I will guide you through the preparation and conduct of a two-day offsite in chapter 2. The event is designed to work through all the phase I and II tasks and finish with an overall organizational assessment as well as a delineation of the future of the organization. Before we get started on the mechanics of developing the strategic plan, meaning the actual process that we will use to develop the plan, I want to devote a chapter to each of the strategic planning approach phases I've outlined in the strategic planning model (SPM). Let's begin phase I to determine your baseline by considering where you are now.

The questions "Where are you now?," "What is your baseline?" and "Why do you exist?" are important ones because you must ask yourself if you did not exist how it would affect your market. How would it affect the environment in which your organization currently dwells? This question applies to all organizations: government, commercial, and nonprofit. You will answer these baseline questions by completing the following phase I tasks:

- ✓ Conducting an environment scan
- ✓ Analyzing the current mission, vision, and guiding principles (MVGP)
- ✓ Conducting a stakeholder analysis
- ✓ Conducting a strengths, weaknesses, opportunities, and threats (SWOT) analysis
- ✓ Conducting a gap analysis
- ✓ Developing the solution set/recommendations

Answering the baseline questions may seem complex; however, such is not the case. Conducting a baseline analysis is a methodical process that yields answers, some of which are good, some bad. Regardless, you will develop those answers into recommendations and then proceed to execute the solutions. Most organizations exist to fulfill a need or a gap in society. Your phase I analysis will determine the viability of that need and the gaps or deficits associated with filling the need.

WHERE ARE YOU NOW?

- ✓ You've read and understood all the Let's Get Started tasks.
- ✓ You've conducted the initial team meeting
- ✓ You're confident you're ready to tackle phase I.
- ✓ You've updated your project plan and annotated your completed tasks.

You're probably thinking, "I have no idea how to accomplish all these tasks, nor do my teams have the expertise." Again, fear not. I will walk you through the process. If you have the financial resources, it is often advantageous to contract a facilitator to help achieve the results of these tasks. Or to reduce costs you may hire a contractor just to conduct your FGOS. In the event you do not have such financial resources, put those thoughts aside and use your field manual: *Strategic Planning: As Simple as A, B, C.*

I want to repeat myself to make sure you understand what you're doing. I am going to discuss all the phase I tasks outlined on the previous page. These same tasks also are

> *TARGET:*
> *We are now discussing phase I of the strategic planning approach (the Approach) and column A of the strategic planning model (SPM).*

shown in column A of the SPM. Once we have discussed all the tasks for both phases I and II, you will conduct a focus group offsite where you will actually complete the tasks, analyze the results, and determine your way ahead with key stakeholders within your organization. But first, I want you to work on these tasks with your team. To get from point A to point B, you must know where point A is. By conducting the phase I tasks you will ascertain where point A is within your organization. As with most projects, you must develop a baseline. A firm grasp of the past is also an important foundation for planning for the future. So let's look at the present and the past. What should you assess? It's rather simple: assess your organization and everything it touches. Assess the internal and external forces that act upon its growth, survival, and relevance. Earlier, in the Preface (Figure 1, Strategic bridge), I displayed an illustration of what you are going to achieve—your vision of the future state. You are moving from the current state to the future state. But first, you must understand your current state.

In Figure 1 are two land masses divided by a gorge. The near side of the land mass represents where you are today (the current, or as-is, state); the far side represents where you want to go (the future, or to-be, state). The bridge that spans the two sides depicts the method you will use to get there. Therefore, as I discussed, phase I really is assessing your as-is state. I urge you not to forgo this phase. In it you will discover facts you did not know and assessments you can include but should not

> *ADVICE:*
> *Setting boundaries is essential for preventing wasted time and energy on matters the customer does not need or want or that the organization does not want to deliver.*

disregard in your strategic plan. As you navigate through phase I, I want you to avoid naive projections based on past trends; rather, find the turning points in the trends. They will serve as critical elements of your strategic plan. Don't fall into the "that's the way we've always done it" syndrome. It's a trap that will keep you in the past.

Conduct an environmental scan

Organizations scan their environment in order to understand changing external forces so that they may develop operative responses that will secure or improve their situation in the future. In order to conduct your gap analysis and a thorough

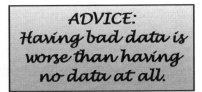

ADVICE: Having bad data is worse than having no data at all.

environmental scan, you must collect information and data. You must examine several aspects of the organization in order to acquire the necessary data for your analysis. Brown and Weiner (1985) defined environmental scanning as "a kind of radar to scan the world, systematically signaling the new, the unexpected, the major, and the minor" (page ix). Aguilar (1967), in his study of the information-gathering practices of managers, defined scanning as the systematic collection of external information in order to: (1) lessen the randomness of information flowing into the organization, and (2) provide early warning for managers of changing external conditions.

Fahey and Narayanan (1986) suggest that an effective environmental scanning program should enable decision makers to understand current and potential changes taking place in their institutions' external environments. According to these experts, environmental scanning consists of combining internal analysis with external analysis. The first step in conducting an environmental scan is to decide which level of scanning commitment is best for your organization. I want you to address the immediate need for information about your organization's internal and external environment. One proven method you should use for scanning the environment is to conduct surveys and submit questionnaires.

The internal and external environmental scan looks at identifying the strengths and weaknesses of your organization. Strategic planning requires that an organization take time out to seriously examine how it scans environments that directly affect its future and how it processes and uses the information obtained. For example, the scan should obtain information on customer satisfaction, marketing performance, capital resources, innovation, internal systems, management functionality, organizational culture, and human resources, among other organizational aspects. This examination is an unceasing process, a loop. There is no single point in the planning sequence at which environmental scanning ends. In that sense, it is a continuous aspect of the planning process. Setting boundaries is essential for preventing wasted time and energy in the pursuit of results customers do not need or want or those the organization does not want to deliver. In conducting an environmental scan for an organization, usually boundaries, authority, and responsibility are well defined; it is thus easier to explore those boundaries, lines of authority, and responsibilities to determine the impact on those employed by the organization. Unfortunately, when the boundaries are not well defined, the environmental scan becomes more complicated as you will have to solidify blurred lines of authority.

> *RECOMMENDATION: Obtain input from customers during the strategic planning process. (For example, does the customer need hardware or software?) It is my recommendation, however, that you not include customers on your planning team. The teams should be neutral and internal to your organization.*

Internal environmental scan

First, you'll examine the internal environment of the organization and complete the tasks identified at the beginning of the chapter. Effective analysis of an organization's internal environment requires:

- ✓ Fostering an organizational setting in which experimentation and learning are expected and promoted
- ✓ Using a global mind-set
- ✓ Thinking of the organization as a collection of heterogeneous resources and capabilities that can be used to achieve creative and exclusive market position

Among the factors to be considered as part of the internal organizational environment are changes in the structure of the organization, in the structure, strategy, systems, processes, and people of the organization, and the organization's strengths and weaknesses. See Figure 1–1, Internal Environment. In addition, the internal environment includes the many structures and systems that are used for day-to-day planning and control within the organization, such as inventory control, product distribution, quality control, and services provided, all of which overlap and interrelate.

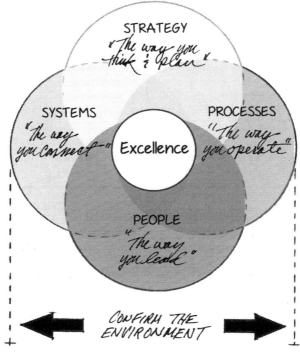

Figure 1–1. Internal environment

Your knowledge of the organizational structure and its horizontal and vertical interactions will assist you in discussions and decisions throughout the planning process and in particular throughout the *determine the baseline* phase.

Before you get started on conducting your internal environment scan, I want you to ensure that you have a full understanding of your organization's structure. By this I mean that you are able graphically to depict the chain of command or the chain of concern within the organization. This chain is often illustrated by an organizational chart or diagram. You must know who is at the top; the functional divisions, departments, and branches below; and the subsets within those divisions, departments, and branches. It is also advantageous to know the relationship among these functional areas within the organization. For example, how does the information-technology division interact and interface with and support the other functional divisions (such as operations) within the organization?

I also want you to be cognizant of your organizational type. For example, is it a functional organization, a matrix organization, or a blend to form a composite organization? Most organizations are functional. According to *A Guide to the Project Management Body of Knowledge (PMBOK Guide)*, functional organizations consist of a hierarchical structure where each employee has one clearly designated supervisor. In such a structure, staff members are grouped by specialties such as operations, marketing, human resources, resource management, and the like. Specialties may be further subdivided into research and development, production, and acquisition functions. Each specialty area or department in a functional organization does its work independent of other departments. Thus, each department is "functional." See Figure 1–2, Functional Organization Structure.

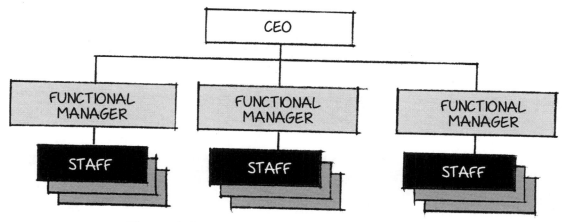

Figure 1–2. Functional organization structure

Matrix organizations have both functional and project-oriented characteristics. Weak-matrix organizations retain many of the characteristics of a functional organization, in which the project manager is more of a coordinator or expediter than a true project manager. Later in the book I will discuss the importance of project management and action plan project manager (APPM) responsibilities. Strong-matrix organizations have many of their projects linked to the organization and often have full-time project managers with considerable authority and a full-time administrative staff. While all matrix organizations recognize the need for a project manager, they do not provide him or her with full authority over the project and project funding. See Figure 1–3, Matrix organization.

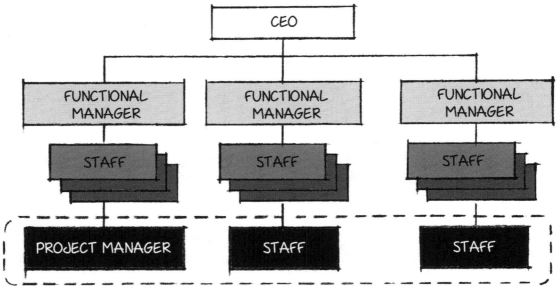

Figure 1–3. Matrix organization

Many organizations encompass all these structures at various levels and are known as composite organizations. For example, even a functional organization may create a special team to handle a critical project. Such a team may include full-time staff from different functional departments, may develop its own set of operating procedures, and may operate outside the standard, formal reporting structure. See Figure 1–4, Composite organization.

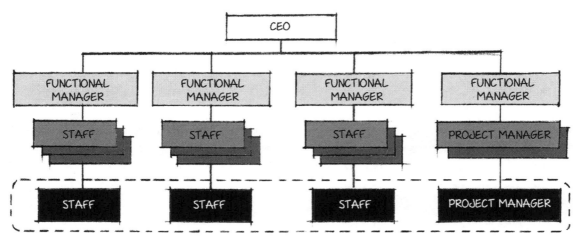

Figure 1–4. Composite organization

In summary, you should know the type, boundaries, authority, and entities within your organization. The more clearly you define them, the easier it will be to conduct an environmental scan and develop your implementation plan.

Exercise #1: Organizational Structure

Print out my graphic or create your own of your organizational structure. Study the lines of authority. Ascertain your organization's type. Then make a list of the functional areas that are critical to the organization's mission. Do you have adequate representation in the SPC? Are your functional areas geographically dispersed? Will the SPC include virtual team members? If you do not understand any part of the organizational structure, do some research and determine its connection to the strategic plan. In addition, ensure that the CPT has a strong understanding of the organization and its internal and external linkages.

Analyze the mission, vision, and guiding principles (MVGP)

Your next task is to conduct an analysis of the current organization mission, vision, and guiding principles (MVGP). The MVGP guides how your executives, managers, and employees behave in the present and the future. In setting an agenda for creating mission, vision, and guiding principles, you will focus on:

- ✓ Defining mission, vision, and guiding principles
- ✓ Reviewing the mission statement (revising as necessary)
- ✓ Reviewing the vision statement (revising as necessary)
- ✓ Reviewing the guiding principles (revising as necessary)

Although mission, vision, and guiding principles statements are often grouped together, each contributes uniquely to the organization in helping it execute the strategy. It is extremely productive for the strategic planning teams to hold a brainstorming session to analyze the MVGP. The agenda for the session will depend on the group's internal working relationships, how long the members have been with the organization, and how much each member knows about the full spectrum of the organization's activities. Most individuals will carry out Abraham Maslow's law of the instrument: "I suppose it is tempting," he famously said, "if the only tool you have is a hammer, to treat everything as if it were a nail." Take note, however, that overreliance on a familiar tool is not good behavior in group sessions. We will discuss brainstorming and other focus group techniques later in the chapter and in appendix H. First, let's take a look at the mission, vision, and guiding principles of your organization.

Developing your mission statement

The mission statement must be a concise and direct declaration of the reasons for your organization's existence. It must also specify what sets your organization apart from its competition and other similar organizations. The mission does not need updating unless your organization undergoes a major change or reconfiguration. For example, customer shifts, product change or expansion, or operational restructuring may necessitate a change in mission. In governmental organizations, the mission seldom changes because most missions are mandated by laws and regulations.

A mission statement gives the organization a framework for devising the services, products, and programs it will offer its customers in fulfillment of that mission. In this step, I will give you the tools for creating or revising your mission statement. As you develop specific tactics and techniques in crafting a strategy, the mission statement actually delivers what the organization needs. It's the vision driver that powers everything your organization does.

The mission statement:

- ✓ Captures the essence of why the organization exists—what it is and what it does
- ✓ Explains the basic needs the organization fulfills
- ✓ Expresses the core values of the organization
- ✓ Is concise, brief, and to the point
- ✓ Focuses on one common purpose
- ✓ Conveys the nature of the organization and its role that differentiates it from other organizations
- ✓ Is fixed or directed to a specific outcome

The mission statement should be formulated to answer four or five questions: what, who, how, and why, and, seldom, when.

What function or functions does the organization perform for its customers? That is, what needs or gaps is the organization attempting to fill? Be aware of marketing myopia—organizational nearsightedness that defines "what" in terms of the products or services the organization provides rather than in terms of customers' needs. Successful organizations try to identify value-satisfying products and services that meet the needs of their customers and include these considerations in their mission formulation. In addition to describing the functions the organization performs, "what" defines the qualities or attributes of the organization that set it apart from its competitors.

Who is your organization's customer base? Is it a specific demographic group? Is it a group involved in a specific activity, such as training or technology? This aspect of mission formulation identifies the segment of the market the organization is attempting to serve. For example, the customer base for government organizations is the taxpayers.

Why does your organization exist? What is its value for its customers, its stakeholders, and its community? Why does your organization perform the functions it does? "Why" is an important question for all organizations—for-profit, not-for-profit, and governmental.

How does the organization carry out its tasks? This question addresses how the organization attempts to achieve its goals. For example, what technologies will be used by the organization to meet the needs identified by its customer base? "How" may involve a marketing strategy, such as becoming the low-cost producer or providing the most innovative or reliable products; it may involve a distribution strategy, such as providing real-time cargo tracking, adding local distribution centers, or offering technology-repair services through computers; it may involve direct-mail marketing, door-to-door selling, or telemarketing. The question to consider is how the organization is, or will be, different from the pack. Its distinctiveness may be a function of its market niche as, for example, would be a charitable organization focused on animals.

> *EXTRA:*
>
> *As a question, When is often used in military operational mission statements. Such statements are concise and focus on one event. For example: the 3rd Infantry Battalion (Who) will attack in force (How) no later than 15100013 (military date/time grouping) (When) in order to secure objective Bravo (What) for the follow-on phase of the operation (Why). For your purposes, (When) will not be a focus of your mission statement. However, you may find a need for it at the operational and tactical levels of your organization.*

In addition, the mission statement should be well known to all members of the organization and understood by all.

Let's dissect the mission statement for Advance Auto Parts. Their mission statement reads: *It is the mission of Advance Auto Parts to provide personal-vehicle owners and enthusiasts with vehicle-related products and knowledge that fulfill their wants and needs at the right price. Our friendly, knowledgeable, and professional staff will help inspire, educate, and problem-solve for our customers.*

W*hat*: provide vehicle-related products and knowledge
W*ho*: vehicle owners and enthusiasts
W*hy*: fulfill the customer's wants and needs
How: to inspire, educate, and problem-solve for customers

The following are some other excellent mission statements:

- ✓ AGCO: Profitable growth through superior customer service, innovation, quality, and commitment.
- ✓ Bristol-Myers Squibb: To discover, develop, and deliver innovative medicines that help patients prevail over serious diseases.
- ✓ ConocoPhillips: To use our pioneering spirit to responsibly deliver energy to the world.
- ✓ The Dow Chemical Company: To constantly improve what is essential to human progress by mastering science and technology.
- ✓ The Mutual of Omaha Companies: To build a corporate culture that respects and values the unique strengths and cultural differences of our associates, customers, and community.

Developing the vision (bringing it into focus)

Envisioning is the process by which you develop a vision or dream of a future state for your organization that is so sufficiently clear and powerfully evident as to stimulate and sustain the actions necessary for that vision to become

> *"Vision is the art of seeing what is invisible to others."*
> *(Jonathan Swift)*

reality. Vision, in other words, is nothing less than an attempt to bring the organization into focus. Once envisioned, the focus is then translated into a declaration known as the vision statement.

Given the critical role envisioning plays in the planning process, you may be wondering exactly how this envisioning occurs. Envisioning can appear in a number of places in the process. Sometimes an individual—often the CEO—or a group of individuals develops such a vision, one that stems from a desire on the part of that individual or group with an interest in strategic planning to develop a process to

> *Envisioning is a creative act. Some of the current literature on leadership suggests that vision should emerge fully developed from the head of the leader, typically after a pilgrimage to a mountaintop.*

share and implement that vision. It should be noted, however, that the final decision on the vision is the responsibility of the CEO or the overall leader of the organization. In a military organization that individual would be the commanding officer; in a commercial company, the CEO; in government it would be the director of the given agency. For example, the commissioner of the Food and Drug Administration (FDA) would be the driving force in setting the vision for the FDA. It is his or her vision of where to take the agency. As noted before, that person can certainly solicit input from small groups and have discussions on what is best for the organization and what the vision should be for the next five to ten years. Ultimately, though, the responsibility for the final vision statement rests in the leader's hands.

The vision statement tends to remain relevant for only three to five years. Even so, you're still looking five to ten years into the future. The statement describes where the organization is going (the to-be state)—how the future is imagined—and tends to be more idealistic and inspirational than does the mission statement. The environment, both external and internal, is continually changing, so, therefore, the vision statement should adapt and adjust to those changes. In several organizations where I've helped shape the vision and guiding principles statements, the end products were formed in select, small groups, usually about three to five key leaders. In one case the group consisted of the CEO, the vice president, the second vice president, and me, as the strategy advisor. We met in a conference room and brainstormed ideas until we arrived at the vision. The CEO wanted to drive the process but with input and guidance from an inner circle. This is just one approach, and depending on the culture of your organization, you may want to consider others.

In detail, this is how that small group developed the vision. First, we examined and discussed the essential requirements that the organization felt it must fulfill. For example, we obviously had to execute the organization's mission. But the underlying questions were: Where did we want the organization to be in the next five to ten years? What did we want the organization to look like? And what culture did we want in the future? At the same time we developed a tagline that embodied what the organization stood for. After much discussion, we decided on: Responsive, Reliable, and Relentless. This earned favor because it focused on the organization's customers. When customers spoke of the organization, we wanted them to say that it was Responsive to their needs, was Reliable, and would be Relentless in pursuing every avenue to ensure that their requirements were met and delivered in the right place at the right time and in line with their expectations. So, based on those principles, we could say that the organization was world class in providing responsive, reliable, and relentless service to its customer base. Next, we produced two vision statements: "Synchronize and develop unrivaled, full-spectrum medical solutions" and "Provide the best-value, end-to-end medical solutions anytime, anyplace, and on time." Of the two statements, the latter one was the runner-up. Finally, we considered the question of how we would achieve this vision. I will discuss this in later chapters.

An organization's vision describes what the organization should look like as it successfully implements strategies, fulfills its mission, meets its mandates, creates significant and lasting public value, and in general achieves its full potential. In determining the vision, these questions should be answered:

> OPINION: Vision creates anxiety, but that's its purpose.

- ✓ What is the organization's mission?
- ✓ What is the organization's value to the public?

✓ What are the organization's basic philosophy and guiding principles?
✓ What are the organization's basic strengths?
✓ What objectives should the organization fulfill or create? How will fulfilling them make the world a better place?

To be effective, a vision statement should be:

✓ *Motivational.* It should keep everyone in the organization moving forward to attain the vision's goals.
✓ *Daring.* It should take an organization beyond its current capability.
✓ *Incorporated.* It should build on the organization's established core—its strengths, capabilities, history, niche, and other assets.
✓ *Future oriented*. It should paint a picture of what the organization will look like years ahead.
✓ *Ambitious*. It should give employees a sense of purpose, that they are an important part of the organization. After all, the people who actually do the work are the most important.
✓ *Simple.* It should be easy to interpret and understand.

There may be few vision statements more perfect than *Star Trek's* "To boldly go where no one has gone before," a simple but clear statement about what is to be achieved. Examples from other notable entities:

✓ National Multiple Sclerosis Society: A world free of M.S.
✓ Amazon: Our vision is to be earth's most customer-centric company; to build a place where people can come to find and discover anything they might want to buy online.
✓ Make-A-Wish Foundation: Our vision is that people everywhere will share the power of a wish.
✓ Kellogg Company: To enrich and delight the world through foods and brands that matter.
✓ Heinz: To be the world's premier food company, offering nutritious, superior-tasting foods to people everywhere.
✓ Alzheimer's Association: Our vision is a world without Alzheimer's.

Regardless of what it is called—a purpose, a goal, a vision, or a dream—the positive consequences of having a vision are clear. It provides members of the organization with a view of the future, a sense of direction, a

"Vision without action is a hallucination; action without vision is random." (Thomas Edison)

55

mobilization of energy, and a feeling of being part of something important. In a word, a vision is essential.

Resistance to envisioning

Owing to rules that set the boundaries of people's daily routines, there is fear of stepping out of the "status-quo box" because doing so disturbs those with a vested interest. You may encounter such negative distracters

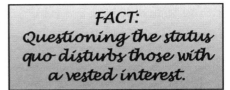

FACT:
Questioning the status quo disturbs those with a vested interest.

during the planning process. In my own work, I have learned that this resistance is particularly prevalent in government organizations, where I repeatedly encounter individuals and even coalitions that spawn tension and put in place obstacles to block a new vision. Regardless of the landscape of your organization (be it government or commercial), do not let naysayers sway your resolve. My advice is to listen and move on. Utilize one of my top-ten staff rules: "Always nod your head in approval." What's of critical importance is that if you do not create a vision, your vision of the future will be the same as your view of the past. And you do not want to be stuck in the past.

Developing the guiding principles

Before we explore the above topic, I want to discuss the differences, to the extent they exist, between values and guiding principles. Values constitute a value system of consistent principles used for the purpose of ethical and ideological integrity, a kind of moral code. They are rules that govern our ethical standards as we apply values in relation to our behavior and our interactions with our colleagues and clients as we go about the "business" of executing our mission. Values are a set of beliefs about good and bad, right and wrong, and about many other aspects of interacting within and outside of an organization. Values serve as a guiding force, providing a sense of direction to an organization. In the workplace, values work best when they are aligned with the organization's strategic vision.

Ralph S. Larsen, when he was CEO of Johnson & Johnson, offered this classic elucidation of his company's core values: "The core values we choose might be a competitive advantage, but that is not why we have them. We have them because they define for us what we stand for. We would hold them even if they become a competitive disadvantage." Larsen is saying that core values are the constants of the organization, that they drive the culture and remain part of it regardless of the existing environmental situation.

Guiding principles, although similar to values, can be described as rules or laws that are universal in nature. Such principles concern the overall behavior of an organization and how the organization interacts within its community and within the organizational environment. Guiding principles, in short, are "any principles or precepts that guide an organization throughout its life in all circumstances, irrespective of changes in its goals, strategies, type of work, or top management." Do you see the similarity between this definition and Ralph Larsen's? In reality, they both consider the same points.

Guiding principles can be seen as guidelines that drive behavior or a mind-set when executed as part of the strategic and operational plans that can lead to an organization's success. Some key elements of guiding principles include:

- ✓ Enduring, passionate, and distinctive core beliefs
- ✓ That which the organization does and stands for
- ✓ The follow-up of words by deeds
- ✓ The deeply held convictions, priorities, and underlying assumptions that influence attitudes and behaviors
- ✓ The importance of these to members of the organization

Both values and principles serve important roles in the birth, growth, and longevity of an organization while dealing with its environment, social issues, and global norms. Values are a set of beliefs about subjective traits, an ideal, while principles are universal laws and truths. Principles are an anchor for an organization when confronted by rough seas, while values allow the organization to move ahead with confidence as though in calm waters. Yes, there are some differences between values and guiding principles, but they are negligible. Throughout this book, therefore, I will use the term guiding principles rather than values as you work on developing the strategic plan.

An organization's guiding principles typically are organized and codified into a philosophy of operations that explains how the organization approaches its work, how its internal affairs are managed, and how it relates to its external environment, including its customers. This type of formal statement integrates the organization's principles into the way it does business. Some organizations have written or unwritten codes about how things are done, such as a formal statement of policy. For their part, these statements of policy or guiding principles identify the traits, behaviors, and qualities that typify an organization's actions. These principles should:

- ✓ Define how employees, managers, and executives behave
- ✓ Reflect the values of management, the board of directors and trustees, and any others, such as stakeholders, who ultimately decide the organization's actions
- ✓ Define the foundation of the organizational culture (how all members will "walk the talk")
- ✓ Drive organizational decisions

> *Values: commitment, service, integrity, collaboration.*
> *Guiding principles: respect, diversity, equity.*

As an example of what I mean, in the most recent strategic plan I worked on, my client and I created these guiding principles (note there are only five):

- ✓ Maximize effective support to the customer
- ✓ Provide a trained and ready organization
- ✓ Be efficient without sacrificing effectiveness
- ✓ Adopt an enterprise culture
- ✓ Take care of the health and welfare of the organization's people

Exercise #2: Assess the MVGP

As part of your internal environmental scan, together with your CPT and the SPC, review the organization's MVGP. This can be accomplished by scheduling a brainstorming session with the teams—first, the CPT alone and then the CPT and the SPC together. Note: CPT meetings and sessions often serve as preparation for other events such as meeting with the SPC, briefing the leadership, discussions with stakeholders, etc. Such meetings serve as a forum to ensure that planning details are in place before moving to the next level of

> *ADVICE:*
> *Send an information packet to all planning-team participants that includes relevant reading material from this book along with the briefing "slide deck" prior to conducting this exercise.*

action. Based on our previous discussion of the MVGP, you should extract key points to include in your brainstorming session presentation in order to provide background for the session itself.

Before taking the next step of analyzing the MVGP, read the pages on brainstorming in appendix H. This will provide valuable pointers for undertaking exercise #2 and for other group sessions you will host. Use a dry-erase board or chart paper to write down key ideas and recommendations. If you are acting as the facilitator for this session, have someone else do the note-taking on the board to speed up the process.

Your first task is to analyze the mission. Does it fit the characteristics and principles we discussed earlier? Is it still relevant? Does it need to be changed? As we discussed before, a change of mission takes place only rarely. More often it's deemed necessary to make only minor changes, which, if needed, you should not hesitate to make. I would recommend you post or show the current mission statement to the team members. Then begin the discussion to ensure that it incorporates all the principles of the mission statement we discussed earlier. Does it fit? Is it in sync with the discussion earlier in the chapter? Does it answer the what, who, why, and how (and maybe when) questions? Remember, anything you revise or change must be approved by the leadership. This will be done at the FGOS. I now want you to read the section on prioritization in chapter 2. This will help in conducting exercise #2 and other exercises.

Next, analyze the vision. Again, ask: Is it relevant? Does it need to be changed? Assuming that you want to develop a new vision or make changes to the vision statement, generate some discussion within the group and solicit recommendations for the new version. Of course, this discussion will also take place again at the FGOS with the key leaders of the organization present. At that time, you may want to present the recommendations that the planning team members developed. Again, review the previous material on developing a vision statement and share that knowledge with your brainstorming group.

The final step of the exercise is to dissect the existing, or develop new, guiding principles. Are the current ones relevant? Do you even have guiding principles? If not, develop some. This effort utilizes the same processes that you used with brainstorming the mission and vision.

Bear in mind that the point of this exercise is not to create the final MVGP but to come up with recommendations to present at the FGOS. For example, you may want to present three or four different vision statements and perhaps five or six guiding principles. The decision to finalize the MVGP belongs to the senior leaders of your organization. During the FGOS, you'll run a similar exercise, though on a smaller scale. However, it is your responsibility to ensure that viable options exist for leadership's consideration and discussion during the offsite.

Stakeholders

A stakeholder is any person, group, or organization that can place a claim on the organization's resources, production of output, or effect on internal structuring. Identifying stakeholders is a process of identifying all the people within the organization who are affected by the strategic plan and documenting the relevant information regarding their interest, involvement, and impact on strategic planning success. Stakeholders may also exert influence (positive or negative) on the devising and shaping of the plan's final outcome. Stakeholders may be at different levels within the organization and may possess different authority levels, or may be external with levels of influence or authority over the organization, or perhaps may even be the reason for your organization's very existence.

Key stakeholders:

- ✓ Are limited to those who will make significant contributions to the organization
- ✓ Should be people from different areas of the organization
- ✓ Must understand the organization's long-term strategy
- ✓ Must be dedicated to putting that strategy into place

For successful planning, it is critical to identify the stakeholders early in the process and to analyze their levels of interest, expectation, importance, and influence. A strategy can then be developed for each stakeholder, depending on the degree and timing of his or her involvement, to maximize positive influences and mitigate potentially negative ones. Most strategic planning efforts usually include a large number of stakeholders. Since, as the team leader, your time is limited and must be used as efficiently as possible, stakeholders should be quickly classified according to their interests, influence, and involvement in the strategic planning process. The process for conducting this classification is called a stakeholder analysis. You should use the results of the analysis to determine who can assist you to ensure success and who may contribute to failure.

Take a hard look at your environmental scan. Who are the people who have influence on your planning process? The CEO, for example, will have significant influence on creating the vision. Therefore, the CEO is a key stakeholder. Another key stakeholder is your set of customers. You must know their priorities and needs. It should be noted, however, that understanding your customers and meeting their expectations will only result in success if your performance exceeds that of the competition.

Some important customer expectations include:

- ✓ Product: What is it that you supply? Does the customer need cars or just tires?
- ✓ Process: How do you deal with the customer? Where and what is the non-"value-added" time in the process?
- ✓ People: What is the quality of service offered by those dealing with the customer?
- ✓ Price: Is the cost to the customer reasonable?

Stakeholder analysis

According to *PMBOK Guide,* a stakeholder analysis is the technique used to systematically gather and analyze quantitative and qualitative data and information to determine whose interests should be taken into account throughout the strategic planning process. The analysis identifies the interests, expectations, and influence of stakeholders and relates them to the purpose of the strategic planning process. It also helps identify stakeholder relationships that can be leveraged to build coalitions and potential

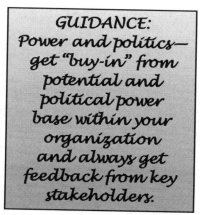

GUIDANCE: Power and politics— get "buy-in" from potential and political power base within your organization and always get feedback from key stakeholders.

partnerships to increase the probability of planning success. A stakeholder analysis is the means of identifying an organization's internal and external stakeholders and analyzing their impact on the organization. An analysis asks such questions as: How do stakeholders evaluate the organization? How do they influence the organization? What does the organization need from them? And how important, in general, are they to the organization? A stakeholder analysis is particularly useful in providing information about the political situation facing the organization, which is an important reason why, as part of your assessment, you must identify the stakeholders within your organizational environment (both internally and externally).

You're now aware that you have to identify and closely analyze stakeholders. Yet how do you know exactly who the stakeholders are? Let's leave this chapter now and go to appendix I, Stakeholder Analysis. This will provide greater detail and answer your questions about all facets of what it means to be a stakeholder as well as instructions on completing exercise #3 below. Understanding your stakeholders and meeting their expectations will only improve your chances of planning success.

Exercise #3: Stakeholder analysis, parts 1 and 2

Before we begin, conduct the stakeholder analysis exercise in appendix I. You may choose to share the results of the exercise with the FGOS. At a minimum, you should share the results with the strategic planning champion and, of course, with your teams.

Surveys

Surveys are an essential tool for research and data collection. Stakeholders know this. Thus, they will typically make more of an effort to help with a survey than they would to help with a sales call because the information can be used for their own

ACTION: Assess your organization's strategic thinking by polling your stakeholders.

edification. The purpose of a survey is to define and measure the quality of a product or service and to identify the gaps between minimum, desired, and perceived levels of the product or service. A survey also serves as an excellent data point for conducting an environmental scan and gathers information to assist in finding areas that need improvement. The key to any survey is to be found in its purpose. And obviously the purpose of a survey depends on what the survey is used for. I want you to conduct a survey to gather information/data from your stakeholders to help shape your organization's future and the construction of its strategic plan. Appendix J, Survey Information, provides more information about conducting surveys.

As mentioned earlier, your most important stakeholder is the customer. Customer input is critical in shaping your strategy and planning. It is imperative to know the customer's priorities and needs. A survey makes known to you the "voice of the customer." It does not matter whether yours is a product or service. Feedback from your key stakeholders, your customer(s), is critical.

Exercise #4: Conduct the survey

Develop a short survey to gauge your key stakeholders' mind-set, being sure to include some noncustomer participants in the survey pool. They can be personnel within the organization or external personnel who you feel can provide constructive feedback, or both. Study the environmental concentric-circles graphic (Figure 1–6, Concentric circles). Read the section on the external environmental scan to gain greater insight into developing your list of survey participants. Ask the questions: Who in this environment can provide feedback that is the most beneficial to the planning process and the future of the organization? Who can give clear, unbiased feedback on the as-is state of the organization? In completing this exercise you will develop your target population for the survey. The results of the survey will be briefed to the participants at the offsite.

Guiding principle questionnaire

Leaders and employees are led by certain guiding principles that describe an organization, both "as it is" and "as they want it to be." They want their decisions and actions to demonstrate these guiding principles. The fundamental vitality and strength of an organization lies in its people. Putting guiding principles into practice creates long-term benefits for stakeholders, clients, employees, suppliers, friends, and the communities in which they and the organization operate. The guiding principle questionnaire (appendix L) is a method to measure both the satisfaction and the importance of your customers to your guiding principles. With this questionnaire you may discover, say, that customers are satisfied with your marketing but do not consider it important, a sign that you may be spending too much money on it. The questionaire should begin with an opening paragraph that describes its purpose and asks questions on the topics below:

- ✓ Dedication
- ✓ Passion

- ✓ Integrity
- ✓ Innovation and creativity
- ✓ Reliability and accountability
- ✓ Financial responsibility
- ✓ Excellence
- ✓ Empowerment
- ✓ Customer service

Exercise #5: Conduct guiding principle questionnaire

Distribute the guiding principle questionnaire to key stakeholders, specific employees, and key individuals in the organization's internal and external environment. In the way that you developed the survey analysis, do the same for the guiding principle questionnaire. Just as with the survey results, the results of the questionnaire will be briefed to participants in the FGOS. Go to appendix L for a sample guiding principles questionnaire.

WHERE ARE YOU NOW?
- ✓ You've conducted the organizational structure exercise.
- ✓ You've conducted the MVGP exercise.
- ✓ You've conducted the stakeholder analysis.
- ✓ You've conducted the survey and its analysis.
- ✓ You've conducted the guiding principle questionnaire and its analysis.
- ✓ You've discussed the outcome of all the above actions with your teams and the SPC and have formulated a synopsis of "what does all this information mean?"
- ✓ You're ready to go to your project plan, check off all the completed tasks, and update the plan as necessary.

Organizational culture

One of the most important building blocks for a highly successful organization and an extraordinary workplace is "organizational culture." Organizational culture is a set of shared beliefs, truths, assumptions, and guiding principles that operate in organizations. Essentially, it is how people behave when no one is looking. An organization's assumptions about the way the world works, its members' individual values, the values of the organization as a whole, and its philosophy of operations all come together to produce the organization's culture, which in turn ties people of the organization together and gives meaning to the purpose of their work. At the heart of the organization's culture are its lineage, rites, rituals, and ceremonies, which help to define the organization's expectations for employees.

Organizational culture is everywhere. It directly affects what happens or does not happen within an organization or any group. Many scholars believe that organizational culture is the primary determinant of that which separates the "champion" from the "runner-up" organization. In their classic book *In Search of Excellence* (1982, 75–76),

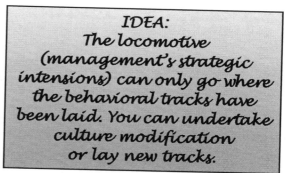

IDEA:
The locomotive (management's strategic intensions) can only go where the behavioral tracks have been laid. You can undertake culture modification or lay new tracks.

Peters and Waterman claim that a strong and consistent organizational culture is of paramount importance if the organization wants to be successful. It should help the organization operate in a better and more effective way, and its employees should display a high level of involvement and loyalty. A definition of organizational culture I particularly like is that it's a social system based on a central set of beliefs and values or guiding principles. An organization's culture provides the social context in which the organization performs its work. It is imperative for you, and your team, to ascertain and understand your organization's culture.

Early models developed by Deal and Kennedy (1982) proposed that one of the key drivers for the success or failure of an organization is corporate culture. By examining cultural elements across organizations, the authors identified distinct types of culture and marketplace factors that in turn influence these distinct types of cultures. The elements are:

✓ The degree of risk associated with a company's key activities
✓ The speed at which companies learn whether their actions and strategies are successful

Deal and Kennedy believe that the risk involved in making a poor decision and the time it takes to find out whether a decision is the right one are reflective of an organization's culture. Both of these dynamics have a bearing on how cultural elements develop and influence an organization's employees. The researchers present the factors in a 2 x 2 matrix that identifies four culture types, as shown in Figure 1–5, Deal and Kennedy 2 x 2 Matrix and Cultural Model. The following are their four generic organization cultures.

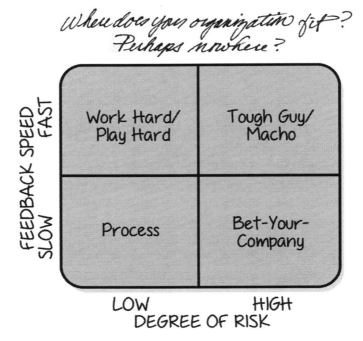

Figure 1–5. Deal and Kennedy 2 x 2 Matrix and Cultural Model

Tough Guy/Macho. This culture includes individualists who enjoy risk and who get quick feedback on their decisions. An all-or-nothing culture, it is where successful employees are the ones who enjoy excitement and work very hard to be stars. The entertainment industry and advertising are great examples of this culture type. Teamwork is not highly valued in this culture, and it's a difficult environment for people who blossom slowly. These factors produce a higher turnover, which impedes efforts to build cohesiveness. Thus, individualism prevails.

Work Hard/Play Hard. This culture includes the environment of sales. Employees themselves take few risks, but the feedback on how well they are performing is almost immediate. Employees in this culture have to maintain high levels of energy and stay upbeat. Stars in such cultures are high-volume salespeople. In this culture one person alone cannot make the organization. Everyone knows it is a team effort and thus is driven to excel.

Bet-Your-Company. Here, the culture is one in which decisions are high risk, but employees may wait years before they know whether their actions have actually paid off. Technology companies are an obvious example of this culture, as are oil and gas companies and organizations in other large, capital-intensive industries. Because the need to make the right decision is so great, the cultural elements evolve such that values are long-term focused, and there is a collective belief in the need to plan, prepare, and perform due diligence at all stages of decision making.

Process. In this culture, feedback is slow, and the risks are low. Large retailers, insurance companies, and government organizations are typically in this group. No single transaction has much impact on the organization's success, and it takes years to find out whether a decision was good or bad. Because of the lack of immediate feedback, employees find it very difficult to measure what they do, so they focus instead on how they do things. Technical excellence is often valued here, and employees will pay attention to getting the process and the details right without necessarily measuring the actual outcome.

An alternative model is offered by Harrison and Stokes (1992); it also involves four generic types of organizational cultures. They are:

The Power Culture. This culture is based on the assumption that inequality of resources is a naturally occurring phenomenon; that is, life is a zero–sum game with clear-cut winners and losers. A strongly managed culture diffuses these inequalities and maintains the overall balance of the system. Badly managed power cultures, on the other hand, are ruled by fear, with power abused for personal advantage for the leaders and their followers, often with much political intrigue and infighting.

The Role Culture. The role culture substitutes rationally derived structures and systems for naked power. Role cultures provide stability, justice, and efficiency. The basic assumption is that structured work is best. Rules, procedures, and job descriptions are the main components. Organizations with such culture can be successful in a measured environment because they are slow to react and difficult to change.

The Achievement Culture. The basic assumption of the achievement culture is that people want to make meaningful contributions in their work and to society and enjoy their interaction with both customers and coworkers. The main strategic objective of this culture is to bring the right people together in order to achieve organizational goals.

The Support Culture. The support culture's basic assumption is that mutual trust and support must be primarily based on relationships among the people in the organization. People must be valued as human beings, not just contributors to work or occupiers of organizational roles.

Effects of culture and planning

Organizational culture's impact on both the process of planning and the results of the strategic plan is considerable. This impact can be either direct or indirect, but in either case it needs to be both understood and managed for the planning process to be successful—that is, that a viable plan emerges from the planning process.

First, and perhaps most important, there's the question of whether the culture even allows the organization to consider engaging in strategic planning. Second, the influence of the corporate culture on the planning process relates to the practicality of the process. Organizations with a culture that ordinarily avoids confronting harsh realities will find a need for objective soul searching in the assessment phase and gap analysis of the process difficult, if not impossible, to achieve. Third, an organization with extensive experience in dealing with its environment will likely have preconceived notions about its mission—for example, what it is, how it will be achieved, and what its operational goals are. Fourth, in terms of internal processes, organizations will have established procedures about how dissemination of the strategic plan should or should not be included in the planning process and how to reward or punish employees for participation or nonparticipation.

I want you and your teams to discuss the section on organizational culture. It's up to you to design a planning process and use techniques that tap into cultural characteristics that advance planning and rein in those who would hinder it. This approach will result in strategies and actions that won't be zapped in their implementation by a culture that is deep-seated and counterproductive, a culture, in other words, that is difficult to overcome. However, if this counterproductive condition exists in your organization, include this as a gap (a goal) to close in your strategic plan.

Exercise #6: Organizational Culture

The purpose of this exercise is to get a better understanding of your organizational culture. Measurement of your culture is critical because culture affects everything you do strategically. You must measure culture, but how? First, go over with your teams the Deal and Kennedy 2 x 2 Matrix. Review their four cultural types and discuss where your organization fits into the model. Second, review Harrison and Stokes's four types of organizational culture. Discuss with your teams where you think your organization fits there. Third, use the results of your discussion to help formulate questions about the guiding principles questionnaire and survey results to determine their implications for your organizational culture. Do the survey and questionnaire give the sense that the culture is not conducive to the organization's goals and mission? Do the survey and questionnaire link your organization to any of the cultural models discussed earlier? Finally, discuss the questions below. Based on the answers to the questions and your discussions about Deal and Kennedy and Harrison and Stokes, paint an overall picture of your organization's culture. As this will be a discussion topic during the FGOS, make sure your administrative assistant takes copious notes throughout the exercise.

The questions to be discussed:

- ✓ Do all of the organization's members have a clear understanding of the mission and purpose of the organization and their roles and responsibilities in achieving organizational goals?
- ✓ What balance does the organization strike, particularly in its reward systems, between future-oriented behaviors, such as planning and long-term investment, and short-term planning and projects?
- ✓ What type of diversity is evident within the organization, whether it's people, environments, opinions, clothing styles, etc.?
- ✓ What "control" mechanisms are used within the organization and are they "tight" (e.g., formal rules with small or zero tolerance) or "loose" (free to do what you want)?
- ✓ What types of "manners" do employees show to "outsiders"? (And not just to people outside the organization; it could be people outside their department or work group but still inside the organization.)
- ✓ How do people treat each other? Is respect demonstrated among coworkers?

- ✓ Is there a sense of emotional and interpersonal openness inside the organization?
- ✓ Are the organization's physical surroundings made available to employees?
- ✓ What styles are used by organizational members for internal and external communications (e.g., assertive/aggressive versus cordial/ tender), and how easy is it for outsiders and newcomers to be admitted and integrated into the organization? (Are there cliques?)
- ✓ Do organization members demonstrate an understanding of the broader business, or are they only given insight into their own small part of the operation? Do they have information they need from across the organization?
- ✓ Is the organization pragmatic (i.e., flexible and adaptable) in dealing with its external environment, particularly its customers (i.e., does the organization have a "customer orientation"), or is the approach more rigid?
- ✓ What decision-making style is evident? Do multiple people seem to share perspectives and participate, or does decision making seem more centralized?
- ✓ Are people fearful—of bosses, competitors, expectations, failure, something else?
- ✓ What are the expectations of organizational members regarding the distribution of power and status within the organization, as well as member opportunities to participate in decision making regarding organizational goals and objectives?
- ✓ What is small talk like before, during, and after meetings? How much bad-mouthing of others goes on when someone leaves the room or isn't present?

External environmental scan

The primary method you will use to examine your external environment is the strengths, weaknesses, opportunities, and threats (SWOT) analysis. In order to conduct the SWOT analysis, you must ascertain your markets as well as the competition and the environment. Understanding your environment or your business landscape is essential. Think of your landscape as a series of concentric circles where your organization is at the center, and the external environment is in the outer rings. Figure 1–6, Concentric circles, depicts an organization's external environment or landscape.

The Macro Environment

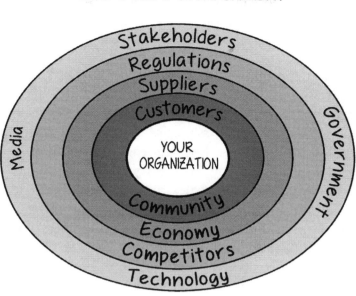

Figure 1–6. Concentric circles

Before moving forward, you must know your landscape, meaning you must have a deep understanding of it, both within and outside of your organization. Obviously, some organizations are more complex than others. Yet due diligence is required no matter the size and scope of your environment. Do not skimp on this! If so, it may lead you onto a path that steers you away from customer satisfaction and profitability.

The center circle of Figure 1–6 represents your organization; the outer rings represent customers, competitors, regulations, technological change, the economy, and other forces that affect your organization. The center circle encompasses all the aspects of your internal organization discussed earlier in the chapter. You must understand that your business environment is dynamic, that it will change over time. These changes will ultimately affect operations, personnel, and culture. For example, a federal regulation may force the organization to implement restrictions that lower production. This affects your bottom line and, more important, your customers. It is extremely important to understand the needs of the customer and how those needs will affect your organization, not just today but in the future.

The economy and technological developments, both political and societal, have an impact on almost all organizations but in different ways and to different degrees. Organizations that monitor societal changes and integrate such changes and their impacts into the planning process obviously have a competitive advantage. This is especially true given today's globalization and social-media boom.

Among the factors to be considered as part of the environmental scan are changes in the structure of the industry, how the industry is financed, the degree of governmental overreach in the industry, the processes and typical products used in the industry, the industry's current state of outsourcing, the current industry innovations, and the marketing strategies employed in the overall industry environment. To clarify the nature and meaning of the external environment, mandates may be imposed that the organization is required to meet. Mandates may be expressed formally or informally and should prescribe what must or ought to be done under the organization's current policies and procedures under federal, state, and local laws, codes, and regulations. Mandates may come to life in public election results, internal culture and belief systems, or in community or key stakeholders' expectations.

Some organizations have support and service responsibilities as well as regulatory oversight responsibilities. While such organizations sometimes use mandates to their advantage, the proper balance between service and support on the one hand and control and enforcement on the other is one that should remain paramount. My experience is that usually one aspect of such responsibility dominates the organization's culture, and so one type of mandate gets most of the attention, which may or may not be in either the organization's or the public's best interest.

Exercise #7: Environmental scan, parts 1 and 2

Part 1 (Internal scan): On a dry-erase board or a large sheet of butcher paper, replicate Figure 1–1, Internal environment. Discuss the four components of the internal organizational environment. Ask questions such as:

- ✓ What are the ways in which the organization thinks (*strategy*)?
- ✓ Do our communications and the way we interconnect *(systems)* result in effectiveness and efficiency? If not, why not?
- ✓ Is the way we operate *(processes)* simple and fluid?
- ✓ Are we learning and leading (people) to be relevant and successful? Do our people experience growth and job fulfillment?

After discussion, capture the key points that indicate a gap in your internal environment. These gaps will be used later to form a more detailed assessment of your internal environment.

Part 2 (External scan): Draw a series of circles as illustrated in Figure 1–6. Ask team members to provide ideas on forces that affect your external environment, both positive and negative. You may want to start the discussion by providing an example, such as a federal regulation. As team members provide recommendations, note them on the concentric circles. At the point where you believe there is sufficient input, discuss each of the recommendations to determine which ones should be eliminated and which kept. Ensure that you take extensive notes so that you can articulate each recommendation's impact on your organization. For example, if you cite federal regulations, you must be able to articulate precisely which federal regulations and how they affect the entire organization or even just a segment of it. Next, arrange in order which entities have the greatest impact on your organization. Place these in the circle closest to your organization and continue to rearrange the entities so that the ones with the greatest impact are the closest to the innermost circle (your organization). This will give you a series of concentric circles with an ordering of greatest to least impact on the organization. You should be able to link the impact of the external environment to the overall productivity and bottom line of the organization's MVGP. Again, the results of this exercise will be presented to participants in the offsite.

Conduct strengths, weaknesses, opportunities, and threats (SWOT) analysis

SWOT stands for strengths, weaknesses, opportunities, and threats. Conducting a SWOT analysis is a simple, frequently used strategy that can help to prepare or amend plans in problem solving and decision making. The SWOT analysis is an all-purpose technique and can be applied

> **ADVICE:**
> Use a SWOT analysis to identify opportunities. You want to build on strengths and reduce weaknesses. Focus on what you do best.

across diverse functions and activities, but it is particularly appropriate in the early stages of planning. Performing a SWOT analysis involves generating and recording the strengths, weaknesses, opportunities, and threats as they pertain to your organization. It is customary for the analysis to take account of both internal resources and capabilities (strengths and weakness) and factors external to the organization (opportunities and threats).

In addition to providing a framework for identifying and analyzing strengths, weaknesses, opportunities, and threats, a SWOT analysis can provide numerous other benefits, a few of which are listed below. A SWOT analysis can:

✓ Be an impetus for analyzing a situation and developing suitable strategies and tactics to attain a favorable outcome
✓ Provide a basis for assessing core capabilities and competences
✓ Provide evidence for, and a cultural key to, change
✓ Be a stimulus for participating in a group experience

As part of your baseline assessment, you will conduct a SWOT analysis. Appendix M (SWOT Analysis) provides a how-to method for conducting a SWOT analysis. By breaking down your internal environment into capabilities, resources, and processes, you can begin to assess your organization.

Exercise #8: SWOT analysis, parts 1, 2, 3, 4, and 5

Conduct the SWOT analysis exercise in appendix M. This exercise serves as a pilot for the SWOT analysis presentation you will conduct at the offsite. The results may differ when you solicit input at the offsite, but that is not an issue.

Conduct gap analysis

A gap analysis is a technique that organizations use to determine what steps need to be taken in order to move from their current state to their desired, future state. It is also called a need-gap analysis, needs analysis, and needs assessment. Gap analysis forces organizations to reflect on what they are and ask what they want to be. The approach you will take for your gap analysis is to utilize the SWOT principle.

In order to conduct your analysis and a thorough environmental scan, you must, as previously discussed, collect information and data. There are several facets of the organization you must examine in order to acquire the necessary data for your analysis. Thus far you have collected data from:

✓ The exercises you have completed
✓ Your internal and external environmental scan
✓ The SWOT analysis
✓ The stakeholder analysis
✓ The survey
✓ The guiding principle questionnaire

All information collected from the above list is essential for conducting your gap analysis.

The gap analysis consists of:

✓ Listing characteristic factors (such as attributes, competencies, performance levels) of the present situation ("as is")
✓ Listing factors needed to achieve future objectives ("to be")
✓ Highlighting gaps that need to be filled to move from the "as is" to the "to be"

Although there are often more challenging moments in drawing up the strategic plan, the gap analysis is typically the moment of truth, a moment that can cause distress to even the hardiest members of the planning team. It is necessary to identify the gaps between the current performance of the organization and the performance required for successful realization of the organization's strategic goals. Furthermore, the gap analysis requires the development of specific strategies to close each identified gap. In fact, if the gap analysis reveals no disconcerting discrepancies between the organization's future goals and its present performance, then the planning process was inadequate: the planning team simply did not reach far enough in its envisioning. See appendix M, Gap Analysis, for more information on gap analysis.

Exercise #9: Gap analysis exercise

Go to appendix M and complete the gap analysis exercise.

Develop the solution sets/recommendations

When you have identified all your findings, identify those you consider most important. You identify them by isolating specific variables that you think are important for the development of the planning strategy and then determine if there are any "second- and third-order effects," by which is meant that if you do something, then something else will occur. It's the "something else" that you want to discover. For example, if you give up a strong management program that emphasizes leadership, then you will not create a pool of strong leaders within your organization. Without strong leadership, the organization becomes dysfunctional—thus, a second- and third-order effect.

Conclusions should be in the context of your interpretations of important findings. What do the findings mean relative to the strategic plan? You may decide that before you interpret the meaning of a key finding, you need to sort the data differently. You may need to sort them by various demographic groups to determine if the findings are true across the organization, or if they pertain to just one or two groups. What's important is that you have all the relevant information in hand before drawing a conclusion.

Validating the findings determines if they are accurate, stable, and repeatable. Can you trust the numbers? Is the information being used as it was intended in the methodology, or have you altered the numerical findings so that they lead you to a mistaken conclusion? For example, if 85 percent of those responding to a survey indicate that they prefer taking tea with "some sugar," you can't claim findings that all respondents prefer tea with sugar.

Upon completion of your solution sets and recommendations, produce a short report on your findings. The report should be concise and to the point, two to three to pages (500 to 750 words) at most, to ensure widespread

> *CAUTION:*
> *Ignoring the assessment conclusions results in a flawed strategic plan.*

readership. The report may be distributed to key stakeholders, business partners, sponsors, members of the strategic planning group, and, if appropriate, participating customers. It is not recommended, however, that final findings be included until after the offsite convenes.

Leadership training: *Leadership must win internal and external support for the strategic plan.*

I want to leave the planning discussion for now and talk about leadership decision making. I've discovered in some organizations that leadership, in particular the CEO, is sometimes reluctant to "pull the trigger" and approve elements of the MVGP. In one organization where I worked, the

CEO kept postponing a decision on what the final vision statement should be. Obviously, this caused significant delays in moving forward with the strategic plan. In cases such as this, it is best to develop leadership training on strategic planning for the organization's key leaders. It is important to note that for organizations to remain competitive, they must view change as inevitable. Thus, the need for leaders, managers, and executives to effectively spearhead change, inspire esprit de corps, and overcome obstacles to ensure that undisruptive change occurs, which is why, in order to motivate leadership to make decisions on change, leadership training may be necessary.

Strategic decisions are, almost by definition, nonroutine. They involve both the art of leadership and the science of management. Routine decisions are based on how to efficiently manage resources according to established procedures and clearly manifest objectives as part of the technical work of management. Such decisions are normally within the purview of supervisors and middle-level managers possessing the authority and responsibility to take action. These decisions affect the day-to-day operation of the organization. Nonroutine decisions, on the other hand, require what Harvard professor Ron Heifetz refers to as "adaptive work," in which senior leadership must consider the broader implications of the situation, take an active role in defining the problem, creatively explore potential solutions, and apply judgments as to what should be done. Sometimes such leadership requires training to realize and implement this work.

Leadership training should focus first on helping participants identify their own leadership styles and then match the styles to the needs of their employees. Participants should also be taught the specific leadership skills needed to work with and influence others, envision the future of the organization, and drive policies to attain the vision more effectively. The United States Army War College defines strategic leadership as the process of "influencing the organizational culture, allocating resources, directing through policy and directive, and building consensus within a volatile, uncertain, complex, and ambiguous global environment that is marked by opportunities and threats." Excellent leaders possess this skill.

At a minimum, leadership training should focus on the following:

✓ How can you be more efficient as a leader and manager armed with greater self-awareness and a personal leadership development plan?

- ✓ How can you increase your impact on personnel to accept organizational norms?
- ✓ How can you determine where you want to take the organization?
- ✓ How can you build excitement, commitment, and passion in your people?
- ✓ How can you build an organization with vision and purpose?
- ✓ How can you develop the skills needed to meet the challenges of leadership, organizational change, and problem solving?

WHERE ARE YOU NOW?
- ✓ *You've conducted all chapter 1 exercises.*
- ✓ *You've developed proposed solution sets to your gap analysis.*
- ✓ *You have a good sense of your organizational baseline—the as-is state.*
- ✓ *You've gone to your project plan, checked off all the completed tasks, and updated the plan as necessary.*

Leadership training is normally conducted by hiring a consultant to offer his or her expertise to your organization's people. Such training, if necessary, is something you should conduct early in the strategic planning process, such as early in phase I, well before the offsite. Be aware that you and your organization cannot really move forward without an approved MVGP. Therefore, leadership training is a venue to "nudge" leadership decision making as it relates to the MVGP. Given that leadership and, in particular, the CEO, routinely face significant time constraints, this training should be limited to between four and eight hours in length.

Chapter 2
Determine the Azimuth

Where are you going? What is your future state?

In chapter 2, you will focus on the second phase of the strategic planning approach, *determining the azimuth* of the organization. You will also define the organization by revisiting and solidifying your mission, vision, and guiding principles (MVGP) and determine if you need to restate any or all of them. Chapter 2 will answer two important questions: Where are you going? And what is your future state? Answering these questions will be accomplished by completing the tasks below. I will discuss them in this chapter, and you will put them into action during the focus group offsite (FGOS). In completing the tasks, you will:

- ✓ Prepare and conduct the FGOS
- ✓ Develop the restated MVGP
- ✓ Outline the future state
- ✓ Develop goals and objectives
- ✓ Prioritize goals and objectives
- ✓ Link goals and objectives to strategic alignments

Conduct strategic planning focus group offsite (FGOS)

I will discuss this task in two steps. First, I will walk you through the preparation required to conduct the FGOS. Second, I will outline and teach you the actual execution of the FGOS. The overarching purpose of the FGOS is to determine, via analysis, the weaknesses and gaps within the organization. I will also help you develop recommendations and solutions to turn those weaknesses into strengths and build a bridge for the gaps. Another key outcome of the FGOS is to solidify all the information required to develop a plan of action and milestones (POAM) and write the strategic plan.

Let's get started on planning and conducting the offsite, for which, it should go without saying, the first action should be to schedule its date and location. This should be completed in accordance with your project plan. As shown in the project plan, the offsite should be scheduled about sixty days prior to its start date. There are numerous tasks that require completion before the actual offsite. Your goal is to have all tasks completed no later than five days prior to that date. Take a look at appendix N, Strategic Planning Focus Group Offsite, to get a "feel" for some of the offsite preparation and execution tasks.

Focus group preparation

As we discussed earlier, you will conduct a two-day offsite where all the phase I and II tasks will be discussed and firm decisions made to shape the strategic plan construction. You must anticipate that stakeholders and partners of the organization will have information you need in order to increase your data pool. Thus, the offsite will serve as a forum for qualitative research in which the participants provide input about their perceptions, opinions, beliefs, and attitudes toward the organization's future and its strategic plan. Questions will be asked in an interactive group setting where everyone can talk freely with other group members. This occasion will be the major muscle movement of phases I and II. This is where you bring everything together for both phases.

Exercise #10: Conduct the FGOS

Conduct a two-day offsite where you discuss and derive solutions for all the topics discussed in chapters 1 and 2. This offsite is without doubt your greatest challenge in developing the strategic plan. You may decide to hire from the outside or appoint from within your organization a facilitator to conduct this session rather than do it yourself. Whoever it may be, this person must have skills in facilitation. If not, the results can be disastrous. *This is important.* The offsite will involve key organizational personnel and stakeholders, to include your CEO. You do not want to be responsible

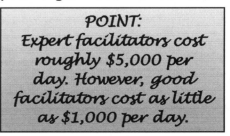

POINT:
Expert facilitators cost roughly $5,000 per day. However, good facilitators cost as little as $1,000 per day.

for a disorganized, haphazard event. It is only two days long. You want every minute to be value-added time for all attendees. One approach for conducting the focus group would be to use two facilitators—one to ensure that the session progresses smoothly and solicit input from the audience, the other to ensure that all the topics are covered. I highly recommend you take this path. You and a trained facilitator can fill these roles.

Focus groups are defined as "carefully planned series of discussions designed to obtain perceptions on a defined area of interest in a permissive, nonthreatening environment" (Krueger & Casey, 2009). Focus groups can or may:

- ✓ Help you get information about attitudes, beliefs, feelings, and emotional reactions.
- ✓ Help you generate new ideas.
- ✓ Allow you to get both individual and interactive opinions on how your subjects react to one another.
- ✓ Allow you to record both verbal and nonverbal behaviors. They also allow you to learn about the language (jargon) your participants use to describe your topic of interest.
- ✓ Provide ideas and opinions, all of which have value (i.e., no right or wrong answers).

Focus group weaknesses

As with any research method, focus groups are not without weaknesses. Challenges associated with focus groups are most often attributed to two main factors: the facilitator and the basic nature of group discussions (Calder, 1977). Some examples of focus group weaknesses are:

- ✓ Lack of an end state or successful and identifiable conclusion.
- ✓ Lack of a well-trained facilitator. I've seen this on numerous occasions. The results were always a nonproductive focus group session.
- ✓ Lack of the right participants.
- ✓ Lack of proper planning and preparation.
- ✓ The possibility that participant attitudes can become more zealous, which could in turn result in greater unification of group opinions or polarize participants. Trained facilitators can deflect this.
- ✓ The possibility that views and values of participants may render certain topics off limits. Participants may also convey information

that may portray them "more favorably," which could slightly distort gathered information.

✓ The possibility that emotionally charged issues may result in argument. A skilled facilitator and adequate advance planning can lessen and possibly eliminate some of this weakness.

✓ Lack of focus.

✓ Conformity to the "voice of leaders"—meaning that whatever the boss says is gospel.

✓ Not be especially useful for gleaning information about sensitive topics that people are uncomfortable sharing in a group setting, or for providing detailed and in-depth responses.

FGOS preparation

Ample planning for the focus group engagement is crucial for a successful outcome.

Focus group information should be gathered in a setting where participants are free to interact with other group members. While group interactions create a more natural, conversational experience than one-on-one interviews, the focus group must still generally maintain a certain degree of structure and control via the facilitator's tools and techniques.

When a venue for the session has been secured, it is a good idea to invite the desired participants as soon as possible. As the time frame is heavily dependent on the availability of the participants, the session should be scheduled at a day and time that is ideal for all. It may be necessary to identify ideal times from each participant and then determine a time that works best for the majority of the group. When inviting participants, consider the level of detail provided to them. It is usually a good idea to inform candidates of the focus group's goals in general terms, but not the specific details of discussion topics and questions. This will prevent participants from becoming sensitized to the subject matter between the time of the invitation and the session. Providing a basic level of information will satisfy curiosity and ensure that potential participants are interested and willing to participate. It is somewhat of a fine line in that you want to provide enough information so that they are prepared to actively participate.

After making decisions about the participants, it is time to focus on the session itself. The most useful resources for mapping the required logistics are through an agenda and a timeline.

The agenda is the schedule used by the facilitator and others involved in executing the offsite and should highlight all materials, activities, and schedules for each topic. The agenda and the timeline should include all activities from the preparation time needed to set up the meeting space to the session wrap-up and closing remarks. Appendix N, TAB 1 provides a sample offsite agenda. Figure 2–1, Focus Group Planning Timeline, provides a possible timeline, with sequencing of the major tasks.

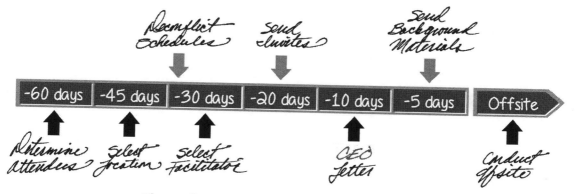

Figure 2–1. Focus group planning timeline

There are some basic steps in conducting the focus group. They are:

- ✓ **Preparation: preparing the room and acquiring the resources.** Arrange tables as needed, set up flip charts for capturing notes, set up tape recorder, set up laptop for note taking, arrange chairs so that participants can see each other, provide name tags. Appendix N, TAB 5, Required Resources and Conference Room Checklist, shows a list of additional required resources along with a conference room checklist.
- ✓ **Registration.** Welcome participants as they enter the room. Have them sign in, distribute any relevant handouts, direct participants to refreshments, and invite them to be seated. In most cases the handouts are in a bound binder consisting of all the material that will be used during the two-day event.
- ✓ **Execution.** Conduct the focus group by adhering to the agenda: welcome participants and thank them for attending, review the purpose for the session, introduce facilitators, provide a brief overview of the

focus group process, establish any ground rules to encourage positive participation, and have participants briefly introduce themselves. The following are some of the key features that will guide the focus group:

- *Theme.* Why are we here?
- *Mission statement.* Does it fit? Does it need to be restated?
- *Vision.* What should the organization look like as it successfully implements strategies, fulfills its mission, meets its mandates, and creates significant and lasting public value?
- *Guiding principles.* Review the guiding principles. Are they in sync with the current organizational culture?
- *SWOT analysis.* What are the root-cause assessment and gaps?
- *Key-results areas and goal setting.* What are the goals for achieving the mission and vision?
- *Strategic objectives.* How are the goals broken into objectives?
- *POAM.* What are the manageable actions for achieving goals and objectives?

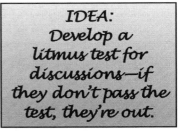

IDEA: Develop a litmus test for discussions—if they don't pass the test, they're out.

Here are some strategic-issues questions you should ask:

- What business should we be in?
- How do we ensure adequate financial funding to fulfill our mission?
- How do we reorganize and manage the organization in order to fulfill our mission effectively?
- How do we influence public policy from strategic to tactical levels to ensure an empowering climate for our products and services?
- What should our role be in meeting the increasing needs of our business environment?
- How do we ensure quality of care or build capacity?
- What is our role in ensuring active participation in planning and systems development?
- How can we attract and retain high-caliber management?

✓ **Conclusion.** This is an opportunity for the facilitator to ensure that all points have been captured effectively and comprehensively. Highlight key points of discussion, answer any final questions, describe how results will be used, inform participants if (and how) study results will be made available, thank colleagues for their participation, and remain in the room until everyone leaves.

In preparation for the focus group, you will seek to answer the following questions (not an inclusive listing):

✓ *What do you want to achieve at the offsite?* The purpose of the offsite is to develop prioritized goals and objectives that will bridge the gaps, strengthen the organization's weaknesses, and create the blocks upon which the strategic plan will be built.

✓ *How will you sequence the events and actions?* You and the facilitator will sequence the tasks based on your day one and day two agendas. As you can see in appendix N, TAB 1, Offsite Agenda, the first day is primarily concerned with working through gap analysis exercises while day two is focused on developing strategies to bridge the gaps and shortfalls from the exercises.

✓ *How much detail do you want to solicit?* A primary goal is to stay on schedule. You have two days to accomplish many tasks. You want details; however, you do not want to be mired in data. You or your trained facilitator will know when to call for some "hard braking" to keep the train from speeding up and running off the tracks. Remember, I recommend a two-facilitator approach.

✓ *What is the mix of qualitative and quantitative questions?* There's no right or wrong answer to the mix of qualitative and quantitative questions. Each analysis will generate its own mix of questions. For example, you may rely more on quantitative questions to conduct the SWOT and survey analyses and qualitative questions to discuss the vision.

✓ *What idea(s) should be the central focus?* The overall theme of the offsite is the principles of knowledge sharing, knowledge transfer, and decision making. Those principles are essentially volumes of data that are imported into your analysis to determine the gaps within the organization. One of the offsite foci is on determining the gaps and developing the solutions for bridging those gaps. Finally, commit to the solutions so that they can be included in the strategic plan. Remember from your preparation exercises conducted earlier with your teams that you already have proposed answers to some of the issues and gaps as seen in your previous research and surveys analyses.

Chapter 2

Why a focus group?

The focus group is a critical step in the strategic planning process. It yields resolution and final decisions on key factors that will drive the organization's future and the strategic plan construction. It employs a committee-style approach so that key members and stakeholders of the organization can have direct input into the construction of the strategic plan.

What are you doing?

You are conducting a brainstorming focus group session to determine and lay out key elements of the organization's strategic plan. Those elements include mission, vision, guiding principles, goals, objectives, and strategic alignments. You want consensus on the organizational issues and the solutions to fix them. You are conducting three stages during the focus group execution: stage 1, generating ideas on each topic; stage 2, narrowing the ideas down; and stage 3, analyzing the results of those ideas. A facilitator should apply all three stages to each topic discussed.

A strong start to the session is important as it will help the group set itself up for success. You will use a customary approach to successful meeting facilitation, which involves:

- ✓ Making introductions
- ✓ Checking for expected and unexpected outcomes and concerns to identify and address any issues that could prevent a successful meeting
- ✓ Reviewing agenda items and time allocations
- ✓ Determining ground rules (e.g., process-evaluation methods, conflict-resolution guidelines, and participation rules, such as no stepping on someone's conversation)
- ✓ Defining roles of key players
- ✓ Creating a "parking lot" for issues that arise that are not within the scope of the meeting

During the meeting, the facilitator will listen carefully to what the participants are saying and periodically summarize their comments to make sure everyone is following along. As the various agenda topics are discussed, the facilitator should ask questions to broaden and/or deepen the conversation, as necessary, to reach the intended outcome. I've found from first-hand experience that videotaping focus group sessions can be extremely beneficial, primarily because it allows for better documentation in the post-offsite data analysis. If videotaping, use discretion; a visible camera may hinder participation. Whether you videotape or not, your strategic plan administrative assistant will be responsible for manually recording (for example, taking notes on a computer) discussion and action items so that they can be revisited throughout the day and be available for the daily wrap-up session.

Task #9: Determine attendees (sixty days before FGOS). Who should attend?

Unlike the classic, quantitatively based random sample, with the FGOS you are not looking for a broad mix of variables. Rather, you want participants with certain characteristics. Therefore, you should target individuals who can provide value-added contributions to the strategic plan. As an example, revisit the outcome of your stakeholder analysis exercise. Ensure that the stakeholders in the Keep Satisfied and the Monitor Closely quadrants are attendees. Your key stakeholders are "must-attend" participants. You want individuals with decision-making authority and influence within the organization. For example, I once held a focus group that targeted individuals with a strong IT background. In that forum, I focused on solving IT-related gaps. In your focus group, you want a cross-section of functional areas within the organization, a sampling of every part of the organization with a vested interest in its future state. To help make this a reality, ensure that your recruiting materials are positive—use phrases such as, "You are important to us; tell us what you think!" or "Share your thoughts with us!"

Developing strategic issues is an activity best attempted in small groups focusing on a specific set of strategic organizational concerns (e.g., resource mobilization, sustainability, program development, expansion, strengthening the organization, improving outreach and global participation, and partnering). Again, all key stakeholders should attend the offsite to provide their insight on strategic concerns. Key stakeholders include the CEO, vice presidents, department heads (such as marketing, operations, human resources, and resource management), CPT and SPC members, and selected key stakeholders from your stakeholder analysis. On several occasions while conducting strategic planning focus groups, I have invited a few lower-tier employees (such as a tier-1 computer specialist, a mail clerk, a junior-grade manager, or a low-grade employee from the operations department) so that I could get a bottom-up perspective on developing the plan. The choice of additional attendees is yours to make and the strategic plan champion's decision to carry out. Keep in mind that you do not want a large group since this is sometimes uncontrollable. Social scientists differ about the optimal number of participants to include in a group. Too few people may not generate enough active conversation, while too many may lead to some participants not having an opportunity to express their opinions. Furthermore, though not always possible, it is ideal to select individuals who do not know one another, a situation that tends to encourage participants to speak more freely and not censor certain information. A total of twenty to twenty-five attendees is optimal. Your final count may differ depending on the size of your organization. Remember, less is more. For large organizations, I use a 1:8 rule of thumb: one participant per eighty employees.

Task #10: Schedule location (forty-five days before FGOS). When and where are you conducting the offsite?

As mentioned before, scheduling should fall somewhere around the end of the fourth month of your six-month plan and noted on the updated project plan. I strongly recommend not conducting the focus group at one of the organization's onsite locations. The site of the meeting should be convenient to participants, as well as provide a point of neutrality. For example, if participants may be against a local ordinance to be discussed, it might not be a good idea to hold the focus group in a nearby government office building. Also consider that the focus group does not have to occur in a formal conference room setting. A casual setting, such as a winery or a country club, can also be suitable. Go off site!

When negotiating for conference rooms with a facility staff member or manager, ensure that you have your specific requirements documented in the contract. This is a business event. Treat it as such. At this time I also want you to "pin the rose" on someone to be responsible for all the operational and logistical requirements of the entire two-day event. This person is your offsite coordinator, and it should be his or her only responsibility. Do not let yourself become bogged down in minor logistical issues—your focus should be the topics of the FGOS. At the same time, do not fail to make occasional supervisory checks. Ensure that your coordinator uses the Required Resources and Conference Room Checklist at appendix N, TAB 5. While this list is not all-inclusive, it does provide a framework to ensure that the environmental setting is conducive to brainstorming, discussions, and a fluid process. Ask your coordinator questions so that you get a sense that all the details have been addressed.

How are you doing it?

The offsite is conducted in several stages. Some tasks are completed prior to the event (preparation), others are conducted during the event (execution), and still others are performed after the event (conclusion). The tasks outlined in this chapter will guide you through each stage of the FGOS. The most important aspect of FGOS preparation is to ensure that you are prepared to discuss each topic on the agenda. For example, on day one you will review the MVGP. In order to accomplish this, go back to the MVGP exercises you conducted with your teams. Determine if what you did in exercise #2, Assess the MVGP, will be the same as what you will do at the offsite. If so, script out exactly what you will say and accomplish. Identify who will assist you and the roles of your team members for each topic. Then rehearse the script with your assistants. You will have to go through the same process for every agenda topic. Allocate ample time to prepare for each topic well before the offsite. Some topics may require you to conduct briefings, while others will require you to conduct exercises. You must ensure that each topic is well-thought-out and rehearsed before the offsite. *This is important!* I want you to look at all twenty-four activities to be completed at the offsite. You need to be at the top of your game in orchestrating each one. Remember, it is best to keep each topic brief and to generally hold to a time frame of one to two hours. *This is per discussion topic.* That would mean, for example, that you would spend about two hours on the SWOT analysis.

> *THIS IS IMPORTANT:*
> *Everything you do at the FGOS will have already been done with your teams in the form of exercises. These exercises served as your data gathering and rehearsal for the engagements at the FGOS.*
>
> *THIS IS MORE IMPORTANT:*
> *Do not cut corners in your offsite preparation. Rehearse every topic. Procure all necessary human resources and train them. Anticipate questions and comments and have responses ready.*

Task #11: Clear schedules (thirty-five days before FGOS)

As we stated before, some of the key stakeholders may have conflicts with the proposed dates of the FGOS. Therefore, it is important that you ensure that schedules are "clear" as early in the process as possible so that you "lock in" key stakeholders. For example, ensure that the CEO and senior leaders are scheduled and committed to attend—without them, the FGOS would be almost futile.

Task #12: Select a facilitator (thirty days before FGOS)

It is best to choose a facilitator similar to the focus group participants in age and gender. In cases of great differences in demographic characteristics, you need to consider:

- ✓ Letting someone of a similar demographic background to that of the subjects conduct the facilitation.
- ✓ At the very least, having someone of a similar background serve as an assistant facilitator (Fern, 2001). I have a slightly different approach than Fern—namely, that it is helpful for the assistant facilitator to have a similar background, but it is not necessary. Not only that, sometimes it is advantageous to have a facilitator with minimal or no experience or background in the organization's given niche. Such an individual can contribute to unbiased and unpreconceived solutions.

Securing an effective facilitator for the focus group is extremely important. Facilitating is an activity that may be perceived as being easy, but it requires experience and skill to be effective. A good facilitator needs a balance of time-management skills and flexibility, the ability to probe deeply into topics, and the experience to effectively manage diverse personalities. An added bonus is if the facilitator has at least a basic awareness of the subject at hand to further engage participants and improve the quality of the resulting information. This is why it's important to ensure that the facilitator has adequate time to study the material and prepare for the offsite. It usually takes me one week of preparation for each day of facilitation. In some instances, the strategic plan team leader serves as the focus group facilitator, but this is not always the case. The team leader may not have the experience necessary to lead the session or may impose certain biases on the group that reflect desired outcomes. In these instances, it is critical to find another individual who can be an effective facilitator.

You want a person who is acceptable to all the members of the group, who is functionally neutral, and who has no substantive decision-making authority—a person, that is, who diagnoses and intervenes to help the group improve how it identifies and solves problems and makes decisions.

The following are some of the functions the facilitator will carry out. He or she will:

- ✓ Gauge the quality of the participant input to determine what factors are influencing validity and reliability and to ascertain bias whereby respondents have a strong desire to influence their own ideas
- ✓ Serve an enabling role
- ✓ Help the group deal with small-group-process issues that are vital to a successful planning process
- ✓ Help the members deal with issues that otherwise might be avoided, overlooked, or swept under the rug
- ✓ Ensure that reluctant participants are involved in the process and that consensus rather than compromise is the primary method of decision making
- ✓ Ensure that necessary group norms of openness and confrontation develop and that the group process enhances rather than blocks the development of a functional strategic plan that will provide the vision for directing the organization's future
- ✓ Keep the group upbeat and positive
- ✓ Keep the session focused and on track in accordance with the agenda.
- ✓ Describe an issue completely and accurately
- ✓ Discuss the factors (mandates, mission, and internal or external environmental factors) that make an issue strategic
- ✓ Discuss the consequences of failure to address an issue
- ✓ Recognize that strategic issues can be about addressing problems but also about capitalizing on opportunities

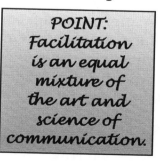

POINT: Facilitation is an equal mixture of the art and science of communication.

- ✓ Ensure that the statement of the strategic issue includes or provides useful clues about how to resolve the failure to address the issue.
- ✓ Focus on what is truly important
- ✓ Focus on issues, not answers
- ✓ Always frame the strategic issue as a question

✓ Ensure that participants also use all of the tools developed during planning, such as the environmental analyses, the SWOT analysis, and the other tasks and exercises

Developing effective questions—*Good question design is the key to collecting good data.*

Social methodology research has provided great insight into how best to develop and arrange questions to be used in focus groups. While there are various approaches, certain elements are common to the process. The bottom line: you want to develop simple questions that minimize bias and variance. The following is a general sequence that is customarily followed in the question-development process.

1. *Determine focus group purpose and goals.*

While it seems an obvious first step, it is important to consider purpose and goals before developing the focus group questions. With your goals (focus group outcome) in mind, consider the following elements:

✓ What information will specifically benefit this session (as opposed to benefitting someone's own personal interests)?
✓ What are the high-priority items for which the information is needed?

2. *Determine what information is currently available.*

A great benefit to focus group participants would be for you and the facilitator to seek out information that currently exists before developing your list of questions. In most professional fields, managers are a very busy consortium, and time is a precious commodity. In order to conserve time, the facilitator should minimize redundancy of topics and questions, an effort that will help to reduce the level of "tiredness" associated with the focus group's topics. If the facilitator has a clear understanding of what information is available before the session, then fewer questions and engagement activities may be required. Use the data already collected from your previously completed exercises and tasks. This is why I want you to select a facilitator early in the planning process. I want him or her to execute a "deep Dumpster dive" into already known information about the organization so that time is not wasted trying to get information that's already available.

3. Draft a preliminary list of questions.

With a clear understanding of the project objectives and a firm knowledge of currently available information, draft a comprehensive list of questions. You and your teams could, for example, use the survey and the guiding principles questionnaire results for this. What questions can be gleaned from them? This technique should be used for each topic that will be discussed. At this point, do not limit the length or number of questions. This can be done later. The most important element of this step is to put these thoughts on paper (or keyboard) to be later evaluated and prioritized. Do not go into the offsite cold—ensure that your staff is prepared.

4. Obtain feedback on the draft questions.

Once a preliminary collection of questions has been drafted, it is important to have the questions reviewed by other members of the planning teams (CPT and SPC) as well as by someone outside the teams. Look to your strategic plan champion for guidance. This step is an important one since it will help decide which questions are most important and which ones are candidates for removal. The process is similar to a pilot survey, in that the planning team will see if the questions are easy to understand and are interpreted as intended.

5. Revise the list of questions.

At this point, revisit the list of questions and consider the feedback obtained in the previous step. It is here that the final focus group questions will begin to surface. As the feedback is incorporated, the number of questions under consideration should become fewer. The following suggestions are adapted from Krueger (2000):

- Use only open-ended questions. For example:
- "What do you think about the proposed mission statement?"
- "Where does one get relevant information on the mission statement?"
- "What problems do you see associated with the statement?"
- Avoid dichotomous questions, since they yield minimal response. For example,
- "Are you in favor of the proposed mission statement?" (Yes/No)
- "Should the vision statement only originate with the CEO?" (Yes/No)

- ✓ Ask "why" questions only rarely. As an alternative, consider asking about specific components that directly relate to the project.
- ✓ Use "think back" questions to provide contextual information. Highlight a past event or a past experience common to all participants.
- ✓ Use a variety of questions to encourage participant involvement. Questions may include perceptions, preferences, rating scales, and case examples.
- ✓ Order questions in a sequence that goes from general to highly specific.
- ✓ Budget time for unanticipated questions and answers.

Pre-FGOS tasks to accomplish

The following tasks must be accomplished before the FGOS. Take a hard look at your project plan for the appropriate sequencing of these tasks.

Task #13: Send invite to attendees (twenty days before FGOS)

Craft a draft e-mail for the strategic plan champion to send to all FGOS participants. The contents of the e-mail should be similar to that which the CEO sends out with regard to the beginning of the strategic planning process. The e-mail serves as a notification to participants of the FGOS and provides details of how and when they will receive guidance and additional materials. Remember, you've already cleared schedules with the key stakeholders. Therefore, this e-mail should not be a "this is the first I'm hearing of this" surprise.

Task #14: Assess survey results (twenty days before FGOS)

You must have the survey completed by this time. The survey analysis should also be completed and put into a briefing or document that provides specifics on the outcome of the survey. This will be one of your discussion topics during the FGOS. Appendix N, TAB 2, Sample Survey Results Briefing, provides a sample briefing of survey results. I've found this template to be simple, brief, and results focused.

Task #15: Assess guiding principles questionnaire results (twenty days before FGOS)

About three weeks before the offsite, ask all focus group participants to complete a guiding principles questionnaire. Some may have already done so since you disseminated the questionnaire as a chapter 1 task. Use the same dissemination, analysis process, and briefing template that you used with the survey. Then develop a short briefing for presentation at the offsite.

Task #16: CEO letter (ten-fourteen days before FGOS)

Draft a letter for the CEO's signature and ensure that it is distributed to all participants about ten to fourteen days before the FGOS. The letter will explain the purpose of the session and what is expected of the participants as well as provide a point of contact (POC) person for questions. Most likely, the POC will be you. See appendix N, TAB 3, Sample CEO Letter.

Task #17: Distribute background material (five days before FGOS)

You must create a packet containing background materials and distribute it to all attendees. The packet should be in their hands no later than five days before the FGOS. Be cognizant of the time requirement if you have to send packets via the mail. Identifying the goals and objectives (the "big-picture outcome") at the onset of preparations is essential to getting meaningful results by the end of the offsite. Prior to the meeting, send out all materials for prereading (a "read-ahead") and for providing action items to attendees to generate greater productivity. I strongly recommend that all the information be neatly packaged and professional in its presentation. Such a presentation will help set the tone that the offsite is an important event for the organization. This also is a good time to print out hard copies of the material to hand out at the offsite.

At a minimum, the package should include:

- ✓ Survey results
- ✓ Purpose and goals of the offsite
- ✓ Methodology of what will happen and what is expected of the participants
- ✓ Guiding principles questionnaire and survey results

> **IMPORTANT:** Conduct pre-execution checks of all FGOS events—check, check, and double-check everything before you start. Ensure that your offsite coordinator has all operational and logistical requirements "wired."

✓ Previous strategic plan, if completed
✓ Offsite agenda
✓ Current MVGP
✓ Any completed analysis
✓ CEO letter
✓ Map of the FGOS location and surrounding areas
✓ Any special requirements (e.g., security, handicap access, etc.)
✓ Layout of the conference room

WHERE ARE YOU NOW?
✓ *You've completed all phase I tasks.*
✓ *You've completed all operational and logistical requirements t for conducting the offsite.*
✓ *Now go to your project plan, check off all the completed tasks, and update the plan as necessary.*

Focus group offsite execution

Let's proceed to day one of your offsite. The following is a synopsis of the main sessions you will conduct at the event:

DAY ONE

✓ Review survey and guiding principles questionnaire results.
✓ Conduct environmental scans.
✓ Conduct MVGP exercise.
✓ Conduct SWOT analysis exercise.

DAY TWO

✓ Finalize MVGP statements.
✓ Adopt strategic alignments.
✓ Conduct gap analysis.
✓ Develop your goals and objectives.
✓ Prioritize and finalize your goals and objectives.
✓ Link those goals and objectives to your strategic alignments.
✓ Assign responsibility.

DAY ONE, Activity #1, Registration

You want this event to be conducted in a professional manner. Therefore, you should pay attention to the specifics—the devil is in the details. From registration to the closing remarks, each action should flow smoothly into the next. Think through every facet of the offsite and brainstorm with your CPT where "Murphy" might strike. Your primary responsibility during the registration process is to ensure that the organization's leadership is properly accommodated and that their time is not wasted. For example, have two people operating the registration table. You can speed up the process even more by having one person register participants whose last names begin with A through L while another registers those from M through Z. Also, providing nametags—with titles—is a plus. Another professional touch is to have members of your team serve as ushers to show participants to their seats and to answer questions. Day one registration begins at 8:00 a.m., which ensures at least one hour for registration, participant "icebreaker," refreshments, and final adjustments to your setup. Finally, make sure that there is enough food and drink for all. Set the tone up front—this is a big event. You're selling a product; do it right.

DAY ONE, Activity #2, CEO Remarks

After the participants are seated, welcome them by introducing yourself and the strategic plan champion. Next, have the strategic plan champion introduce the CEO. The CEO's remarks should articulate the importance of the next two days and how the outcome will drive the future of the organization. It is important that the CEO stress participation and contributions from everyone so that there is a wide variety of perspectives in determining the current state of the organization and where it wants to be in the future. I recommend you write a draft introduction for the CEO and provide it to his staff about ten days before the offsite.

DAY ONE, Activity #3, Introductions

After the CEO's remarks, introduce your teams. Explain the functions key team players will have during the offsite. For example, Mr. Franklyn Harricharan is introduced as the facilitator. Then go around the room and have participants introduce themselves and their position within the organization. Next, explain the "rules of engagement." Some items to cover include the importance of:

✓ Attaining consensus on the issues
✓ Staying focused on organizational interest
✓ Ensuring "balance" in perspectives and strategies
✓ Staying on schedule
✓ Reminding participants that this is a nonattribution/nonretribution event

> *IDEA: Sometimes I show an unrelated, humorous video, usually two to three minutes in length, to break up the monotony.*

DAY ONE, Activity #4, What is Strategic Planning?

For this activity, you will give a short presentation on strategic planning. This is primarily an orientation briefing to inform the audience about what has been accomplished to date along with providing them with an information briefing (PowerPoint) about the strategic planning approach and the strategic planning model. See appendix N, TAB 4, Opening Briefing, for a sample briefing. This briefing is, again, similar to the orientation briefing you gave to the leadership and your teams. At a minimum, the first part must lay out the purpose, mention your teams, and describe the project plan. The second part should outline the two-day offsite agenda as well as the theme, goals, and what will constitute success for the offsite. Consider including what you've accomplished to date, what is expected at the offsite, and what are the steps that will be taken postoffsite.

DAY ONE, Activity #5, Survey Results

Provide the briefing you previously built on the survey results (see appendix N, TAB 2, Sample Survey Results Briefing). Have the facilitator open the discussion on some of the main findings of the survey. At a minimum, answer the questions, "What did you learn from the survey?" "What are the gaps?" and "What needs to be fixed now?" Remember, as the briefing is taking place the facilitator is asking questions, promoting discussion, and noting key points on the parking lot. At the same time, your recorder is taking notes on the entire discussion. The recording of the discussion is essential. It will drive your goals and objectives development on the following day as well as ease your end-of-day wrap-up presentation.

DAY ONE, Activity #6, Guiding Principles Questionnaire

Provide the briefing you had previously built on the guiding principles questionnaire results. Open up for discussion some of the main findings of the questionnaire. As you did with the survey results presentation, answer the questions, "What did you learn from the questionnaire?" "What are the gaps?" and "What needs to be fixed now?" among others. The facilitator should again generate discussion on some of the results. Remember that you are looking for gaps—holes that preclude the organization from "being the best it can be." The key is promoting discussion to generate, gaps, ideas, and recommendations.

DAY ONE, Activity #7, Environmental Scan

Share the principles of Brown and Weiner (1985), Aguilar (1967), and Fahey and Narayanan (1986), which we discussed in chapter 1 (exercise #7, Environmental Scan), with the FGOS participants. Conduct an overview of the internal and external environment. I want you to replicate the exercise you conducted earlier in chapter 1 but at a reduced level. Certainly use the concentric circles exercise and allow the participants to provide their input as to what are the internal and external environments' impacts upon the organization. As with every event you will conduct

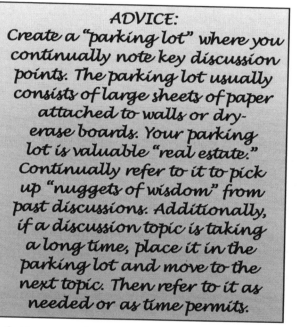

ADVICE: Create a "parking lot" where you continually note key discussion points. The parking lot usually consists of large sheets of paper attached to walls or dry-erase boards. Your parking lot is valuable "real estate." Continually refer to it to pick up "nuggets of wisdom" from past discussions. Additionally, if a discussion topic is taking a long time, place it in the parking lot and move to the next topic. Then refer to it as needed or as time permits.

at the FGOS, document the input of the participants and ensure that the facilitator is asking pertinent questions. When you believe you have enough input, "walk through the drill" with the participants and delete the inputs that do not have significant relevance for the organization. You just want to discover "the nuts and bolts" impact of the environments on the organization.

DAY ONE, Activity #8, Mission, Vision, and Guiding Principles (MVGP)

Revisit and analyze your current MVGP. Walk through the same steps you walked through with your teams in chapter 1, exercise #2, Assess the MVGP, discussing each step (mission, vision, and guiding principles) separately. First, discuss the mission statement, then the vision, and last the guiding principles. You may want to include some of the passages from this book on the MVGP in the participants' read-ahead packet. Open the discussion with the current mission statement. Does it need to be reworded? After the group discussion, show, if appropriate, the recommendations the teams developed when you conducted your exercise. Again, you are recreating the MVGP exercise you conducted earlier with your teams. That was your rehearsal for this activity. This is a lengthy exercise, so note your time to stay on schedule.

If the discussion yields a new mission, vision, or set of guiding principles, document the changes and formalize them, for they will be important as you proceed through the remaining phases of the strategic planning process. It is critical that the organization's leadership give final approval of any rework of this bedrock element

> **INSTRUCTION:**
> If changes are made to the MVGP, do not move forward until they are approved by the leadership.

of the strategic plan—the MVGP. The goal of this activity is to obtain final MVGP approval from the CEO.

DAY ONE, Activity #9, SWOT Analysis

As we discussed in chapter 1 and appendix L, there are numerous benefits a SWOT analysis can provide. Give a brief introduction of the SWOT principles and then conduct a SWOT analysis with the participants. Again, you are replicating the previous exercise you conducted with the CPT and SPC. Now you want input from the focus group. As with every one of the activities you will conduct during the offsite, it is important that all the key points are documented. Use the same format and process you used when you conducted exercise #8 from appendix L.

DAY ONE, Activity #10, Day One Wrap-Up, Day Two Agenda, and Closing Remarks

Prepare and present a short recap of the activities that were completed on day one. As there was much information shared and discussed during the day, you should ensure that it is collated and presented in the form of a daily summary. In preparing your wrap-up, use the fifteen-minute break times, the lunch hour, and any free time during the day (see day-one and day-two agendas) to put together your presentation. This simplifies your "crunch work" to get the wrap-up ready for your and your staff's presentation.

I've always made sure that I had someone working throughout the day preparing the wrap-up.

Next, provide day two's agenda and give a brief explanation of that day's work. You also want to briefly talk about some of the key decisions or topics discussed during day one. For example, "The CEO agreed that the mission statement remains unchanged and agreed to the new vision statement and the three new guiding principles that were added."

Finally, turn the floor over to the CEO for closing comments.

DAY TWO

Just as you did on day one, ensure that all participants are well accommodated. Obviously, the requirements are reduced on day two since most of the participants are familiar with the routine. However, continue to check and make sure that all is going according to plan. Murphy's law does not go away on day two.

DAY TWO, Activity #11, Strategic Plan Champion Opening Remarks

It is a good practice to allow the strategic plan champion to open the second day of the FGOS and make remarks as he or she sees fit.

DAY TWO, Activity #12, Recap of Day One's Activities

As you did with your previous day's wrap-up, provide a reminder/summary of the tasks completed on day one and how they will allow you to move into day two's sessions. Keep the summary short and concise and be sure to include significant decisions, such as the agreed-upon MVGP. Then walk through the day-two agenda and provide any additional instructions pertinent to the topics.

DAY TWO, Activity #13, Conduct Gap Analysis

As you did earlier with your teams, conduct a gap analysis with the offsite participants. The strategic gap is a fundamental challenge affecting an organization's mandates, mission, product or services, customers, financing, structure, processes, and/or management. The identification of strategic gaps is at the heart of the strategic planning process. Gap analysis will also have a powerful impact on how goals and objectives are formulated, on how stakeholders assess their interests and weigh the costs and benefits of alternative objectives, and whether specific ventures are likely to be winners or losers in support of various objectives.

Many important gaps are likely to have emerged before this step in the process—from the comments, stakeholder analysis, MVGP discussions, environmental scan, and exercises conducted earlier. Gaps fall into three main categories:

- ✓ Current gaps that probably require immediate action
- ✓ Gaps that are likely to require action in the near future but that can be handled as part of the organization's regular planning cycle (this is the strategic plan execution—phase III)
- ✓ Gaps that require no action at present but need to be continuously monitored

Over the course of the strategy discussions (and in this activity specifically), a number of gaps are likely to emerge that are more operational, or tactical, than strategic. It is important to take note of those operational gaps for three reasons. First, many participants will think that such operational gaps are the ones that have the most impact on their day-to-day work and will want to see something done about them. Second, finding ways to take action on these gaps often energizes the strategic planning process because people see that that action is leading to immediate results that can directly affect their work lives, giving them confidence that the organization is serious about dealing with strategic concerns. Third, addressing operational gaps can often remove barriers to both effectively confronting and dealing with the organization's strategic gaps.

I want you to follow the same process that you followed in exercise #9, Gap Analysis, to determine the gaps discovered on day one and, thus far, on day two. Use the gap analysis worksheet in Figure M-1. Walking through each organizational factor, ask the question, "What are our gaps?" Be sure that the gaps are ones that the organization can do something about and then frame the issue as a question that

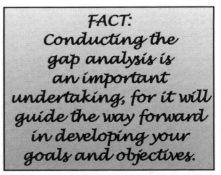

FACT:
Conducting the gap analysis is an important undertaking, for it will guide the way forward in developing your goals and objectives.

invites more than one answer, such as "Why is this issue important?"

"How is it related to the SWOT analysis, goals, and objectives and the organization's ability to meet its mandate and fulfill its mission?" and "What can we do to bridge the gap?"

DAY TWO, Activity #14, Develop Strategic Alignment

The question you must answer is how you determine where you want to go. At the FGOS, you will determine where the gaps are within the organization and, with these "nuggets in your sack," formulate a way forward. First, you must develop the strategic alignments—special focal points toward which an organization directs its efforts. Second, you must decide where you want to develop your efforts. That is, what are the key strategic areas within the organization on which you must focus? Again, refer to your assessment, the final solution sets, and recommendations. How do you bridge these gaps? What were the recommendations based on your analysis?

Strategic alignments are developed to meet specific requirements of the organization. They are created so that managers:

- ✓ Are aware of challenges within the environment and their impact on the organization
- ✓ Have a greater strategic awareness so that they understand how their actions contribute to the organization's sustainability and relevance
- ✓ Can explore the as-is and to-be environments and recognize related challenges and issues and develop new approaches to address the changing environments
- ✓ Can identify performance drivers
- ✓ Can develop a framework for measuring and managing key performance indicators

You can examine some of the more common strategic alignments by reviewing what you've accomplished thus far. The strategic alignments you will develop are based on your final recommendations from the assessments during phases I and II of the strategic planning model. Those assessments were as follows:

- ✓ Environmental scan
- ✓ Current mission, vision, and guiding principles (MVGP)
- ✓ Stakeholder analysis
- ✓ Strengths, weaknesses, opportunities, and threats (SWOT) analysis

  ✓ Gap analysis
  ✓ Focus group, teams, and external input
  ✓ Solution set/recommendations

Take a look at the list above. What are some of the strategic alignments that you will gain in completing these tasks? What are the most important focal points for ensuring your organization's survival? You would agree that stakeholders are important to any organization. The results of your stakeholder analysis solidify the importance of stakeholders—primarily, your customers—to the organization. Without customers the organization would have no reason to exist. Therefore, *stakeholders* would be a strategic alignment. Again, strategic alignments are the focal points toward which the organization directs its efforts.

When you developed your MVGP, dissected the strengths and weaknesses in your SWOT, and conducted the gap analysis, you were taking a deep dive into your organization's internal processes. Again, you would agree that internal processes are important to any organization. They are the operational tempo that creates and provides your product or services. Therefore, *internal processes* is another strategic alignment.

In phase I, you explored cultural attitudes within organizations. You also discussed in the stakeholder analysis the importance of personnel within an organization. The main contribution of an organization's personnel is their intellectual capital. Given today's rapid change in technological advancement and competitive challenges, continuous learning and employee growth are critical to your, and any, organization. Continuous learning equates to growth and intellectual capital. This in turn equates to a successful organization. Therefore, *learning and growth* is a strategic alignment.

What is the most important resource required to build that bridge from the as-is state to the to-be state? You would doubtless say financial and human resources. You should realize the truth: without resources you cannot move forward in an organization. Therefore, *resources* is the final strategic alignment.

Putting it together, you have built four strategic alignments: *stakeholders, internal processes, learning and growth,* and *resources*. What you have just developed is the basis for what is called a balanced scorecard, the concept developed by Harvard Business School professor Robert S.

Kaplan and management consultant David P. Norton as a performance-measurement framework that adds strategic, nonfinancial performance measures to traditional financial metrics to give managers and executives a more "balanced" view of organizational performance. Figure 2–2, Balanced Scorecard, illustrates the balanced scorecard (BSC).

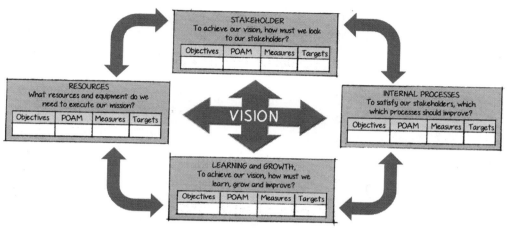

Figure 2-2. Balanced Scorecard

You will use the balanced scorecard in chapter 5 as I discuss how to monitor and apply metrics to your strategic plan. However, at this juncture you will utilize the BSC as a tool that will help translate your strategy into operational objectives that drive both behavior and performance. You will do this by using your strategic alignment as pillars on which to build your goals and objectives in order to achieve your vision and accomplish the organization's mission.

Goals

A goal is a broad statement of what you will accomplish. A goal is general, intangible, and abstract. A goal involves the final impact or outcome that you wish to bring about. To have a balanced holistic strategy, organizations must have goals that feed off each other.

As long-term organizational targets or foci of development, goals are what the organization wants to accomplish or become over the next several years. Goals provide the basis for decisions about the nature, scope, and relative priority of all projects and activities. Everything the organization does should help move it toward reaching its goals.

The purpose of compiling a list of goals is to identify the six to eight things you must do to keep your organization running. You can state your goals qualitatively, but I recommend that you state them quantitatively, if possible. Goals take the notion of vision, which you articulated in your strategy, and orient it toward results. The key, again, is to give meaning to goals. Each goal should have its own "swim lane" and unique approach associated with it. Study the graphic in Figure 2–3, Cascading goal pyramid.

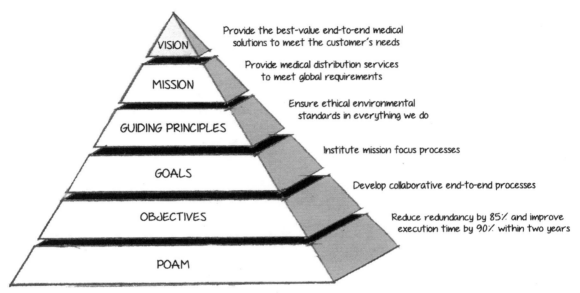

Figure 2-3. Cascading goal pyramid

As you can see, goals cascade from the top of the strategic pyramid (the vision). They are forged from the strategic analysis you previously conducted. Everything is linked and connected for a tight, end-to-end model for directing strategic execution.

Goals should drive the organization's strategic direction and close the performance gaps. Goals:

Are built on strengths and shore up weaknesses

- ✓ Describe a future end state—a desired outcome supportive of mission and vision
- ✓ Shape the way ahead in actionable terms
- ✓ Are best applied where there are clear choices about the future

> *"If you don't know where you're going, any road will get you there."*
> *(George Harrison)*

✓ Are a means to put strategic focus into the organization—assigning ownership to someone

Organizations, like people, typically have several goals at the same time. "Goal congruency" refers to how well the goals combine with each other. Does goal A appear compatible with goal B? Do they fit together to form a unified strategy? "Goal hierarchy" consists of the nesting of one or more goals within another goal or goals. One organizational approach may involve short-term goals, medium-term goals, and long-term goals. In this approach, one can expect to attain short-term goals fairly easily: they stand just slightly beyond one's reach. This is sometimes referred to as "low-hanging fruit." At the other extreme, long-term goals appear very difficult, almost impossible, to attain. They are sometimes referred to "big, bad goals" (BBG).

Using one goal as a stepping-stone to the next involves "goal sequencing." A person or group starts by attaining the easy, short-term goals, then steps up to the medium-term, then the long-term goals. In an organizational setting, the organization may coordinate goals so that

> *ADVICE:*
> *For goals, there is no exact answer as to the right number. (But not a lot: six to eight.)*

they do not conflict with each other. That is, the goals of one part of the organization would mesh easily with those of other parts of the organization. I've seen organizations where each functional area pursues nearly identical goals. There are two mistakes here. First, the organization's goals were not in sync with the overall strategic plan goals. And second, each goal was vying for resources to accomplish the same result, producing organizational confusion, dysfunction, and waste.

Take, for instance, the goal of profitability, something you'd routinely want to achieve. This is a goal you would want to realize every year. You don't say, "We made money last year, so we don't need any this year." That doesn't make sense (or cents); profits are a constant goal. When you state your goals, they must include the elements that are necessary for success. Keep the list as short as possible. I recommend the following generic list of goals to consider as a starting point:

✓ Profitability
✓ Intensified research and development
✓ Customer satisfaction

✓ Internal efficiency and effectiveness
✓ A strong financial position
✓ Dominance of a particular market
✓ Competitively priced, quality products and services
✓ A motivated and innovative organizational workforce

Your list can be shorter or longer (though it shouldn't be too much longer); these are only possibilities. Every organization is different, and some will find other components they need to be successful from year to year. The more you can quantify things and write down exactly what you expect, the more your goals can take real shape. You don't want your goals to be amorphous. You want tangible goals, so you set targets. The targets should be consistent with your strategies. Goals take the notion of vision, which you articulated in your strategy, and orient it toward results. The key, again, is to give meaning to goals. With quantifiable goals, the idea is to look three to five years ahead and figure out what target makes sense for your strategy. For some organizations, this means looking forward to being at 100 percent operational capability five years down the road. For others, it means looking at a percentage (perhaps 85 percent) on-time performance that they will meet repeatedly in each of the ensuing five years.

Goal setting

Goal setting is a process of determining what the organization's goals are, working toward them, and measuring progress in accordance with a plan. A generally accepted paradigm

> *"A goal without a plan is just a wish." (Antoine de Saint-Exupéry)*

for setting goals is one that is specific, measurable, achievable, realistic, and timely (the SMART principles). Each of these principles is described below.

Specific. A specific goal has a much greater chance of being accomplished than a general goal. Don't "boil the ocean": try to remain as focused as possible. Without going overboard, provide enough detail so

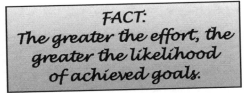

> *FACT:*
> *The greater the effort, the greater the likelihood of achieved goals.*

that there is little or no confusion as to what exactly the sponsor (the individual tasked to develop the goal) should be doing.

Measurable. Goals should be measurable so that you can gauge progress for adjustment as it occurs and if necessary. A measurable goal has an outcome that can be assessed, for example, on a sliding scale (1–10), as a hit or miss, or a success or failure. Without measurement, it is impossible to sustain and manage the other aspects of the goal framework. Defining the desired end state is accomplished through a set of questions used to draw participants into the process to meet your SMART principles. After top managers have set the organization's overall goals, they then establish performance measures (discussed in chapter 4) for the various divisions and functions, as follows:

- ✓ The measures specify the level at which divisional and functional managers' units must perform if the organization is to achieve its overall goals.
- ✓ Divisional managers then develop a business-level strategy (a POAM) they anticipate will allow them to achieve those goals.
- ✓ In consultation with functional managers, the divisional managers specify the functional goals that managers of different functional areas need to achieve to allow the division to accomplish its goals.
- ✓ Functional managers in turn establish goals that first-line managers and nonmanagerial employees need to achieve to allow the particular function to accomplish its goals.
- ✓ Managers ensure that goals set at each level harmonize with the goals set at other levels.
- ✓ Goals should be set appropriately so that managers are motivated to attain them.
- ✓ The best goals are specific, difficult goals that will challenge managers' ability but not be beyond their reach.

Achievable. An achievable goal has an outcome that is realistic, assuming the organization's capacity for providing the necessary resources and time. Goal achievement may be more of a "stretch" if the outcome is more difficult to begin with. Ask: "Is what we are requesting of the organization possible?" "Does the organization have the resources to attain this goal?"

> **GUIDANCE:**
> A stretched goal is better than a safe goal. You should not be afraid to increase the desired outcome, meaning if four is the standard, why not stretch the goal to five or even six widgets?

Realistic. Start small and remain sharply focused on what the organization can and will do, letting the stakeholders experience the elation of meeting a goal. Gradually increase the intensity of the goal after having a discussion with the stakeholders to redefine the goal.

Timely. Set a time frame for the goal: next quarter, six months, or one year. Setting an end point gives the stakeholders a clear target to aim for. Planning-follow-up should occur within the six-month period (best practice) but may occur within a year depending on the progress of your plan execution.

DAY TWO, Activity #15, Develop Goals—Outline the Future State

The end state for this activity is to solicit participants' input in populating the goals and objectives that link to each strategic alignment.

Ask participants to articulate several goals based on the discussions during days one and two. Your wallpaper should already be full of points and parking-lot comments. You want to place the goals under their respective strategic alignments. For example, look at Table 2–1, Strategic alignments worksheet; you can create a separate sheet of wallpaper for each strategic alignment so that participants can note their goals.

VISION: provide the best-value end-to-end medical solutions to meet customers needs					
Strategic Alignments	Goals	Objectives	POAM	Measures	Targets
Stakeholder					
Internal Processes					
Resources					
Learning and Growth					

Table 2–1. Strategic alignments worksheet

I suggest using large Post-it notes for this exercise. This will allow you to easily remove duplicated goals and move the goals up and down in priority or simply discard the ones that are not selected. Have the participants write and post their goals under the corresponding strategic alignments. One method I have used is to take a fifteen-minute break in the session and ask participants to write and post their goals while on the break. At the end of the break, discuss each goal with the participants, have them remove superfluous comments, then decide which goals should remain and which should be discarded. The next step is to prioritize the goals that remain.

DAY TWO, Activity #16, Prioritize Goals

You need to create criteria to rank order the needs, or priorities, of your organizational goals, which ultimately helps you make decisions about your implementation plan. By revealing what is most important to the organization, the criteria point you toward the actions that will deliver the best results for your efforts.

Rank ordering allows you to keep your goals at a manageable number. I recall one strategic planning session with an organization in which the planning team listed fifteen different goals. I suggested participants rank order the goals and arrange them as priority one, priority two, priority three, and so on. Then I drew a line after number six and stated that those above the line were the organization's top priorities. The others might be important but not as important. One of the reasons management teams set so many goals is that the organization has so many things to measure, and they all seem important. Managers want to know that each and every machine, during each and every shift, is operating optimally. This is understandable. But the statistics for each and every machine during each and every shift don't belong in the organization's strategic plan. Instead, a composite number representative of the overall production output might be sufficient. Which of your ranked goals will make it into the strategic plan?

Almost always, when leaders tell you to prioritize your goals so that you're working on what's truly important instead of getting caught up in minutiae, they are pushing you to focus on what's best for the organization. However, those same leaders rarely explain precisely how to do this. How do you decide which goals are really the most important at any given time? Are they the goals that are the most urgent, the ones that will earn the most money, and the ones that will produce the greatest long-term happiness? If you don't use an intelligent method of prioritization, you'll lack consistency and bounce from one goal to another with no direction or purpose.

From a purely military (i.e., nonpolitical) standpoint, the goal of any engagement is to achieve victory by inflicting the greatest damage on your enemy with the fewest resources. Wouldn't you say this is the essence of all goals? You want to make the greatest amount of progress with the least amount of effort. For prioritization to have any meaning, it's imperative that you have a clear goal. For the military, the overall goal may be to achieve a decisive victory. Your organizational goal may be a set of goals, such as the mission statement or purpose, or even the state of organizational existence. A consideration in prioritization is the resources you have available. Military resources include troops, equipment, supplies, and so forth. Your organizational resources include time, money, people, and so forth. Time is generally your scarcest resource because it cannot be replenished. In order to prioritize intelligently, you need a method that tells you how to evaluate goals in terms of their overall importance. Prioritizing is often one of the most difficult parts of the strategy-planning process. All strategies and actions produced in a brainstorming session, for example, look important and interrelated, so how to leave anything out and focus scarce resources on the gaps?

To prioritize, the organization has to be clear about what matters most. Prioritizing is an important aspect of all decision making and often needs to be done as a group activity if the results are to be generally agreed upon. The bottom-up approach (discussed in the Introduction and Let's Get Started sections) argues for including low-level members in decision making about organizational strategy and in selection of the priorities to be pursued in the members' functional or specific areas. Much has been written about the importance of setting priorities, but whether in time-management or corporate-strategy planning, the point remains: you must know your priorities and focus on the goals and objectives that represent them. The saying "Do your best and forget the rest" is applicable here. Focus your resources and energy on your best opportunities and set the others aside. The question is: How in the face of competing corporate agendas do you justify your choices? Both prioritization and justification are important steps in an effective corporate planning process.

One model of prioritizing goals and objectives uses hierarchies. The goals may be organized in a hierarchy of means, ends, or numbers called the order of merit list (OML). The OML follows a number ranking such as OML 1, OML 2, OML 3, and so on. It is a simple method for ranking goals. I've used the OML process numerous times. Working with groups, I've used cards with goals and objectives. In this method, each participant placed his or her cards (with a goal from activity #15) in the OML column (1, 2, 3 etc.). Simple tabulation determined what the consensus was for the most- to the least-important goals (OML 1 representing the most important). A graphic format such as OML allows for the prioritizing of options to be simple and visual. After discussing the goal-card placement, the participants discuss their rationale for the placement. Adjustments are made based on the merits of the discussion, and the results provide a listing of the most important goals (OML 1, 2, 3 ...). This prioritized list forms the basis for decision making and strategic plan inclusion.

CARVER prioritization method

A key component of military strategy is selecting the most important targets to attack. But how do you know which targets are the most important? Centuries of warfare have provided us with a reasonably intelligent answer—the CARVER method. CARVER is an acronym for a military method of target selection: criticality, accessibility, recuperability, vulnerability, effect, and recognizability. The CARVER matrix has its roots in the Vietnam War and was developed by the US Special Forces as a method to rank and prioritize the targets to be destroyed. Interestingly, the matrix has now become a popular concept in business and project management. For every potential target, a value of 1 (lowest) to 5 (highest) is assigned for each CARVER factor, thereby creating the CARVER matrix. Then, by adding the six CARVER values, a total score can be calculated for each target. These scores, when compared, produce a target prioritization list. The higher the CARVER score, the more "important" the target becomes.

Let's consider the six CARVER factors and how we can apply them to prioritizing goals and objectives.

Criticality. How critical is the target with respect to your organization's main objective? Will it move you significantly closer to your goal, or is it a relatively insignificant item? An example of a low-criticality goal and objective might be building a bigger snack bar. It would be nice, but it's probably not going to make that much difference in the organization's productivity.

Accessibility. Can you actually reach the target, or is it so well defended that attacking it directly is impossible? Do you have the means to tackle this target immediately, or does tackling it come with preconditions?

Recuperability. In military operations the term recuperability, refers to how quickly the enemy can recoup from the destruction of a target. There's little point in attacking a target that can be rebuilt or replaced with minimal effort. How great is the expected recuperability and return on your commitment of resources?

Vulnerability. How vulnerable is the target? What amount of resources will be required to "take it out?" How vulnerable are the goals and objectives you're considering? Easily achieved goals and objectives will score a high vulnerability rating, while difficult ones will score much lower. Similarly, an inexpensive project is less vulnerable than an expensive one.

Effect. If you successfully destroy the target, how widespread will the impact be? If you successfully complete your goals and objectives, what effect will it have on the longevity of the organization?

Recognizability. Can we see the target well enough to attack it, or is it highly camouflaged or mobile? Are your goals and objectives crystal clear or totally fuzzy? How easy is it to recognize the steps necessary to execute the goals? Have you completed this type of action before, or will you have to figure out the steps as you go along? Clear goals with clear steps will score higher on recognizability than foggy goals with unclear steps.

Look at the example (Table 2–2, CARVER Matrix) of a CARVER matrix that prioritizes certain goals. The 1–5 rankings for each factor are simply for the sake of illustration; your rankings may vary. Keep in mind that the rankings are all relative to your primary goals.

	Criticality	Accessibility	Recuperability	Vulnerability	Effect	Recognizability	Total
Start a Company	2	5	3	1	5	2	18
Enter Politics	1	5	2	5	5	5	23
Buy a House	4	2	3	1	2	4	16
Buy a Car	2	5	5	3	1	1	17

Table 2–2. CARVER Matrix

The numbers tell the story. According to our sample CARVER matrix the most important project to tackle is to enter politics (it has the highest score of 23). While it's among the least critical items and won't necessarily produce a great return for the time invested, it's relatively easy and straightforward to do. Next comes starting a company, which would be a more critical, long-term project but would require a lot more effort to achieve. The worst project is buying a house, its main drawbacks being that it's too fuzzy and ill-defined. It might be wise to replace that goal with a more specific one. Even though we're just using simple addition instead of a more complex weighting of these factors, CARVER does a fairly decent case of spitting out an intelligent prioritization of objectives. It's really good at depicting which goals and objectives are worth the effort and which aren't. It also shows when you should choose a piece of low-hanging fruit rather than initiating a big project.

I use CARVER in making decisions about my consulting business, as, for example, when the matrix indicated it would be better to apply for government contracts than to create a marketplace in the for-profit sector for my skills. Although creating such a marketplace would be more profitable, I saw how CARVER demonstrated that government contracts were more stable. I now adapt the basic concept of CARVER to my goals and objectives prioritization. I sometimes assign extra weight to certain factors or introduce additional ones such as "time" or "ease of completion" to the list. If you choose to follow this approach, just be careful not to get carried away. The point of CARVER is to select a reasonable project and then put it into execution. Don't lose yourself in hours of analysis paralysis. By using a simple system such as CARVER, you'll know which goals and objectives are important enough to deserve your attention and which are, relatively speaking, a waste of your time and energy. You'll benefit from greater consistency in decision making with better results for your efforts.

Other methods for prioritizing

Two other methods are described here, and you can find many more on the Internet or from specialized practitioners such as facilitators and analysts. Both methods are meant for a group of people to collectively rank competing priorities, and both are suitable for a focus group or a meeting.

Decision matrix

Another favorite of the military and similar tool to the CARVER method is the decision matrix. The decision matrix uses a measured criterion technique in which ratings are given for each criterion. The decision matrix is a variation of the L-shaped matrix that utilizes points (usually from 0 to 10) that is predefined per criterion and may vary among criteria depending on its relative importance in the final decision. It evaluates and prioritizes a list of options. For our decision matrix example (Table 2–3), consider the information that follows.

Let's say we've identified criteria C1, C2, C3, and C4 (criteria such as time to complete, cost, personnel requirements, and ease of completion) as playing a role in the final decision, each with weights of 1 through 5. Moreover, we have four prospective courses of action that will constitute the best solution to the problem statement. As shown in Table 2-3, values are assigned to each criterion and then tabulated to mathematically obtain the best course of action (the lowest sum is the best).

"Least Is Best"

Criteria	C1	C2	C3	C4	Total
Weight	.5	1.5	.3	1.8	
Course of Action 1	2/3	5/12.5	3/3.9	2/3.6	12/23
Course of Action 2	1/1.5	5/12.5	2/2.6	5/14	13/30.6
Course of Action 3	4/6	2/5	3/3.9	1/2.8	10/17.7
Course of Action 4	2/3	4/10	5/6.6	3/8.4	14/28

Table 2–3. Decision Matrix

Choosing the right criteria for the decision matrix is critical. The following are key actions for criteria selection:

- ✓ Brainstorm the criteria appropriate to the situation.
- ✓ Discuss and refine the list with your teams or group.
- ✓ Identify any criteria that must be included and any that must not be included.
- ✓ Identify criteria relative to the problem statement.
- ✓ Reduce the list of criteria to those the team believes are most important.
- ✓ Assign a relative weight to each criterion based on how important that criterion is to the situation.
- ✓ Ensure that you adequately define your selected criteria. For example, if C2 equals costs, define costs as "Costs are all costs, including planning, surveying, building, and landscaping the facility. Costs do not include plumbing, electrical, cabling, etc."
- ✓ Make sure that your rating scales are consistent.
- ✓ Word your criteria and set the scales so that the low end of the scale (1) is always the rating that would tend to make you select that option (i.e., greatest impact on customers, greatest importance, least difficult, and greatest likelihood of success).

Stephen Covey Time Management Matrix prioritizing method

In this method, you draw a grid of four squares, with the axes labeled 'Urgent/Not Urgent' and 'Important/Not Important' (as shown in Figure 2–4,

117

Stephen Covey Time Management Matrix). You then collate a list of goals or pick them from earlier documents.

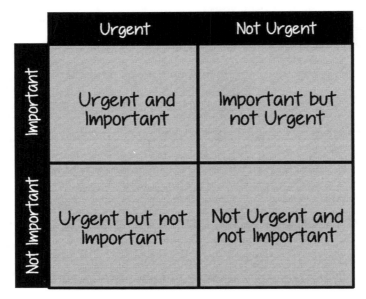

Figure 2-4. Time management matrix

Different colors can be given to goals representing different themes. Place each goal in the grid to indicate its importance and urgency. Finally, you record the solution for further discussion. You can also use the x- and y-axes as scales to allow for more variety. When building the list of goals and assessing their urgency and importance, get the whole of your team involved. People are likely to have differing views on the urgency and importance of some tasks, so allow these discussions but ensure that participants come to an agreed-upon conclusion, as each objective must end up somewhere on the grid. Getting everyone involved in the discussion gives each a stake in the process and means each is more likely to get involved in delivering the final plan.

DAY TWO, Activity #17, Develop Objectives

Following goal setting and prioritization, you will develop new and/or reenergize existing objectives. These objectives must be specific and measurable. A measurable objective must be met on the way to attaining a goal. A goal is only as good as the objective that goes with it. Thus, the objective represents a step toward accomplishing a goal. In contrast to the goal, an objective is narrow, precise, tangible, concrete, and can be measured. Wording of objectives should be clear to enable people to understand it. Having formulated and prioritized your goals, it's time to develop objectives to meet and realize those goals. Look at the goals and objectives in Figure 2–5, Strategic Alignments Linkage.

VISION: provide the best-value end-to-end medical solutions to meet customers needs					
Strategic Alignments	Goals	Objectives	POAM	Measures	Targets
Stakeholder	Provide successful medical distribution	Deliver medical supplies as requisitioned	Improve supply chain management system	99% on-time deliveries	Sept 2015
		Provide best-value solutions	Develop stakeholder satisfaction program	100% survey of customers	July 2016
		Provide total visibility	Implement tracking software	100% accountability	May 2016
Internal Processes	Institute mission-focus processes	Improve business processes	Integrate customer turn cycle	100% customer satisfaction	September 2015
		Develop collaborative end-to-end processes	Reduce redundancy and improve execution time	85% reduction in 90% improvement	February 2016
Resources	Optimize all resources	Articulate and document resource requirements	Develop an advance resource program	Track 100% of resources	June 2016
		Incorporate stewardship, accountability, and internal controls	Integrate IT systems to support cost-efficient program	Ensure 95% efficiency	July 2016
Learning and Growth	Develop high-caliber employees	Recruit, train, and certify employees	Develop an accurate manpower program	100% accuracy	November 2015
		Develop knowledge-and information-sharing environment	Develop a knowledge management (KM) program	100% KM throughout the entire organization	December 2015
		Develop leadership skills at all levels	Develop a mentoring program	95% of mid-level managers have a mentor	July 2016

Figure 2–5. Strategic alignments linkage

For example, the goal in the Learning and Growth strategic alignment is "Develop high-caliber employees." The three objectives developed to accomplish the goal are:

- ✓ Recruit, train, and certify employees
- ✓ Develop knowledge- and information-sharing environment
- ✓ Develop leadership skills at all levels

The formula is straightforward: when you complete projects (meet objectives), your organization moves ahead. Strategic objectives are general areas in which your effort is directed to drive your mission and vision. You can follow this effort from vision to mission statement and on to goals (see

Figure 2–3, Cascading goal pyramid). It all fits together. But now is the time to figure out what it means in terms of implementation: *What are you going to do?* There are certain high-priority projects that you need to undertake in order to drive the organization forward.

Strategy determines those three- to five-year objectives that will really move the organization toward world class. Objectives should:

> FACT:
> *Strategic objectives are general areas in which your effort is directed to drive your mission and vision. However, having too many objectives results in a lack of focus— if everything is important, then nothing is important.*

- ✓ Represent significant change and improvement
- ✓ Require the organization to stretch itself
- ✓ Be characterized as home runs or grand slams
- ✓ Usually require multifunctional effort and teamwork

The link between the organization and the department responsible for executing the goals and objectives is very clear. In most instances, however, it will take several departments to realize the organization's goals and objectives. For example, in a financial services organization, the marketing department has responsibility for creating the marketing program; in a transportation organization, the human resource department is responsible for developing new recruits' safety training.

Objectives communicate your ultimate purpose or intention for devising the strategic plan. They state the direction you will take with the goals you have. As you formulate each objective, answer two questions:

- ✓ Does this objective support our mission, vision, and goals?
- ✓ In fulfilling this objective, will we meet our mission and attain the vision?

Before you begin to write the strategic plan objectives, you need to understand that the objectives are neither your tactics nor the stated responses to the recommendations generated by your analysis. Implementing objectives will come later as you build a specific quantitative POAM for the strategic plan implementation (discussed in chapter 3). To develop the objectives for your mission, you need copies of your mission statement and the findings, conclusions, and recommendations from your assessment in phase I and, more important, the goals you developed. Objectives, as you know, are measurements you'll use to track your success.

Work with your offsite participants to identify at least two to three objectives that support each goal to fill the gaps identified in phase 1. Ultimately these objectives will help you measure how well the organization performs. Strategic planning and decision processes

> *QUESTION:*
> *Based on your SWOT analysis, do you have the strengths to obtain your objectives?*

should end with objectives and a roadmap of ways to achieve them. As you did earlier with goals, use the SMART and SMARTER rule to develop objectives.

SMART and SMARTER objectives

S: Specific—significant, simple, and easy to understand

M: Measurable—manageable and directly supportive of the goal and specific enough to quantify and measure the results

A: Attainable—attainable and realistic; compels the organization into action

R: Relevant—resourced and related to the customer to improve products and services

T: Time related—targeted with an end date

E: Evaluated—with analysis and metrics

R: Referenced—easily traceable linkage to the strategic plan

> *POINT:*
> *Objectives are often focused on the customer.*

The following are examples of objectives that meet the SMARTER rule:

- ✓ Develop a knowledge-management (KM) program in one year.
- ✓ Reduce redundancy and improve execution time to 85 percent in one year.
- ✓ Increase supply-chain response time by 50 percent in two years.
- ✓ Reduce defects and external customer complaints by 99 percent in three years.
- ✓ Improve tracking software to 100 percent visibility in eighteen months.

Difference between goals and objectives

Once you learn the difference between goals and objectives, you will realize how important it is that you have both of them. Most think of "goals" and "objectives" as meaning the same thing. However, if you want to convert vision into results, there is an important difference. As discussed before, a goal is elastic and general. It is something that that can be described subjectively, with no pressure to be specific. For example, *"My goal is to be a successful author"* is nonspecific and qualifies as a goal. An objective, on the other hand, is a specific description of what must be achieved in order to realize a goal. Objectives are usually more descriptive and quantifiable than goals—for example, *"My objective is to write one chapter every month and complete a book by July 5."* I used the SMART principle to develop this objective before I began writing. The objective is **s**pecific, **m**easurable, **a**ttainable, **r**elevant, and **t**ime related. (See Table 2–4, Goals and objectives differences.)

GOALS	OBJECTIVES
Very short statement, few words	Longer statement, more descriptive
Broad in scope	Narrow in scope
Directly relates to the mission statement	Indirectly relates to the mission statement
Covers a long time period (such as 5 years)	Covers a short time period (such as a 1 year budget cycle)

Table 2-4. Goals and objectives differences

Thus, goals express the physical and emotional outcomes you seek to achieve while objectives describe the specifics that your action or implementation plan is designed to achieve.

DAY TWO, Activity #18, Prioritize Objectives

Use the same methods for prioritizing goals discussed earlier to prioritize objectives. You may use one method to prioritize goals and a different method to prioritize objectives. For example, you may choose to use the OML for goals and the CARVER matrix to prioritize objectives.

DAY TWO, Activity #19, Finalize Goals and Objectives

After a comprehensive analysis of your organization's as-is landscape, you have now developed new or updated existing goals and objectives to reach the to-be end state—the vision attainment. My experience suggests that when organizations establish numerous and complex goals, very little is achieved. With that in mind, I limit the number of goals so as to ensure that the organization possesses the resources to accomplish those goals. For each strategic alignment, look at your rank-order list of goals. Draw a red line under the second or third goal. (You decide where to draw the line, but remember that least is best. As you can see in Figure 2–5, I only have one goal for each strategic alignment. Really, one is all you need.) This means that you will only execute goals above the red line. Certainly others should not be ignored. They may be assigned to a functional area if they are determined to be important and low-hanging fruit. These are your prioritized goals with their supporting objectives. This is now one of the key drivers of your strategic plan—goals to be accomplished. Remember, it's critical that you gain approval from the CEO that these are the appropriate organizational goals for the strategic plan because they might set in motion significant changes in the organization's daily routine.

DAY TWO, Activity #20, Link Prioritized Goals and Objectives to Strategic Alignments

Now that you have the goals with their supporting objectives, it is time to link them to the strategic alignments. Earlier we identified our four strategic alignments: *stakeholders, internal processes, resources*, and *learning and growth*. These alignments are incorporated into your balanced scorecard. Using the diagram in Table 2–1, Strategic alignments worksheet, as a template, ask participants which goal and objective should be linked to which specific strategic alignment. For this, study the matrix in Figure 2–5, Strategic alignments linkage. On the far-left column are the strategic alignments. The next column shows a goal that supports the strategic alignment and the objectives that support that goal. For example, in the *stakeholder* strategic alignment, the objective of "deliver medical supplies as requisitioned" supports the goal "to provide successful medical distribution." To round out the matrix, you see several POAMs that support the objectives, measures for the POAMs, and target-completion dates. I know that earlier when you developed goals you did so by linking them to a strategic alignment. The purpose here is to ensure and finalize that everything was done correctly; Activity #20 serves as a check on what was previously accomplished. Do not be concerned with the POAM, measures, and targets at this point. I will discuss them in chapter 3, and their development will become the responsibility of a tasked functional area.

In order to complete this activity, you will need to recreate the strategic alignment worksheet on a large wall. Then invite the participants to write on the worksheet or use large Post-its as to which goals apply to which strategic alignments and which objectives support which goals. It may be advantageous to place worksheets on two walls in order to move people along at a quicker pace. Remember, you are using the finalized and prioritized goals and objectives you developed in Activity #19. This is not the time to pile on "another good idea." Show concern but don't act on concern—just note any new ideas in the parking lot. Once you have determined that the participants have adequately input data into the worksheet, have an open discussion to conduct a "sanity check." The sanity check will determine the following:

- ✓ Do the linkages make sense? That is, are the objectives linked to the goal, and are the goals linked to the strategic alignment?
- ✓ Do you need to sculpt away objectives? (Remember that three to five objectives per goal is optimal.)
- ✓ Do you need to sculpt away goals? (Remember that one to three goals per strategic alignment is optimal. Again, I recommend only one.)

DAY TWO, Activity #21, Balanced Scorecard (BSC)

Provide a short briefing on how the balanced scorecard will be used. The BSC is discussed in greater detail in chapter 5. This briefing is for informational purposes only. Show the diagram in Figure 2–2, Balanced Scorecard. Inform the participants how the goals and objectives that were linked to the strategic alignments will be tracked on the BSC. This will serve as the metric to determine how well, or how poorly, you are executing the strategic plan.

DAY TWO, Activity #22, Assign Goals

Now that you have determined your strategic alignments and prioritized goals and objectives, it is time to fix responsibility for the functional areas that will execute the goals and objectives. I want you to place the completed strategic alignment worksheet so that it is visible to the entire group. Next, "walk down" the list, begin discussions, and attain judgments on which functional area within the organization is best suited to implement the objectives. For example, the objective "recruit, train, and certify employees" (*learning and growth* strategic alignment) would see the best results if assigned to the human resources functional area. Or the objective "improve business processes" (in the *internal processes* strategic alignment) would be best suited for the operations functional area. I would suggest that you accomplish this activity by first providing your recommendation as to whom the objectives should be assigned, then soliciting discussion, and finally gaining approval from the CEO.

DAY TWO, Activity #23, Outline Strategic Planning Next Steps

The next steps in the strategic planning process are outlined in chapters 3, 4, and 5. They will provide a short briefing on the major tasks, to include:

- ✓ Writing the strategic plan
- ✓ Developing a (POAM)
- ✓ Developing performance measures
- ✓ Linking the budget to objectives
- ✓ Fixing responsibilities
- ✓ Applying resources
- ✓ Executing the POAM
- ✓ Conducting an implementation review
- ✓ Refining goals, strategies, and processes

DAY TWO, Activity #24, Debrief Session and Closing Remarks

The debriefing is a wrap-up of the key events and discussion points of the last two days. One debriefing technique involves walking through the agenda and discussing the salient points of each topic. Articulate the criteria for success and whether those criteria were met.

When you've completed the debrief session, turn the podium over to the strategic plan champion or the CEO for closing remarks. I would highly recommend that the CEO close the session by strongly advocating for his or her desire to continue the strategic

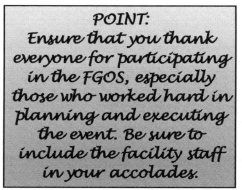

POINT:
Ensure that you thank everyone for participating in the FGOS, especially those who worked hard in planning and executing the event. Be sure to include the facility staff in your accolades.

planning process and for all functional areas and key stakeholders to provide the resources required.

You have now completed one of the major tasks in developing the strategic plan. However, your work is far from complete. You, your teams, and all participants have put significant effort into the offsite. But this is just one game during the season. Now it's time to start planning for the next game. A significant amount of information and data points was produced from the offsite; you and your teams will analyze the data before moving on to phase III.

Focus group analysis

At the collective level, focus group data can sometimes reveal shared understandings or common views. However, there is a danger that a consensus can be assumed when not every person has spoken: you will need to consider carefully whether the people who have not expressed a view can be assumed to agree with the majority, or whether they may simply be unwilling to voice their disagreement. This is where the facilitator is most beneficial. Skilled facilitators are trained to detect personality traits and bring out discussion from the entire group. The offsite was about discussion, brainstorming, and developing sound ideas for building the strategic plan. Therefore, the analysis of focus group data presents both challenges and opportunities when compared to other types of qualitative data. Some authors have suggested that such data should be analyzed in the same manner as interview data (quantitative analysis) while others have said that the unique features of focus group data—particularly the opportunity that it provides to observe interactions among group members—suggest that it should be analyzed in a quantitative manner. Data analysis can take place at the level of the individual or the group and provides the opportunity to analyze the strength with which opinions are held. If the opinions are opposed or directly challenged, the individual may either modify his or her position or defend it. Bringing together all the comments that an individual makes can enable you to determine whether the individual's view changes in the course of discussion and, if it does, further examination of the transcript may reveal which contributions by other focus group members brought about the change. The data provide the opportunity to analyze the input as part of your gap analysis and, eventually, vision-goal- and objective-setting decisions/recommendations. Data analysis is discussed in appendix N, TAB 6, Focus Group Data Analysis.

After reading TAB 6, consolidate all data points from the offsite, including, for example, completed worksheets, parking-lot notes, and completed exercises. These contain important information that will assist in writing the strategic plan.

WHERE ARE YOU NOW?
- ✓ *Congratulations! You've completed one of the most difficult strategic planning tasks: executing the FGOS.*
- ✓ *You've gathered all the data and feedback from the FGOS for further analysis.*
- ✓ *You can go to your project plan, check off all the completed tasks, and update the plan as necessary.*
- ✓ *You're ready to digest and document all the data from the offsite.*

Chapter 3
Convert Strategy into Operations

How are you going to get there? What is your plan to get there?

Chapter 3 will focus on the development of the plan of action and milestones (POAM) to answer the questions:

- ✓ How are you going to get there?
- ✓ What is your plan to get there?

You will also answer the important question, How are you going to get there with the resources you have? The key tasks for this chapter are to:

- ✓ Produce the strategic plan document
- ✓ Communicate strategies and the new strategic plan
- ✓ Develop the implementation plan
- ✓ Develop the POAM

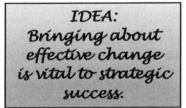

IDEA:
Bringing about effective change is vital to strategic success.

Produce the strategic plan

Now it is time to carefully write the strategic plan itself. The plan should be:

- ✓ Simplified and specific
- ✓ Concise—not a huge book that no one reads
- ✓ Easy to understand
- ✓ Comprehensive but not ponderous

One of the core charges when drafting a strategic plan is to develop it in a way that is easily translatable into action. Most strategic plans address high-level initiatives and overarching goals but don't get articulated (translated) into the day-to-day projects and tasks required to achieve the plan's goals and objectives. Terminology, word choice, and the level at which the plan is written are examples of easy ways to fail at articulating your strategic plan in a way that makes sense and is executable by others. Often, plans are filled with conceptual terms that don't tie into day-to-day realities for the staff expected to carry the plan out. Recently, I read a plan, and I really could not understand the message. It read well, but I could not grasp what the planners were trying to accomplish. Terms such as "paradigm shift," "vigorous reengineering," and "holistic approach" were in the plan, yet they had very little meaning for me—and perhaps for many others.

Desired planning outcomes

The desired outcome of a strategic plan is a document that provides a foundation such that the organization can implement goals and objectives to achieve the strategic direction. Some additional desired outcomes are:

✓ Organization-wide agreement on the strategic plan among key decision-makers and a firm decision from leadership to adopt the plan and proceed with implementation.

✓ Provisions for the necessary guidance and resources for implementation. It is important that the funding necessary to implement the plan be identified and allocated to the fullest extent possible. Nothing is more disruptive to the credibility of the planning effort than to have insufficient resources for implementation.

✓ Substantial support from internal and external stakeholders who can strongly affect implementation success. Review the stakeholder analysis you conducted earlier to determine where you have the most support.

✓ A widely shared sense of excitement about the substance and symbolism of the plan.

> *TRUE STORY:*
> *In the most recent three organizations for which I helped develop a strategic plan, fewer than 30 percent of the goals were implemented. Why was that? They were not executed because of the very reasons I gave in the Introduction. Two of those reasons I want you to be cognizant of when writing the plan are: Lack of simplicity. Complexity = catastrophe. Lack of effective communication strategies.*
>
> *As you write, keep it simple so that the plan is easily understood and communicated.*

I would suggest that you develop a theme for your overall strategic plan construction, an approach, I have discovered, that has advantages throughout the process. For example, in the last strategic plan I developed, the theme was "simplicity and brevity." I chose this theme because I wanted every member of the organization to understand the strategic plan. It should not be complicated or a burden to read. If the lowest-ranking member of the organization cannot understand the strategic plan, the probable outcome will be miscommunication, confusion, and, almost always, failure. As with most written documents, the message must be fully understood by readers at every level. I once encountered the theme "a picture is worth a thousand words." Here the planner used pictures and graphics with minimal text to successfully convey his message.

Regardless, the theme should be present from the beginning and should exist as a unifying thread throughout the entire process and in the final document. Another way to plan your writing is to consider how to develop the document and how to display its complexity and unique facets throughout the planning process. Ask, "What do I want to achieve?" Then ask over and over, "What else do I have to say about that?" Although the execution of the strategic plan may prove to be a complex process, the end document itself (the strategic plan) should be short and encompass what you're trying to communicate in about fifteen to twenty pages.

Task #18: Research Other Completed Strategic Plans

There are numerous examples of completed strategic plans. Simply search the web and look at the various examples. Take note of word usage, layout, graphics, front and back pages, and so forth. If you like a certain style, fashion your document in a similar manner. There is no crime in admiring and adopting another's format.

A word on branding

Considering the sometimes worldwide spotlight on corporate identities, their design and message can be some of the most important decisions an organization makes. Branding must be highly customized and focused on an organization's internal and external environment. Brand identity is an essential component of the strategic plan and vision of an organization. Whether you are launching a new program or reenergizing a current program, a brand facelift and/or creation is highly recommended. Customers recognize products and services by a brand, and vital to a successful organization is building that brand identity. Understanding relationship marketing (marketing based on customer relationships) is a key component of management and becomes a necessity for understanding how to develop and guide your mission. As you put your strategic plan document into final form, consider the need for a branding makeover. In one organization on whose strategic plan I worked, we rebranded the logo and tagline, using new colors and shapes. The redesigned logo and tagline were then placed on every document and presentation the organization made. Along with an updated strategic plan, they became the new face of the organization. The changes had a positive impact on customers and on the culture of the organization, where they were seen as "out with the old, in with the new." Consider these benefits of an organizational branding or rebranding:

- ✓ Increase workplace morale
- ✓ Provide organizational visibility
- ✓ Have high impact internally and externally
- ✓ Are low cost
- ✓ Offer perception of change for the better

Task #19: Write the Strategic Plan

Writing the strategic plan involves outlining an organization's purpose, goals, and methods used to reach those goals. (You may wish to revisit the Preface and Introduction in order to refresh your thoughts on strategic plans.) In writing the document, you want to identify what the organization stands for, what it hopes to accomplish, and what methods and processes it will use to realize those accomplishments. Remember the *A, B, C* approach:

A = Where are you now?
B = Where are you going?
C = How will you get there?

The *A, B, C* approach is the core foundation of your strategic plan. The elements of the question "Where are we now?" are derived from the assessments conducted in chapters 1 and 2. This is where you defined the baseline. You may want to include the results of some of these assessments in the plan. These assessments, and the tasks in chapter 2, provided you with the MVGP, which should be included in the strategic plan. You should answer the question "Where are you going?" by giving the CEO's vision statement. Here you will discuss the goals and objectives produced at the FGOS. Knowing what you must do to reach your vision is the major muscle movement of your strategic plan document and tells how you will get there. You may choose to discuss how your goals convert to strategic objectives and then to specific performance targets.

I would recommend that you structure your strategic plan with the topics listed in the sequence below:

- ✓ **Leadership message**. This topic consists of three to four paragraphs written by the CEO that discuss the journey on which the organization is about to embark. The message should also discuss the commitments of the CEO and the responsibility of everyone in the organization to provide his or her full support for implementing the plan. Most important, the CEO should articulate his or her vision in his or her own words. For example, "My vision is for X-Ray Corporation ..." (*Note: X-Ray Corporation is a fictitious company.*)
- ✓ **Introduction**. The introduction typically consists of a few paragraphs about the organization, including its reason for existence, historical significance in the marketplace, partnerships, affiliates, and the like.
- ✓ **Progress since last plan.** This is an optional entry in the strategic plan and should include some of the major accomplishments of the organization since the last strategic plan. It also provides some insight as to the value of strategic planning and the overall relevance of the organization to its stakeholders and its community.

- ✓ **Mission, vision statements, and guiding principles.** Here are included the mission, vision statements, and the guiding principles. Discuss the vision and how it synchronizes with the future environment. You may include future organizational alignments, new customer bases, and impacts from the external environment. Keep this to one page. Include graphics as filler if necessary. Look at the mission as your nucleus and the vision and the guiding principles as its electrons energetically orbiting the mission.
- ✓ **Strategic relationships**. Discuss your key stakeholders. Who are your customers? Who are your strategic partners?
- ✓ **Strategic priorities (i.e., goals and objectives)**. Describe the goals and objectives and their linkage to the strategic alignment. The goals and objectives should explain how the organization will manage and influence its primary business lines to provide the best support to customers and stakeholders. List each goal and its supporting objectives as well as the strategy to accomplish the objectives. Refer to Figure 2–5, Strategic alignments linkage, for an example of how the vision cascades into action.
- ✓ **Strategic alignments**. Included in this topic are your four strategic alignments: *stakeholders, internal processes, learning and growth,* and *resources.* Provide a definition of each and how they link to the organization's strategic framework.
- ✓ **Implementation of strategic alignments**. Describe the organization's acknowledgment that a successful strategic plan is an ongoing process of change. Provide a brief explanation of your implementation plan and the organization's commitment to provide the resources to execute the plan. Also, include how the organization will track implementation of these important objectives and continue to measure performance.

✓ **Summary**. You may choose to provide a few paragraphs that summarize the key points in the strategic plan.

Let me wrap this discussion up with a sample table of contents. In the text box on the right, you will see a table of contents for a sixteen-page strategic plan. Use this as a guide.

Review and evaluate the plan

Now that your plan is written out and completed, it is time to evaluate it. Did you produce the theme you intended to produce? You certainly put a lot of time into the document. You now have to take a close look at it to ensure that you did not overlook any errors. As you conduct your review, answer these questions:

✓ Does your plan connect your mission to your vision?
✓ Are the goals and objectives aligned with your vision and in support of your mission? Look at Figure 3–2, Cascading linkages. Does everything cascade from the vision? You may want to use Figures 3–1 and 3–2 as illustrations in your final strategic plan document.
✓ Is your plan achievable and realistic? Is your plan integrated? Ensure that all facets of the plan support each other. Look at the illustration Strategic Alignments (Figure 3–1). Note how each strategic alignment is integrated with the overall vision and how each pillar connects the current to the future state.
✓ Is your plan synchronized? Ensure that there is a good balance among *stakeholders, internal processes, learning and growth, and resources* strategic.
✓ Is the document clean and fluid? Is it easy to read? Does it flow logically, and is every word understandable and not open to interpretation?

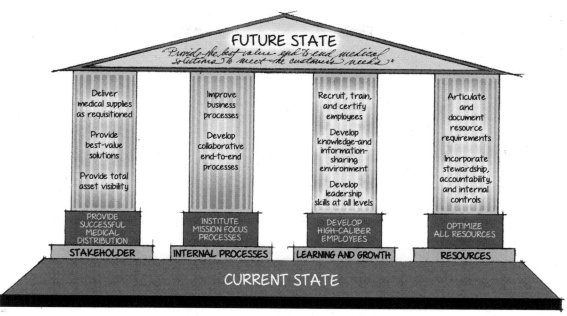

Figure 3-1. Strategic alignments

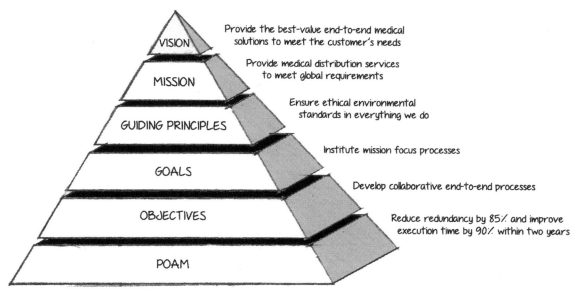

Figure 3-2. Cascading linkages

The final product

The completed strategic plan should be a ten- to twenty-page booklet printed in an easily read 8-by-11 format. It should include pictures, illustrations, and graphics, easily visualized and interpreted at a glance. You may visit our website at www.allonscg.com for more instructions on creating the final document. Another approach is to create a trifold brochure showing the key points of the plan. This could be distributed at organizational symposiums and conferences and to customers.

As you can deduce from this book, I like graphics. I believe a picture can be an effective tool for telling a story. Be careful not to go overboard, however; have just enough to make the plan easier to read and understand. To get the most out of your graphics component, I strongly recommend retaining a graphic artist and designer to lay out the document.

Task #20: Proofread and Obtain Final Approval

> ### WHERE ARE YOU NOW?
> ✓ You've completed the post -FGOS analysis.
> ✓ You've written the draft strategic plan.
> ✓ You've updated your project plan and annotated your completed tasks.

I want you to edit, edit, edit, and proofread, proofread, proofread the document. Have key stakeholders review it for recommendations and feedback. On several occasions, I have given draft strategic plans to lower-tier employees to read and then asked for feedback. In particular, I am looking at whether they understand what the organization is planning. You may want to use this as a feedback technique for your own plan.

Once you believe you have a good draft, schedule a meeting with leadership, including the CEO. Present the document to them and carefully walk them through it. You will need the CEO's approval before "going to print." The approval may require several sessions with leadership. Make any changes and recommendations they request until they are satisfied with the final product. Ensure that the draft version is the same one you send to the printers—the same graphics, stock, colors, font, and design as the proposed final strategic plan document itself. Once you've obtained approval from the CEO, finalize the document, and print copies as desired.

Communicate strategies and the new strategic plan

As mentioned before, a plan is useless if no one looks at it. A good strategic plan is a living document that becomes part of the culture of the organization. Most organizations have strategic plans at the highest levels but do not communicate them to the lowest level.

ADVICE: Use the open-book management approach with your strategic plan: be transparent and keep employees informed.

It is imperative to get everyone within your organization involved with the new plan—not just leadership. You need to spread the word about the new strategy so that everyone understands what the organization is trying to accomplish. All employees must understand the vision—where the organization is going and the necessary steps to get it there. An important approach is to develop a simple communication plan with a systematic method for spreading the word. Use the entire media spectrum available to the organization, including newsletters, e-mail, posters, graphic boards, and other means to disseminate the vision, goals, and objectives of the strategic plan. Place a link on your organization's Intranet to provide updated information and progress on the planning and implementation process. Also, show any "quick wins" that have been completed to date. Develop additional links to more information and documents for employees and stakeholders to download (for example, a link to the survey results).

Task #21: Strategic Plan Dissemination

Now that you have a strategic planning document, it's time to distribute it. Develop a fluid distribution approach. This ensures that you can store and distribute the plan in an efficient manner—providing the right amount of materials to the right people at the right time. Conduct an organization-wide (or all-hands) meeting and/or webinar to discuss the contents of the plan. Begin with an introduction by the CEO followed by a presentation that lays out all the plan's important attributes, such as goals and objectives and who's responsible for what. This should be done as soon as the plan is released. I have found it extremely productive when leadership, in particular the CEO himself or herself provides an explanation of what's been done, where the organization expects

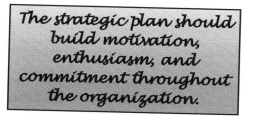

The strategic plan should build motivation, enthusiasm, and commitment throughout the organization.

to be, when it expects to be there, and how it's going to get there. As we discussed earlier in organizational culture, it is important that the strategy becomes part of the culture. In many cases, the CEO provides a briefing to the entire organization explaining the new strategic plan. This can be done in person, via video presentation, or by a combination of both. I strongly endorse having the CEO articulate the plan to the entire organization. As a commanding officer at several levels of the military, I conducted numerous "talks to the troops" (TTT). In those sessions, I informed my men and women of what we'd accomplished, where we were now, where we were going, and how we could get there.

You must:

- ✓ Communicate the plan to the employees—sell it verbally and in writing. Unfortunately, while most organizations have strategic plans, they do not communicate them to the lowest levels.
- ✓ Make the process ongoing—in group and one-on-one sessions and in meetings.
- ✓ Communicate the strategy to everyone—internal and external alike.
- ✓ Show that the payoff is beneficial to all.

Send copies to all stakeholders. Take the CEO's message from the plan and send it in an organizational-wide e-mail. Distribute a trifold brochure of the important aspects of the plan (MVGP, goals and objectives, and strategies to achieve them). The focus here is a "media blitz" to stakeholders and the entire organization just as if you were selling a product, which, essentially, you are—your strategic plan. Don't stop there; follow up your blitz with monthly updates. Again, use the organization's knowledge-management and information systems (e-mail, newsletters, etc.) to blast out your message, which is: *There is a new strategic plan in place, and we're going to implement it*. Include in your blast the functional departments so that they can further disseminate the information through their department heads with a personal touch and guidance.

> **INSTRUCTION:** *Utilize the organization's means of communicating the strategic aims to the staff; if the means do not exist, create them.*

Implementation plan—Always develop your implementation plan with the rest of the organization in mind.

Now that you know what you want to do—realize your goals and objectives—you need to determine how you will get there. You will get there by developing an implementation plan that consists of actionable tasks to realize the goals and objectives and, ultimately, the organization's mission and vision. Strategic planning, in and of itself, is an academic pursuit, of little direct use to any organization. The payoff of strategic planning is in its application, its execution, and its implementation. This arrangement to develop and implement the goals and objectives was already sanctioned by the CEO at the FGOS. Now is the time to put it into action.

You've expended a lot of energy in creating your strategic plan, but it is not enough. In the best of circumstances the plan will be an agreement about what to do and how, where, when, why, and by whom to do it, negotiated among and committed to by stakeholders and leadership. But for the

> *SUGGESTION:*
> *Indicate by name the individuals to whom you should allocate time and resources when developing the implementation plan.*

plan to be brought to life, an effective implementation process and a set of actions are required. It does not matter how outstanding the strategies and plan are: if there's no capacity or appetite to carry them forward, they're of little value. It is worth repeating that implementation should be considered from the start of the strategic planning process. If you want the strategic plan to be successfully prosecuted, implementation cannot be an afterthought. As the implementation plan is developed and pursued, issues with execution will become the focus of dialogue and deliberation among your teams, the strategic plan champion, and the functional areas. In other words, the dialogue and deliberation at the heart of the strategic planning should continue throughout the implementation process, so that strategic thinking, doing, and learning are continuously fostered, and the organization is helped to fulfill its mission, meet its mandate, realize its vision, and achieve its goals and objectives.

Some critical concepts that together make up the ingredients for successful strategic implementation are:

- ✓ Relevance—making the actions that need to be taken relevant to and understood by those who will execute them.
- ✓ Resources—ensuring that you have the right skills, backed by adequate time and funding, available in the right place at the right time.

✓ Alignment—making sure that throughout the organization all the actions, including the ongoing tasks, support the mission and the strategic alignment.

✓ Accountability—giving everyone who has strategic tasks to implement (at any level) the means to succeed in executing their tasks and holding them accountable for completing the tasks.

Creating an implementation plan is the top priority for making the strategic plan happen. The first step in the process is to break down the strategic goals, objectives, and tasks and assign them to functional areas that in turn will assign the work to teams or individuals who have the resources and motivation to execute them. As you recall, this assignment was already made at the FGOS.

Implementation, like strategic planning, generally does not happen by itself. Leadership is absolutely essential. It involves taking a proactive approach to implementation so that as strategies are implemented and actions taken, the next priorities in line will have already been considered and can thus move to the front and be addressed. A proactive approach obviously includes deliberating with others about ways in which factors affecting implementation success should be handled. Therefore, in implementation, leadership involvement has to be assigned direct roles. The implementation plan should:

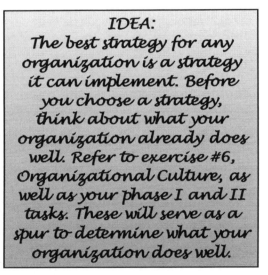

IDEA:
The best strategy for any organization is a strategy it can implement. Before you choose a strategy, think about what your organization already does well. Refer to exercise #6, Organizational Culture, as well as your phase I and II tasks. These will serve as a spur to determine what your organization does well.

✓ Have an implementation strategic sponsor (ISS). In order to minimize personnel requirements, the tasks of the ISS are usually "dual-hat" responsibilities of the strategic plan champion. This individual must have enough prestige, power, and authority to commit the organization to implementing the strategic plan and holding people accountable for the implementation. As stated before, the strategic plan champion is typically a high-ranking member of the organization, often a member of a policy board, cabinet, or executive committee. The implementation's strategic sponsor/strategic plan champion must:

- Have the requisite political will and external and internal support to make any changes, if needed.
- Have the ability to commit the resources necessary to implement the plan in its entirety, or at least critical parts of it.
- Be able to focus on what are agreed to be the highest priorities, or have a strategy for making sure the highest priorities receive timely attention.
- Find ways to move key personnel to change, including such change as, for example, realigning organizational structure and processes.
- Develop ways to change organizational culture and belief systems in the desired directions.
- Hold functional areas accountable to execute the strategic plan's objectives assigned to them.

✓ Have a strategic plan team leader. In many organizations, short-term planning and daily execution tend to take precedence over planning for the future. A short-term operational task, for example, always takes precedence over a long-term one. Therefore, it is essential that you ensure that the implementation of the plan adheres to the established timelines. You, as the strategic plan team leader responsible for both the strategic plan development and implementation, have as your primary responsibilities developing the strategic plan and managing implementation efforts on a day-to-day basis. Other responsibilities are to keep the people executing the plan on track, monitor their progress, and pay close attention to details. You and your teams developed the plan; now it's time to manage its implementation. During the implementation process, the strategic plan team leader should:

- Keep the implementation high on people's agendas
- Think about what has to come together (people, information, resources, completed work) at or before key decision points
- Be vigilant for obstacles that may delay implementation
- Keep rallying participants and pushing the implementation process along
- Assist in developing implementation action teams
- Be sensitive to power differences and be able to engage all implementers in finding ways to share power in order to increase the chances of implementation success

- Involve the strategic planning committee in all facets of the implementation plan
- Act as a sounding board to assist action plan project managers (APPM) in implementing the plan
- Be the implementation "go-to button" for strategic issues

✓ Ensure that the CPT has an implementation mandate that includes at least the following responsibilities and requirements:

- To serve as a forum for deliberation, consultation, negotiation, problem solving, and buffering the organization, units, groups, or persons involved in the implementation process
- To ensure that all members allocate the quality time necessary to implement the plan
- To record all decisions or recommendations in writing and share them with key stakeholder groups
- To approve, where appropriate, recommendations and decisions made by the teams or to serve as an advisory body to formal decision makers or policy=making bodies regarding implementation issues
- To track and ensure adherence to implementation plan timelines
- To establish and execute all interim progress reviews (IPR).

Implementation Action Team (IAT). The primary purpose of the IAT is to execute the POAM. The IAT is comprised of the APPMs, who are designated by their functional area supervisors, department heads, and anyone with supervisory authority over them. More about APPMs can be found in chapter 4. The diagram in Figure 3–3, Implementation Organizational Structure, shows the IAT hierarchy.

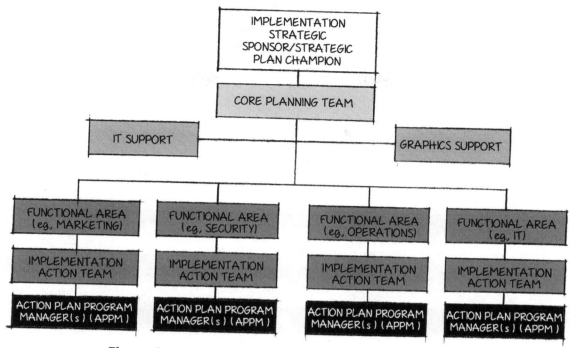

Figure 3–3. Implementation organizational structure

At the top is the implementation strategic sponsor/strategic plan champion. The CPT is undergirded by the functional area IATs. The APPMs are selected personnel who will develop a POAM to meet the end state of a given objective. For example, if the APPMs were assigned the objective "develop a knowledge- and information-sharing environment," those individuals would be responsible for ensuring that all parameters of that objective were met. Review appendix O, Plan of Action and Milestones, for more information on the APPM and developing a POAM. The IAT is responsible for:

✓ Reviewing strategic alignments, goals, and objectives
✓ Creating a list of actions required to realize the objective
✓ Developing a POAM to meet the objective's intent
✓ Providing leadership and the CPT with a gauge of the strategic objective implementation and whether the objectives are being achieved to realize the vision

Chapter 3

Transformational and operational strategies

There are, essentially, two kinds of strategies: transformational and operational. A strategy is transformational when the organization faces significant uncertainty, aims to change the game in the industry, or must address substantial customer or competitive challenges. Strategies are operational if an organization faces relatively low uncertainty and is mostly attempting to "play the game" better than the competition.

It takes vastly different skills to execute these two kinds of strategies. For the operational approach, an organization must focus doggedly on conventional measures such as capacity utilization or throughput and on such basics as customer service. Transformational strategies, by contrast, require an organization to use what amounts to inadequate information to make timely options-based decisions about product or market priorities, investments in technology, configuration of business systems, and industry partnerships. From running a factory at world-class levels to knowing how to close on an acquisition target, neither kind of strategy will work if an organization lacks the skills needed to implement it. Moreover, the skills needed to execute operational and transformational strategies, while not mutually exclusive, are rarely present in a single organization. After all, these strategies require top management to focus on fundamentally different things: building exceptional internal capabilities in the case of operational strategies and gaining unusual insight into the evolution of an industry and market-based opportunities in the case of transformational ones. They also call for different kinds of organizational support (distinctive frontline behavior or excellent strategic decision making, respectively), different approaches for implementation (highly linear or options based, respectively), and different ways of monitoring progress (highly structured tracking of targets or event tracking and contingency planning, respectively). More important, once an organization has distinguished itself in one set of skills or the other, the skills cannot be reversed overnight because they are so dissimilar. This is why the alignment between a strategy and an organization's real strengths is a critical, though often neglected, factor in determining whether strategies succeed.

> *ADVICE:*
> *Ensure that all new ideas are tested in a business-case context. "There is nothing more wasteful than becoming highly efficient at doing the wrong thing."*
> *(Peter Drucker)*

Task #22: Develop an Implementation Plan

An implementation plan should be a brief summary of the who, what, when, where, and how of the strategic plan's implementation. Consider Figure 2–5, Strategic alignments linkage. In the strategic alignment row of Learning and Growth, you see the goal "Develop high-caliber employees." Let's use the objective "Develop knowledge- and information-sharing environment" as an example. The following questions should be answered:

- ✓ **Who?** The who are the individuals, functional areas, and APPMs responsible for this objective. For example, they could be the organization's IT division.
- ✓ **What?** The what is to develop a knowledge- and information-sharing environment to provide high-caliber employees and increase learning and growth within the organization.
- ✓ **When?** The when is the completion date of December 2015.
- ✓ **Where?** The where is at the organization's headquarters in Washington, DC.
- ✓ **How?** The how is to build an IPT to develop a POAM, courses of action, and a project plan; to acquire resources and financing; and to execute the POAM.

The implementation plan must answer these questions for every approved goal and objective stated in your strategic plan document. The implementation plan allows you to track each objective with the who, what, when, where, and how approach. Your final implementation plan should be a short document that outlines the purpose, processes, responsibilities, and reporting requirements of the functional area or areas assigned to execute the objective. By and large, use the text from this chapter in your document. Again, the mantra is "least is best." Below is a suggested framework for your implementation plan.

Purpose: describes the purpose of the plan and identifies the vision of the organization.

Overview: provides a description of the goals and objectives to be implemented.

Assumptions: describes the assumptions made regarding the development and execution of the plan as well as any constraints. Some items to consider when identifying the assumptions and constraints are schedule, budget, available resources, and required skill sets.

Management: provides a description of how the implementation will be managed (the management approach) and identifies the key tasks involved.

Implementation narrative: provides a description of the planning and execution of each objective.

Point of contact (POC): identifies the responsible functional areas, members of the IPT, APPMs, and anyone else involved in the implementation process. Includes titles, e-mail addresses, and telephone numbers of personnel involved in the implementation.

Key tasks: provides descriptions of the important implementation tasks and adds as many subtasks as necessary to adequately describe all the key tasks. The key tasks described here are not objective tasks; they are generic overall implementation tasks that are required by the CPT to manage all aspects of the implementation. Be sure to include the following information for the description of each task, if appropriate:

- ✓ What the task will accomplish
- ✓ Resources required to accomplish the task
- ✓ Key person(s) responsible for each task
- ✓ Criteria for successful completion of the task

Key tasks include, for example:

- ✓ Overall planning and coordination for the implementation
- ✓ Appropriate training for personnel
- ✓ All needed assistance, including such assistance as that from the ISS to allocate more funding resources
- ✓ Assurance that all requirements are synchronized across the organization to support the APPMs

Implementation schedule: provides a schedule of activities to be accomplished and shows the required key tasks in chronological order, with the beginning and end dates of each objective. I recommend using a Gantt chart, as in appendix B, Project Plan.

Security (if applicable): includes overview of security requirements that must be followed during the implementation.

Implementation support: describes the support, facilities, and materials required for the implementation, as well as the resources and training requirements; and discusses in detail the number of personnel, length of time needed, expertise, and any necessary security requirements.

Implementation impact: describes how the implementation is expected to affect the organization's internal and external environments.

Performance monitoring: describes the performance-monitoring tools and techniques and how they will be used to help determine if the implementation is successful; discussed in chapters 4 and 5.

WHERE ARE YOU NOW?
- ✓ You've finalized and printed the strategic plan.
- ✓ You've developed and begun implementing the communication plan.
- ✓ You've developed the implementation plan.
- ✓ You've developed a sample POAM.
- ✓ You've updated your project plan and annotated your completed tasks.

Risks: identifies the risks and specific actions to be taken in the event one or more objective implementations fail or need to be altered at any point and includes the factors used for making the decision; often referred to as a risk-management plan.

Task #23, Develop Plan of Action and Milestones (POAM)

Task your APPMs to develop a POAM for each objective. Appendix O provides more information and a sample POAM.

Chapter 4
Employ Change

How will you employ change?

> *"A good plan, violently executed now, is better than a perfect plan next week." (George Patton)*

Chapter 4 focuses on the tools and techniques that ensure successful implementation of the strategic plan. The main tasks in the chapter are to:

- ✓ Develop performance measures
- ✓ Fix responsibilities
- ✓ Apply resources
- ✓ Execute the plan of action and milestones (POAM)
- ✓ Develop training

Develop performance measures

The following definitions are used to assist the development of this portion of the strategic plan:

Goal. A goal is a broad statement of what the organization hopes to achieve; it is qualitative in nature.

Objectives. Objectives are specific, achievable, and measurable statements of what will be done to achieve goals within a designated time frame and are typically reached through a plan of action and milestones (POAM).

Performance measures. Performance measures are quantitative or qualitative characterizations of performance that are used to evaluate progress toward executing objectives. Respectively, they quantify and describe the organization's efficiency and effectiveness in conducting the business lines of operations. Implementing the performance measures that relate to each objective provides a basis for ongoing measurement of the objective's success as it is implemented. My research at the University of Arizona turned up

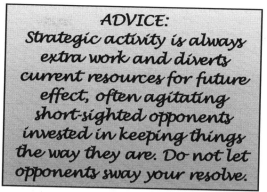

ADVICE:
Strategic activity is always extra work and diverts current resources for future effect, often agitating short-sighted opponents invested in keeping things the way they are. Do not let opponents sway your resolve.

some characteristics of good performance measures. Such measures can be characterized as:

- ✓ Meaningful—significant and directly related to the mission, vision, and goal.
- ✓ Responsibility linked—matched to an organizational functional area responsible for achieving the measure.
- ✓ Organizationally acceptable—valued by those within the organization.
- ✓ Customer focused—reflective of the point of view of the customers and stakeholders.
- ✓ Comprehensive—all key aspects of the organization's performance included.
- ✓ Balanced—several types of measures (e.g., outcome, efficiency, and quality measures) included.
- ✓ Timely—data (measurable metrics) used and reported in a reasonable time frame.
- ✓ Credible—based on accurate and reliable data.
- ✓ Cost effective—based upon acceptable data collection and processing costs.
- ✓ Compatible—integrated with existing financial and operational systems.
- ✓ Comparable—useful for making comparisons with other data over time.
- ✓ Simple—easy to calculate and interpret.

Performance standard. The performance standard is the level that the performance measure should meet so that the objective is attained.

Performance measurement is the ongoing monitoring and reporting of accomplishments and progress toward achieving approved goals and objectives. For many objectives, requirements can be met through performance measurement, which includes collecting data on the level and type of activities (inputs), the level of activity conducted (process), and the direct products and services delivered by the objectives (outputs). Simply put, performance measurement is a determination of what an objective accomplishes and whether desired results are being achieved. It measures the system-wide effectiveness of an organization's mission accomplishment and vision attainment.

Once established, performance measurement provides organizations with a valuable tool that gives leaders and managers a method of determining progress toward a specific, defined organizational objective and ultimately the strategic plan. While high-performing organizations may have sophisticated and complicated performance measurement systems, basic performance measurement techniques can be used in all organizations regardless of size, complexity, or mission.

Why measure performance?

The saying, "What gets measured gets done" has been attributed variously to Peter Drucker, Tom Peters, and Edward Deming, among others. Certainly, what is measured (and briefed to the leadership) gets attention. However, organizations should ensure that measures reflect the "right things" and focus on what really matters. In production, it's easy to identify important goals such as "on time" and "lower costs," which can be measured and then lead to changes in processes. Identifying important "strategic business-side goals" is more difficult, particularly when attempting to relate those goals and objectives to the organization's strategic alignment. Despite the effort required in establishing, maintaining, and reporting, performance measurement has several critical, tangible benefits. First, without some form of standard for achievement, there is no rational basis for decision making. I've found that if you do not measure it, you cannot manage it. On the flip side, to measure performance and then do little with the outcome is just as bad as not measuring at all—it's a waste of your time. Second, performance measurement provides an achievement standard for processes and can help identify areas that are succeeding or failing. Furthermore, things that are not measured usually fall by the wayside and are not done (or done well), so it is critical to include key (if not all) business processes in the performance-measurement system. More important, if an organization measures the wrong thing, it may reinforce the wrong behavior, which will ultimately detract from its ability to achieve its goals. Third and last, it is important not only to measure performance, but to report performance outcomes and reward desired performance. As noted leadership trainer John E. Jones put it, "What gets measured gets done. What gets measured and fed back gets done well. What gets rewarded gets repeated."

Arguably, the two most important measures from a performance audit standpoint are *outcomes* and *efficiency*. Outcome measures assess how well a service or a product accomplishes stated goals and objectives and indicate the quality or effectiveness of that service or product. For instance:

- ✓ Maintenance ratings based on routine and scheduled inspections could describe overall performance of equipment, which can give the organization an overall sense of its "readiness."
- ✓ To gauge success, the IT department might track the success of its "call response" effort using its "call efficiency" rating or frequency of its (customer complaint) rating.
- ✓ Shipping firms can use "on-time delivery" to track efficiency and customer satisfaction.
- ✓ Adequate yearly progress and the results of random parent surveys could be used to determine outcomes of special education services provided.

As a young leader in the military, I recall that we used a simple measurement system to gauge individual proficiency. It was called tasks, standards, conditions (TSC). Every task, event, or training scenario linked to the TSC. The system simply referred to the task to be completed (e.g., qualify with a weapon); the standard by which to complete it (hit forty-six of fifty targets); and the conditions under which to complete it (in darkness without a scope). It was a simple measurement, yet an effective one. In the event the standards were not met, retraining or reworking of the task was conducted. This cycle was repeated until the standards were achieved.

Factors to consider in selecting performance measures

Since performance measures are used to assess progress toward meeting objectives and, in turn, goals, selection of performance measures is closely tied to development of goals and objectives. As Figure 4–1, Relationship between Goals and Performance Measures, illustrates, the performance measure supports the objective, which is linked to the goal.

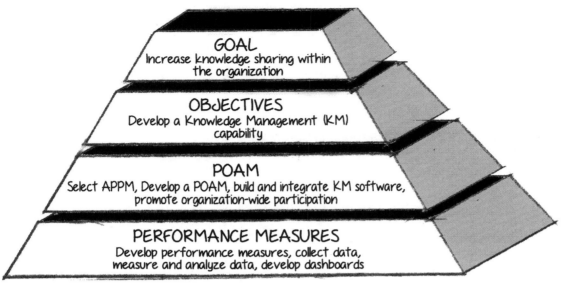

Figure 4–1. Relationship between goals and performance measures

Additionally, Figure 2–5, Strategic Alignment Linkage, depicts performance measures linked to specific objectives. As you can see (Figure 2–5), these performance measures are quantifiable (e.g., "integrate IT systems to support cost-efficient program" or "ensure 95 percent efficiency within one year (July 2016). They set a particular standard that must be achieved to meet the stated objective.

Selecting performance measures requires considering what specific metric will be used and how measurements will be taken. In selecting performance measures, several factors should be considered, including:

✓ **Key Concerns.** The performance measure should play a role in driving the planning and execution and relate clearly to established goals and objectives. Many measures are available and reflect data that can be collected, but it is important to focus on selecting the few that will be most important in influencing decisions that relate to process and output. Measures should be carefully selected to reflect key concerns of the organization. For example, in seeking to gauge congestion at a military base entry point, you could consider a variety of potential measures, such as inbound lanes operating below a certain level of capacity, vehicle delays, military guards' hours of duty, necessary safety obstacles and procedures, and so forth. The selected measure will have important implications for strategies that are chosen to mitigate congestion. For instance, measures of vehicle delay and volume/capacity congestion will tend to favor capacity solutions; measures that focus on person-hours of operation or accessibility via multiple entrances may encourage a broader set of strategies, such as construction of new or wider traffic lanes. Other measurements may drive policies such as relaxing security requirements to improve vehicular flow. It is important to consider tradeoffs associated with selecting different measures or using multiple measures.

✓ **Clarity.** Performance measures are one ingredient that is used for converting broad goals into measurable objectives. The measures should be understandable to the individual executing the task, the stakeholders, and the organization. You must ensure that measures are clear and avoid technical terms as much as possible. The key is to keep it simple. For example,

> *GUIDANCE:*
> *If you cannot initiate a new process while the old process is in place, it's perhaps best to forgo the new process.*

an objective of a city transit system is to "increase ridership on the Red Line by 10 percent in one year." One possible measuring method would be to calculate a baseline of the number of riders passing through the turnstiles on a daily basis (input). Next would be to institute processes to increase ridership by 10 percent (processes). Then, using the same baseline calculation method (output), you would determine if the new processes revealed an increase in ridership.

✓ **Data availability.** You need to consider the feasibility and practicality of collecting, storing, and analyzing data and reporting performance information for the selected measures. Moreover, there should be a reasonable level of confidence that the data will be available for future analyses. The cost of data is also an important consideration. However, while data availability is important, it is also worth remembering not to simply define the measurement based on what data are readily available but to consider what data could be collected that will best reflect issues of importance to the organization, stakeholders, and decision makers. You should be cognizant of the fact that data can sometimes skew outcomes. In one organization, my team and I tracked numerous sets of supply-chain data from a requisition to "pick, pack, ship, receipt, and invoice." Performance measures were developed for each phase of the supply-chain process mentioned above. We saw significant problems with bad and erroneous data. That bad data led to bad assumptions and bad decisions. I strongly urge that you "cleanse" raw data and verify its accuracy and timeliness before using it to draw a conclusion. I've often used data to develop metrics as a basis for comparing alternative courses of action or policies in order to make decisions—for example, using metrics to measure something quantifiable, such as "fifty pieces moved in one week." In the event the objective is not met—"only thirty pieces moved in one week"—the process begins for selecting alternate courses of action that when implemented will attain the desired objective.

✓ **Is the measure something the organization and its stakeholders can influence?** A good measure does not need to be something that an organization controls. As noted earlier, most outcome-based measures of performance reflect system-wide considerations and may be influenced by many external factors. At the same time, it is important to select measures that can be influenced through policy and operational decisions.

✓ **Is the measure meaningful?** While consistency in metrics is valuable, it is also important to make sure that a measure is meaningful to the area or process to which it is applied. For instance, in the above supply-chain example, my team measured transportation fuel consumption when the vehicle was not in motion (e.g., driver's rest stop, but vehicle runs to cool the cab). In reality, fuel consumption cost as a whole had little to do with our performance measure to support the objective. Yet, we "chased that fuel consumption rabbit" despite wasted time and resources.

✓ **Is improvement direction clear?** In some cases, organizations choose measures but do not state clearly whether they desire the measures to increase or decrease, which is particularly problematic when the measures could be interpreted differently depending on one's perspective. You must have a reference for target setting. Metrics are used as the basis for selecting a target that is intended to be achieved. This is sometimes specified in a quantitative measure—for example, as a percent (2 percent defect rate) or a number (fifty widgets).

There often can be value in using multiple measures to address multiple dimensions of a problem. At the same time, it is advisable to start with a limited number of measures

> "Every strike brings me closer to the next home run." (Babe Ruth)

since it can be overwhelming to address hundreds of different measures. My experience suggests it's important to keep the measures simple and few. As has been noted in many places, "Measure what is important; do not measure everything." Again, study the table in Figure 2–5, Strategic alignments linkage. Take note of the suggested quantitative-performance measures that support the objectives. I recommend that you use the same approach.

Fix responsibilities. Put strategic focus into the organization: assign ownership to someone.

The final implementation of the strategic plan involves the initiation of the activities designed at the unit and functional levels and their integration into the operations at the top of the organization. The idea of strategy is not to merely write a story about success. It is to actually succeed. So you need to do something specific—you need action. The test of a successful strategy is converting your objectives into results. That is where the POAM translates the grand strategic objectives into a series of specific, bite-sized tasks, with human and financial resources allocated to ensure success. If you do this right, you will know who is supposed to do what, when.

I've seen far too many times that unless organizations have a specific functional area or individual commitment to do precise things in a POAM, doing those things is deferred. The successful POAM achieves an objective by allocating the time and resources necessary for each step; it develops a timeline to complete each task. The main ingredient of a successful POAM is fixing responsibility to accomplish the objective. Without this, main ingredient objectives are simply a wish list. Thus it is imperative that you fix responsibility to plan and execute objectives. The various approaches used by the organization to hold functional areas and people accountable must reflect the desire to execute the strategic plan.

Murphy's Law and experience have taught me that events never go as planned on a project. And not just because there's a problem. Opportunities present themselves, economies of scale can be taken

> POINT: Do not hesitate to embrace rework.

advantage of, or new technologies become available that can skew the best-laid plans. However, without adequate POAM planning, events can't be completed in a timely manner, if at all; reworking will become standard fare, and the final product may be far from the acceptable performance measure. Your goal is to ensure that responsibility is given to the right individual so that the right actions get done with the right resources at the right time.

In order to fix responsibility, an APPM must be selected for each POAM. This individual must possess the initiative and drive that make a difference. In order to execute a successful strategic plan, you must fix responsibility upon reliable individuals with the intellectual capital to achieve success. Some goals and objectives are complex and require connecting and coordinating structures, processes, resources, or activities across organizational boundaries as required for successful POAM implementation. The APPM may also be required to take action not necessitating high-level approval. In these and most cases, the APPM should have some authority to act independently, thereby curtailing continuous requests for approval. Some of the functions of the APPM are to:

- ✓ Plan, coordinate, and execute the actions required to realize the objectives
- ✓ Select individuals with specific expertise to assist in POAM planning and execution (e.g., develop the IAT)
- ✓ Address all security requirements
- ✓ Focus attention on strategy and the strategic plan objective and develop a POAM to realize the objective
- ✓ Develop and incorporate all required facets of project management (e.g., scope, time, cost, facility, human resources, communications, risk, and procurement management)
- ✓ Make recommendations to the organization's leadership on implementation steps and actions
- ✓ Coordinate all support to execute the POAM (e.g., logistical requirements, human resources, funding, infrastructure upgrades, and IT support).
- ✓ Take action within authorized limits
- ✓ Rally key participants and stakeholders to push the POAM along
- ✓ Offer a setting where important conflicts may be explored and managed effectively
- ✓ Ensure that funding is approved before beginning each execution phase

✓ Develop performance measures
✓ Provide updates and status reports of progress

You must serve as an enabler to assist with your resources (mostly political clout) to ensure that the APPM stays within his or her scope and on schedule.

APPM conflict

In over 80 percent of the cases, the APPM has another job or performs other duties within the organization (primarily in functional organizations). How will this individual effectively allocate his time and resources to both endeavors? In your eyes, the APPM is linked to the strategic plan, and that should be the priority. In the eyes of the individual's supervisor, his or her day-to-day work is critical and must be completed. It is incumbent upon you and the implementation plan sponsor to broker this deadlock and ensure that the APPM stays on course in accordance with the stated mission: to plan and execute the objective. In many cases, the APPM will have to devote the preponderance of his or her time to POAM planning and execution.

Another key component in executing the POAM is applying all the tenets of project management. As mentioned earlier, the APPM must be skilled in the scope, time, cost, facility, human resources, communications, risk, and procurement management spheres. By adhering to these spheres, the APPM will develop supporting plans (e.g., risk management plan, human resource plan, etc.) to ensure that the appropriate tools and techniques are applied, thus producing the desired end state.

Another point I want to reemphasize is teamwork. The APPM must understand and utilize the dynamics of brainstorming, group norms, meeting punctuality, and various other aspects of personnel interaction. I deeply believe that the entire planning project has a greater probability of failure if the APPM is unaware of how to properly conduct, mentor, and guide these social settings and requirements.

Internal conflict

Many years ago I had a person working under me as an APPM. "Mike" was extremely talented and productive but was also extremely disruptive. His ability to cause carnage among the rest of the IPT was legendary. After one extremely aggravating episode, I decided to discuss his performance with him, the result being that I replaced him so that we could move forward and be more productive. Mike was combative and argumentative and a drag on the process such that the team could not progress with him as the APPM. We often fail to realize the impact of disruptive or underperforming individuals on teams. This is not surprising because today's mantra of business success preaches that we need to build teams that feature value and inclusiveness.

While inclusiveness has its place and can be an asset to your organization, I believe that the pendulum may have swung too far. When you value tolerance at the risk of the potentially negative impact of "unique individuals" on the productivity of the team, you may have overegged the pudding. Let me pause and clarify that by inclusiveness I am *not* talking about diversity in terms of race, sex, or other demographics. What I am suggesting is that supporting diversity in the workplace does not mean you should tolerate and accommodate every odd-behaving individual who ends up on your team or, worse, who leads your team. Many of the most talented people in any organization have attributes and styles of interaction that are disruptive and frustrating to the people around them, circumstances that make one wonder if the aggravation they cause is worth the talent and results they bring to the team. At the same time, the individuals or team chosen to implement the POAM must be motivated to achieve success. Every POAM must have a primary person assigned to be responsible and accountable for the overall planning and execution. My point: select an APPM with excellent leadership and management traits and the skill set to perform the technical functions required by the action plan. Remember that vignette in the Introduction about "winning" and "fighting" organizations? The same holds true for teams. Winning teams travel a far easier path to achieve success.

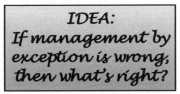

IDEA:
If management by exception is wrong, then what's right?

Execute the POAM—the project plan

As mentioned before, the CPT has the primary responsibility for management of the implementation plan. However, the actions within the POAM are executed by the appropriate functional area. (Refer to appendix O, POAM, for more information.) A comprehensive but detailed operational plan must be developed for each POAM—both new and existing—that survived the gap analysis. The combined thrust of these plans represents the newly established strategic direction of the organization. The POAM should be consistent and clear and have easy-to-understand steps for launching new activities. The following elements should be present in each POAM:

- ✓ A clear description and the actions to obtain the objective
- ✓ The intended outcome or output
- ✓ The resources necessary to develop, produce, and deliver the objective end state

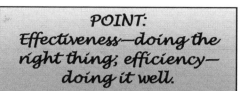

POINT:
Effectiveness—doing the right thing; efficiency—doing it well.

- ✓ A detailed, realistic financial analysis, including revenue projections and fixed and variable costs
- ✓ The milestones (a project plan) for the entire process, from initiation to full operational status
- ✓ A comprehensive implementation plan
- ✓ A fixed responsibility for each task or activity

"Don't fall victim to what I call the 'ready, aim, aim, aim' syndrome; you must be willing to fire."
(George Patton)

The key to a successful POAM execution is project planning. Creating a project plan is the first step that must be done when undertaking any kind of project. Often this step is considered to consist mainly of creating a project schedule or milestones. When the project scope is not well defined, or the project sponsor (assigned functional area manager) has not authorized certain resources and support to be provided for various tasks, or possible known risks have not been considered with alternatives for mitigation, that project is headed for certain failure. Many people fail to realize the value of a project plan in saving time and money and avoiding problems. Use elements from the project plan in creating the POAM for each objective. The POAM (project schedule/milestones) must coordinate independent tasks to ensure that all work is completed in the proper sequence.

Contingency planning

Even though events rarely work out exactly as anticipated, strategic plans need to be developed and executed. The typical planning process focuses, as it should, on the highest probability of success, but this focus can result in an incomplete set of plans that affects that very success. The two key concepts in contingency planning are *highest probability* and *impact*. In other words, contingency plans involve potentially high-impact events that do not have the highest probability of success. You should identify the key indicators that will trigger an awareness of the need to reexamine the adequacy of the current strategic plan. Such a trigger point could be an actual or anticipated increase in the price of a critical raw material, or in the price of fuel, or a sharp, unexpected, positive economic turnaround that offers the possibility for expansion and growth. When trigger points are identified as having been reached, two levels of response are possible:

- ✓ Monitoring. At this level, no participation should be undertaken; in fact, no immediate action may be required.
- ✓ Implementing. At this level, the determination is made that conditions are different, thus an approved contingency plan is implemented, or some aspect of the strategy is modified.

> *FACT:*
> *Why do plans that look good on paper go bad when they are executed? Because of unforeseen secondary and tertiary effects.*

Those events with the highest probability of success are addressed in the basic strategic plan in the form of approved goals and objectives. The most important contribution that

> *"Obstacles don't have to stop you. If you run into a wall, figure out how to go around it." (Michael Jordan)*

contingency planning can make to an organization is the development of a process for identifying and responding to unanticipated or unlikely events. It is possible for any organization to sort out the lowest-probability events that might have significant impact on the organization and to develop detailed plans to respond to them. The APPM must have knowledge of all contingency plans and build actions into the POAM to address any contingency events.

Integrating POAM horizontally and vertically

The final implementation of the strategic plan involves the initiation of the several POAMs designed at the functional-area level and their integration into the planning process at the top of the organization. Once a strategy for closing the gaps (revealed in the gap analysis) of the planning process has been developed and initiated, two important issues need to be addressed. First, each of the various functional areas of the organization—from business to general administration to IT—needs to develop a detailed operational

POAM based on the overall objectives assigned to its functional area. This may, for example, involve new construction, initiation of management to develop technical training, new technology implementation, or increased research and development. Second, these POAMs need to be worked into your implementation plan. Prior to developing functional area POAMs, the strategic plan team leader and the APPM must ensure that the plan is synchronized with established, prioritized goals and objectives in the strategic plan.

Horizontal and vertical POAM integration is critical for alleviating duplication and organizational turmoil. Say, for example, that your IT department is executing a POAM to "develop a knowledge-management program" within the organization. At the same time, the operations department is executing a POAM to "implement tracking software." It would seem obvious that there may be some technological conflicts, synchronization issues, overlapping resource requirements, and other clashes that may arise when implementing actions associated with each POAM. In the same vein, the human resources department objective to "recruit, train, and certify employees" requires input from each functional area along the full spectrum of personnel skills and specialties required to accomplish its mission. You can see from these examples that without integration of POAM planning and execution, the organization will experience some level of conflict that may significantly degrade day-to-day operations. You must ensure that these "stovepipes" are dismantled.

Typically, questions for the strategic plan team leader (to be asked of him/her) include the following:

- ✓ Which POAM gets more attention early in the implementation process and which can wait until later?
- ✓ Are some critical-success indicators more important than others?
- ✓ Where are the POAM integration conflicts and what actions are required to mitigate organizational disruption?
- ✓ Based on integration conflicts, will some strategies be emphasized during the next year or two while others are held for later?
- ✓ What and where is the low-hanging fruit?
- ✓ What is the best program-management approach for detecting early signs of POAM integration conflicts?

Planning for the integration of all project activities

Integration planning starts with the drafting of the POAM by the APPM, who explains the scope of the project and its objectives, names the participants, and defines their roles, responsibilities and the authority of the APPM. Most important, the POAM includes its linkage to the strategic plan (stated goals and objectives) and the functional areas within the organization. The POAM includes all sub-project plans as well as the work breakdown structure (WBS) and project schedule and specifically identifies task interdependencies across functional areas with emphasis on the activities in the project's critical path. As each subplan is created (scope management, risk management, communications management, etc.), the CPT must ensure that the APPM diligently identify tasks that can be conducted in tandem or processes that can be combined to satisfy multiple task requirements within his or her POAM as well as within those being implemented by other functional areas. Since information technology systems touch all functional areas, I have discovered that this is where most redundancies occur.

Executing the integration-management process

Accurately matching resources with schedules and addressing all risks as quickly as they are anticipated or known are keys to the POAM success. This requires active engagement with all stakeholders as you coordinate the timely use of resources to mitigate risks. In other words, the resources used by an APPM to execute the POAM affect the resources of the entire organization. For example, "human resource requirements" is a common need to execute a POAM. It's a given that when several POAMs are being executed simultaneously or in parallel, they will compete for organizational resources. In many cases, these organizational resources (such as funding or IT requirements) are a scarce commodity. Therefore, all POAM activities must be carefully managed and integrated across the organization to avoid duplication. I will restate that: as the strategic plan team leader, one of your critical tasks during phase IV and phase V is integration of the POAM. Remember, your role in implementing the strategic plan includes developing the plan, suggesting ideas for the allocation of resources, coordinating APPM requirements, monitoring POAM progress, and deconflicting issues.

An important factor in the integration-management process of the organization's strategic plan is its strategic management. "Strategic management involves the execution of an explicit strategic plan that has captured the commitment of the people who must execute it; that is consistent with the values, beliefs, and culture of those people; and that they have the required competencies to execute" (Peters, 1984). The acid test for any strategic planning process is the degree to which it affects the ongoing behavior of the organization. Some questions that you should answer to determine the organization's willingness to accept the strategic plan implementation process are:

- ✓ Is your organization accepting of any reengineering of the strategic plan?
- ✓ What are the cultural attitudes of those involved?
- ✓ Are those attitudes positive or negative?
- ✓ Are individuals within the organization accepting of these changes?

Strategic management is similar to program management. *A Guide to the Project Management Body of Knowledge* (*PMBOK Guide*) defines program management as "a group of related projects managed in a coordinated way to obtain benefits and control not available from managing them individually." Strategic management is the centrally coordinated management of programs to achieve strategic objectives and benefits. Therefore, strategic management equates to the management of all the POAMs and projects that are geared toward achieving organizational goals and objectives. Consequently, you and the CPT have the primary responsibility for the strategic plan management function.

Communications management

Communications management is the primary method for gaining and sustaining stakeholder commitment and is therefore a key to POAM success. Organizational change management (OCM) is the umbrella under which communications management operates. Studies of project implementations and other organizational changes have shown that management failure is mainly related to communications mismanagement. The main elements of an OCM program include:

- ✓ Creating and executing viable communications and stakeholder engagement plans
- ✓ Knowledge transfer to fill gaps in skills and education across the organization

✓ Strong communications interchange entailing a multipronged approach to information dissemination for educating and training members of the organization. The specific approaches the APPM uses will depend on the culture of the target community and the availability of technology.

✓ A plan for how to measure whether change is a success

✓ Monitoring of opposition to OCM to implement strategies to counter such opposition

✓ Metrics to determine extent of POAM execution

As noted earlier, identifying the APPM's roles and responsibilities is critical to the overall strategic plan success. You must also document the roles and responsibilities of all personnel in the strategic plan execution and how they are integrated into the organization. At the end of each milestone event, the APPM must document lessons learned to include assumptions, constraints, and risks associated with the completed tasks, as well as those lessons associated with the new process about to begin. Before advancing to the next milestone in a POAM, the APPM functional manager will be presented results of completed tasks for approval at a formal IPR. (IPRs are discussed in chapter 5.)

Apply resources

The best strategic plan will fail when not given adequate resources in the budgeting process. Among all the challenges to effectively implement the POAM, a lack of resources is one of the most significant. Given current economic stresses and national, state, and local resource constraints (the so-called new normal), public and private organizations are wrestling with how to support strategies and actions with the necessary money, staff, facilities, and equipment. It also bears repeating that plan implementation does not need to wait until the plan is completed. Whatever wise, innovative action that can be taken during the planning process should be. Targeting small, low-cost wins (low-hanging fruit) for early action is a way of showing that things are going to change as a result of the time, effort, and resources expended on the planning process; it will also build on ongoing determination and support for the process and make a full-blown implementation effort easier. Such targeting is also valuable not only for the savings and gains affecting the bottom line in a positive way, but also for the morale boost and validation that such quick manifestations of return on investment bring to the organization at all levels. It should be noted, however, that it is not uncommon for the returns to slow to a trickle or even stop altogether after this initial surge of activity.

Strategic plans cannot succeed without people, time, money, and other key assets. Some projects require significant financial and human resources. For example, the objective "Develop Knowledge Management and Information Sharing" (Figure 2–5) may require the developing or buying of expensive software as well as hardware, such as servers and data-storage devices. There may even be a need to build space to house equipment as well as substantial "cabling requirements" to create the network architecture. These requirements are costly and require several months to install. Thus, how an organization aligns its resources to support the strategic objectives is critical to the overall success of the plan.

One method of managing and allocating resources is to establish a budget resource board (BRB). The purpose of the BRB is to prioritize and allocate resources to meet the strategic plan goals. BRBs are unique to their organizational structure. In some cases, the BRB consists of one person while in other cases it numbers ten or more. Normally, the BRB is chaired by the resource management director and comprised of key financial decision makers within the organization. Some of the BRB's functions with respect to the strategic plan include:

- ✓ Allocating funds based on goal prioritization
- ✓ Providing finance and accounting guidance to the strategic plan execution
- ✓ Monitoring and synchronizing interfaces among financial and nonfinancial systems
- ✓ Performing funds analyses to ensure fiscal responsibility in POAM execution
- ✓ Preparing and disseminating financial reports as they pertain to the strategic plan execution on a recurring basis
- ✓ Providing financial and accounting support for the APPM
- ✓ Performing special projects (executing objectives) as required for executing the strategic plan

> *IMPORTANT:*
> *Before undertaking any POAM activities, ensure that all*
> *facets are adequately budgeted. If not, your project may*
> *fail. As the APPM, you will find that financial resources*
> *are your biggest obstacle. Ensure that the BRB allocates the*
> *required funds at the required time to execute the POAM.*

APPM training

You must understand that the better trained your APPM is, the greater the possibility that the POAM will be finished on time and within budget, meet all requirements and expectations of the stakeholders, and improve organizational effectiveness and efficiencies. In executing the POAM, the organization, in particular the APPM, may require training in fields such as project management and operations management along with specific training targeted at the technical requirements of the POAM's objective. This training may also fulfill goals and objectives in the Learning and Growth strategic alignment. For example, if the organization has an objective to produce better program and project managers, APPM training can be woven into that overall POAM to fulfill all or some of those Learning and Growth objectives. The organization should work with the human resource manager to design, develop, and implement a focused project management training program.

The need to design, develop, and implement an organizational project management training program is based on the complexity of the POAM. Your information gathering during phase I and phase II will provide insight as to the level for which you should design your training, the training goals, who will support the training, any types of learning constraints you must consider as you prepare the curriculum, and the training approach and delivery method. Trained APPMs will improve project management effectiveness and efficiencies while executing the POAMs. I highly recommend a curriculum consistent with *PMBOK Guide*. Additionally, you may choose to add a learning management system (LMS) to enroll, manage, and track students and to electronically document their progress.

A Note on Lean Six Sigma (LSS)

Six Sigma, a rigorous, focused, and highly effective managerial concept of proven principles and techniques, incorporates elements from the work of many original thinkers, especially at Motorola, where it was developed, and was used with great success by Jack Welch at General Electric. Six Sigma aims for virtually error-free business performance and focuses on helping the organization improve customer value and efficiency. Lean Six Sigma (LSS), a model that combines lean manufacturing or enterprise and Six Sigma, encompasses activities that focus on several things that matter most to an organization's three constituencies—customers, shareholders, and employees. In some organizations for which I managed strategic planning, I linked specific applications of "Lean" (LSS) to the strategic plan. LSS is a way of managing your organization to deliver maximum value to customers with minimal resources and zero waste. Companies that put it into action become highly competitive, resilient, and adaptive. While an organization's LSS effort is typically focused on prioritized value streams, all aspects of the strategic plan execution can benefit from the application of its principles. In several cases, as an LSS black belt (Lean Six Sigma creates a special infrastructure of trained people within an organization [champions, black belts, green belts, yellow belts, etc.] who are experts in these methods), I utilized LSS methodology to execute objectives. Instead of using a POAM, I developed an LSS project charter and executed the project using the LSS's define, measure, analyze, improve, and control (DMAIC) methodology. In the event your organization chooses to embrace LSS, I recommend executing some of your objectives using this process.

WHERE ARE YOU NOW?

✓ You've developed performance measures.
✓ You've conducted POAM integration.
✓ You've conducted APPM training.
✓ You've fixed responsibilities for executing the goals and objectives.
✓ You've reviewed contingency planning.
✓ You've conducted resourcing with the BRB.
✓ You've updated your project plan and annotated your completed tasks.

Chapter 5
Measure and Maintain

How will you measure success?

Chapter 5 will focus on monitoring and maintaining the strategic plan, including how to:

- ✓ Conduct an implementation review and measure performance indicators
- ✓ Refine goals, strategies, and processes
- ✓ Align the organization to support new strategies
- ✓ Measure, analyze, and improve the strategic plan

Conduct implementation review and measure performance indicators

In order to know whether you are attaining a goal, you must examine the performance indicators that will provide the metrics for measuring progress in achieving the goal and its objectives. The following are some suggestions for how to select measures and indicators that will help you:

- ✓ Identify your starting point—that is, the point at which you begin measuring. Based on the initial database assessment that led to the establishment of goals and objectives, you should provide a starting point or guidance for determining meaningful performance measures and indicators. For example, look at the survey results, environmental scan/ gap analysis results, and other data points, then determine to what extent you want to improve a deficiency.

FACT:
If you don't measure it, you don't mean it.

✓ Monitor and measure progress to determine the methodology you will use to take corrective action while executing the objective (POAM).
✓ Know when you've achieved the goal—clearly defining the end state to obtain the objective.

The core of the planning process begins with the organization's mission, vision, and guiding principles (MVGP). Goals and objectives are the path to the future vision. As we discussed before, and as shown in Figure 5–1, Steps to Vision, specific strategies and plans must be measured and incorporated into day-to-day operational activities in order for the organization to reach its goals and realize its vision.

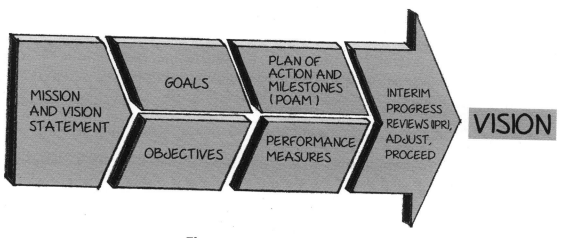

Figure 5–1. Steps to vision

The key to selecting measures and indicators is asking thoughtful questions about how these activities can be measured in an understandable manner, with data that can be collected using a reasonable amount of resources. Developing good planning measures can take some planning of its own.

Strategic plan implementation is a continuous process that requires constant feedback as to how the current strategies are working. Profit levels, returns on investment, customer satisfaction, and sales trends let businesses know when they need to adjust their strategies. In the same vein, performance indicators also provide an organization with comparable information to gauge its performance.

The strategic plan defines the performance (for goals and objectives) to be measured, while performance measurement provides the feedback that keeps the strategic plan on track. The connection strengthens both processes:

> **ADVICE:**
> *Make strategy a continuous habit, not an event.*

- ✓ Performance measurement relies on specified end outcomes—not just tasks, but the results of those tasks. The strategic plan's goals and objectives focus performance measurement on outcomes that define appropriate performance indicators.
- ✓ The performance must be reviewed by the leadership to ascertain whether a strategic course correction is needed.
- ✓ You must regularly revisit and "sanity test" the goals, objectives, and outcome measures. The environment changes. Thus, periodic reporting of performance indicators provides the information necessary to adjust the strategic plan. This information is acquired in terms of the reviews, reports, IPRs, etc., sent to the leadership. These are critical to keep strategic plans on track and to accommodate change.

Not meeting performance methods

Sometimes you do not get the results you want. Say, for example, your performance measure by the end of the third quarter was to

> **HINT:**
> *If you can't measure it, you can't manage it, and vice versa.*

attain 60 percent of the objective. However, when the APPM input the last update into the BSC, you were only at 40 percent of the objective. Despite your best effort, you were not meeting your performance measure. As I discussed before, it is time to analyze. The APPM should gather the team and diagnose the problem. It may take some regrouping to solve it, but it is well worth the time and effort. In essence, you just conducted the measure, analyze, and improve process. Do not dismay; missing targets occurs in every organization at some point.

Measure, analyze, and improve the plan

Strategic planning looks ahead toward reaching desired goals; performance measurement looks back at the achievement of those goals. Combined, strategic planning and performance measurement form a circle—a continuous process of governing for results. As Figure 5–2, Performance cycle, shows, there must be a continuous cycle of measure, analyze, and improve. You must *measure* whether you are meeting the agreed-upon metric (for example, at the end of the third quarter you should be 60 percent completed).

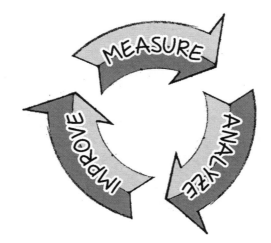

Figure 5–2. Performance cycle

If this metric is not being met or exceeded, you must *analyze* to determine the cause and effect. Once you've analyzed, you must implement activities and actions to *improve*. Then repeat the process … again, and again, and again. Although this is a critical step, it's one that is seldom begun, let alone completed. You've spent a considerable amount of time producing and implementing a strategic plan, and now is not the time to consider your work over and done with. This is a false positive. Effective strategic plans are living documents that change and respond to change both inside and outside the organization. This is why the "final" step does not end.

As mentioned previously, implementation is the difficult part of the planning process. The key point to remember is that you are far ahead of the "power curve" in having developed and implemented a strategic plan. Again, the process is cradle to cradle. You continually want to assess (measure), examine (analyze), and better (improve) your current position. It's acceptable to deviate (flex and pivot) from the plan; it's even recommended. Besides, sometimes, even when all parties are engaged, the anticipated results are just not there. Perhaps, if not seeing significant cost reductions, customer satisfaction, organizational responsiveness, and/or significant achievements established, it is time to change course and make adjustments to the plan. This is the time to drive more analysis and determine what is not working. I mentioned this earlier in a discussion about conducting after-action reviews (AAR). Two important considerations in the AAR are: what you did right in accordance with the plan, and what you did wrong in accordance with the plan. Continue to conduct AARs with the CPT, SPC, APPMs, and the strategic plan champion to perform your sanity check. In addition, do not hesitate to meet on a continual basis with the functional area leadership to discuss and get recommendations for how to improve the planning and execution process and get back on track. After all, in briefing leadership at the monthly IPRs, you will have to give explanations as to why you're not where you should be. The explanations you provide will be based on the analysis conducted. Remember, it's the functional areas that have the "rose pinned on them" to execute the objectives and provide the answers.

The balanced scorecard (BSC)

There are two basic measurement methods I use during phases IV and V of a strategic plan. They are:

- ✓ Key performance indicators (KPI). I use this to monitor the progress of existing daily management systems.
- ✓ Balanced scorecard (BSC). I use this to track progress of the implementation of objectives.

I strongly advocate the use of a balanced scorecard methodology whenever multiple metrics contribute toward overall performance evaluation. In the case of tracking your POAM, you should expect to see multiple metrics being generated for multiple tasks and activities within each POAM. The BSC can look at individual factors from one task, all factors together, or combine them into an overall performance assessment for all tasks. A good performance measurement system will measure multiple dimensions of performance—that is, quality, quantity, timeliness, and customer satisfaction. It emphasizes results of each, based on factual performance indicators rated against a goal or standard, combined in a weighted format to present an overall picture of performance. The BSC is effective as:

- ✓ A framework to organize and report actionable POAM components
- ✓ A sound way to manage the execution of your strategic plan

✓ A way to encourage you to look at different perspectives and take into account cause-effect relationships
✓ A means to improve how you communicate your strategy, which is critical to the execution of the plan
✓ A quantitative focus on accomplishing the mission and meeting the vision
✓ A tool to generate current status dashboards

There are numerous BSC software programs on the market. However, if you have familiar software that is specific to your organization, then I would recommend using it. For instance, some governmental organizations such as 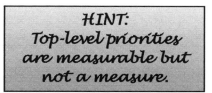 the Department of Defense (DoD) have internal BSC software—the DoD Strategic Management System (SMS) being one such example. Again, use what is comfortable for you and your organization. I prefer a software package that delivers assessment and analytic capabilities.

In order to obtain the maximum benefit of the BSC, you must cascade the BSC reporting structure and align each unit to the tasks it is executing. Each functional area must have an individual BSC so that it can input data relevant to its tasks. After the cascading and alignment have been concluded, automate the required reports within the software tool. This automation will in effect create an overall dashboard for the entire organization. The following is a situation for which I utilized a BSC.

Using the BSC

Using the IT department as a starting point, I built the BSC showing the objective. I then built the "lower decks" to show the status of each task and its corresponding subtasks. The main focus was to develop a BSC to measure and display performance. I tracked progress to keep abreast of the status that enabled my team to quantitatively measure the performance of each POAM task. The first step was to construct the BSC to fit our needs (what we wanted to show the leadership). Thus, the BSC was built to show the strategic alignments, goals, objectives, and status of each task and subtask that made up a POAM. Figure 5–3, Sample Balanced Scorecard, shows a BSC snapshot.

STAKEHOLDER	
S.1 Deliver medical supplies as requisitioned	✔
S.2 Provide best-value solutions	◆
S.3 Provide total asset visibility	✘

INTERNAL PROCESSES	
IP.1 Improve business processes	✔
IP.2 Develop collaborative end-to-end process	✔
IP.3 Eliminate redundencies	◆

RESOURCES	
R.1 Articulate & document resource requirements	✘
R.2 Incorporate stewardship, accountability, and internal controls	✘
R.3 Link decisions to resources	◆

LEARNING AND GROWTH	
LG.1 Recruit, train, and certify employees	✔
LG.2 Develop knowledge-and information-sharing environment	✘
LG.3 Create and develop leaders at all levels	✘

Figure 5–3. Sample Balanced Scorecard

Each quadrant is assigned a strategic alignment with its objectives, with the far-right column providing the current status. For example, the check (usually green) means the objective is on schedule; the diamond (usually yellow), slightly behind schedule; and the X (usually red), considerably behind schedule. Clicking on the objective or the status enables one to drill down to see greater detail for each subtask within the POAM. Additional clicking on a task reveals the status of that task, with remarks explaining possible issues.

These "snapshot" charts were briefed to leadership during our monthly IPRs. Some of the important metric factors we followed with our BSC were:

✓ Measured milestones—short-term outcomes at the POAM level
✓ Measured outcomes of our objectives
✓ Explanations of each task in order to minimize the reviewer's face-to-face meetings with the APPM for clarification
✓ Lead and lag measures to depict cause-effect relationships
✓ Measures using a template to capture critical data elements

Now consider the performance of the "recruit, train, and certify employees" objectives within the learning and growth strategic alignments linkage (Figure 2–5). These objectives were assigned to the human resources (HR) department. After the HR department conducted an analysis of the objectives, it determined the desired performance measures. Once the performance measures were developed, they were included in the POAM. Then, each task and performance measure was input into the BSC. Every two weeks, it was the responsibility of the HR APPM for that particular objective to input updated data into the BSC. This input showed the status of each task/milestone—for example, the measure "obtain baseline of employee knowledge" is only 10% complete. This was lower than the 50% projected measure and thus received a red X. In this manner, all interested parties could log in to the BSC and get a "visual read" and an explanation of why the status was at 10 percent. The benefit was obvious for leaders, APPMs, and stakeholders—they got real-time information on the status of the strategic plan objectives as well as the holistic plan, a textbook example of how the BSC can provide utility for an organization.

Retrieving data; reviewing, interpreting, conducting analysis; displaying performance dashboards; and providing concise solutions are the basic factors of measurement. In order to conduct effective IPRs, you should have the capability of incorporating these basic factors. Integrated intelligent agent (IIA) technology was developed to retrieve and interpret data and display performance dashboards. For example, for another project on which I worked, IIA technology was used as a dashboard to monitor all the events associated with a network that included intrusion detection, patch management, and performance-related information. The alerts were displayed on the dashboard. Here, the IIA technology was backed by a solution that recorded incidents as issues in the IIA; they were marked closed as each was resolved. All events were displayed in near real time. We then interpreted the display data, reviewed for data cleansing, and conducted an analysis so that we could provide actionable recommendations to the leadership. Obviously, you do not need a system this complex to track metrics; however, you do need some type of automation to track the progress of the plan. This automation is your BSC software.

BSC training

You must provide each APPM access to the BSC so that he or she can input his POAM progress and update as required. This allows for:

- ✓ Keeping the plan on track to closely monitor progress in both operational plans and change or modify POAM status
- ✓ Developing dashboards for the entire organization

You must also provide hands-on, classroom-based training in how to use your chosen BSC software. Such training is critical to successful tracking. Simply put, I've seen numerous gaps in BSC updates. In researching why,

I discovered several departments and APPMs did not know how to properly use the software. Obviously, that is a nonstarter. Training on BSC software is a "must-do."

Training should include:

- ✓ Software security and access.
- ✓ Users, groups, permissions, and settings.
- ✓ Navigation through all facets of the software.
- ✓ Scorecards, strategy maps, graphs, charts, and reports.
- ✓ Access to administrative support.
- ✓ Data population and automation.
- ✓ Scorecard owners and updaters. Who should have access?
- ✓ Briefings.

The trainer should meet with each functional area and APPM to:

- ✓ Train each on the full spectrum of the software capabilities
- ✓ Assist each in noting trends, issues, successes, and shortcomings
- ✓ Identify best practices
- ✓ Create reports and dashboards
- ✓ Record each's objectives and accomplishments in the system

As I've stated before, most strategic plans unfortunately never get implemented. The most difficult part of the strategic planning process is to ensure that the goals and objectives are implemented. The best method to gauge implementation is to conduct

> *IDEA:*
> *Quantification is the truth detector of your intentions— it eliminates uncertainty about the interpretation of your strategic intentions.*

monthly status updates to inform the CEO and senior leaders on how well the organization is executing the plan. I have seen numerous episodes of plans that are put in motion and then die after a few months. The primary reason for these failures is a lack of leadership focus or consequences for not completing required actions. I've worked with several organizations that conducted elaborate and expensive exercises. They developed a long list of "lessons learned," only to fail to "put into play" any actions to correct perceived deficiencies. Again, the primary reason for this failure was lack of interest by the leadership and in some cases just poor management. Conversely, I've worked with several organizations that had monthly updates with the CEO to provide reports on how deficiencies were being remedied. These are the IPRs discussed earlier. In one organization, I was even responsible for executing and providing a weekly written status report to a CEO on one of his organization's important goals. This report was followed by monthly briefings to the CEO and his staff on the status of that goal. I am certain that it was the requirement to continually provide weekly and monthly updates that drove the necessity to make progress in executing the POAM. This continuous feedback resulted in goal attainment. I was held accountable and had to demonstrate progress on a monthly and even weekly basis. I certainly did not want to brief the CEO that we'd made no progress in seven, let alone thirty, days. Thus, I was compelled to execute the POAM in a results-oriented manner. This approach vividly demonstrated to the organization that in order to achieve goal attainment, progress must be continually managed and judged. I discussed performance measures in chapter 4, but I now want to tie that discussion together with a discussion of conducting implementation reviews.

Interim progress review (IPR). Without a measurable plan, you'll surrender control.

The IPR is a comprehensive report formatted into sections correlating to each strategic alignment and the administration/execution of such. This report is typically accompanied by a briefing to leadership. Each IPR includes an overall status review that incorporates historical data and metrics, trend analysis, and recommendations to mitigate issues or risk in meeting goals. An IPR read-ahead package that includes charts and summaries of applicable data and issues should be provided to leadership before each briefing. The information contained and presented in the IPR is a compilation of monthly data and should include trend analyses and histograms. Typically, the IPR is 30 percent historical and 70 percent future planning (what's been accomplished to date and what's next). Most BSC software is able to provide numerous dashboards for displaying progress. You can brief the leadership directly from these graphic reports.

At a minimum, you should provide one of the following for real-time reporting and formal project reviews:

- ✓ Monthly status report (MSR)
- ✓ Interim progress review (IPR)
- ✓ Milestone summary

✓ Green, Yellow, Red (G, Y, and R) "stoplight charts"

All of these can display current POAM progress and can be presented at regularly scheduled project-overview meetings. Displayed data should include but not be limited to:

✓ Project description
✓ Percentage of completion for each milestone
✓ Percentage of overall project completion
✓ Perceived issues, risks, and actions to mitigate
✓ Lessons learned

During the IPR, the dashboard template must give leadership a real-time, comprehensive snapshot of the POAM status and performance. A snapshot report should indicate the status of all ongoing projects using the G, Y, and R dashboard signals to denote the health of the overall strategic plan or a project and its various tasks (see Figure 5–4, Sample stoplight dashboard).

GOALS	STATUS	COMMENTS
OVERALL	G	
Provide successful medical distribution	R	Software prototype requires patches
Institute mission-focus process	Y	Need identification by Aug 30, 2015
Optimize all resources	Y	Working with NCA and HBR to determine what and when
Develop high-caliber employees	G	Course in development Recruitment strategy in place

Figure 5–4. Sample "stoplight" dashboard

Review and refine goals, strategies, and processes

Many organizations incorporate strategic plan maintenance into their strategy as they create it. They know that, with rapid changes in technology and global expansion, an organization will evolve over, say, a period of three years. Therefore, it is necessary to regularly revisit the plan as a whole. The first step in refining the current goals, strategies, and processes is to review the mission statement to determine if it still defines the organization. As I mentioned earlier, an organization's mission statement is usually stable unless there have been dramatic changes in its customer base, product, services, or the marketplace in which it operates.

After the mission statement review, it is important to look at any changes in strategic goals and strategies. You must consider whether the internal and external environment has changed in such ways as to merit reshaping your strategic goals and strategies to achieve those goals (as well as objectives). There are typically three phases in a product or service life cycle: introduction, growth, and decline. Even though, or sometimes because, your product or services may not change in these phases, the market (external environment) certainly will. You must heed the decline phase, for it is in this phase that your strategies will require reworking. At this point in the overall planning process, you should have enough information to identify what maintenance is needed. Is it simply readjusting existing strategy? Or do you need to create a completely new strategy? What should you do if the need falls between the two extremes? Or does the organization simply require an operational-process change? Maintenance of your strategy need not take a great deal of time—as little as a few weeks a year. However, if a complete overhaul is needed, it may take as much time as it would to develop an entirely new strategic plan. The length of time required depends on how much change has occurred since the plan was first developed or last updated. If required changes are minimal (that is, if customer demographics, types of product and service, and mission remain the same), then maintenance will focus mostly on new goals and objectives. However, if your mission or other aspects of the organization have changed in a material way, obviously the change will require a large-scale strategic (re)planning effort.

A strategy review should be scheduled just as any other task should be. You can, for example, set a mark on the calendar for every six months to review the planning process and identify changes. Another method is to use a set of flags or triggers and review matters as required. If you're in a fluid, fast-paced organization, you probably would link much better to the triggers or flags approach. A more stable organization (such as a government agency), on the other hand, might be better suited to the scheduled approach.

External triggers affecting strategy might include such occurrences as an increase in fuel prices, political upheaval, massive technology change, or altered customer expectations. Internal triggers—changes within the organization—might include a corporate reorganization introducing new leadership philosophy or a change of goals and objectives. Changes—be they external or internal—on these orders of magnitude would require a major review of the strategic plan. Being aware of changes happening within and beyond the organization's environment is half the battle of staying current. Organizational changes are the most frequent internal trigger, so it's important to ensure that your strategy continues to be linked to your core functions and capabilities should such changes occur. This is why it is best to allocate time to conduct your sanity check and "adjust fire" as necessary to stay on course.

(Almost) last but not least …

The strategic plan is the DNA of your organization. Ensure that all facets of the plan are linked, synchronized, and connected to your end-to-end process for driving strategic execution.

Finally

You have completed one of the most difficult tasks in organizational management—developing and executing a strategic plan. Congratulations!

WHERE ARE YOU NOW?

- ✓ You've established processes to measure, analyze, and improve the strategic plan implementation.
- ✓ You've, if applicable, returned team members, to their respective place of duty.
- ✓ You've provided appreciation letters to team members.
- ✓ You've completed a lessons learned document on the entire planning and execution process.
- ✓ You're continuing to monitor and analyze performance indicators and adjust strategy as necessary.
- ✓ You've begun planning the next comprehensive strategy review.
- ✓ You've updated your project plan and annotated your completed tasks.

Appendix A
CEO "All-Hands" E-mail

Dear Colleagues,

This year marks the tenth anniversary of the establishment of X-Ray Corporation. I can think of no other organization or cause that lines up more perfectly with our mission to provide on-time medical distribution services for those in need than our company. Never has our purpose been more apparent or more important. You have been a critical part of our success for the last ten years.

I want to ask for your support in the reengineering of our strategic plan as we begin the process of developing X-Ray's vision for the next five years by preparing a plan to get us there.

Hannah Ellen will serve as the strategic plan champion, and Randy Etter will be the lead planner for our effort. Ms. Ellen is my designated appointee to make all resourcing, allocating, and implementing decisions. She will speak for me throughout this entire endeavor. As the lead planner, Mr. Etter will be responsible for developing and executing our plan. He has my full confidence and support in this role. I urge you to give him your support as well.

I know this planning effort may result in some disruption to your operational responsibilities at X-Ray, but strategic planning is critical to our long-term success and survival in a very competitive global environment.

As we begin our second decade of providing to those in need, I invite you to join me in making this a planning event in whose success we can all take pride.

Thank you.

Most cordially,

JH
Jim Hodge

Appendix B
Project Plan

The project plan below is represented in a Gantt chart format. As you can see, the strategic planning process begins on 1 June (row 2) and ends on 16 November (row 35) when the plan is distributed. Within the six-month period (with a ten-day buffer), you will complete all the tasks required to conceptualize, construct, publish, and distribute the strategic plan. The tasks following row 35 are phases IV and V tasks. As mentioned in chapter 4, the duration of these tasks is dependent upon the scope of the objectives. This project plan is available at my website (www.allonscg.com) in an editable version of Microsoft Project.

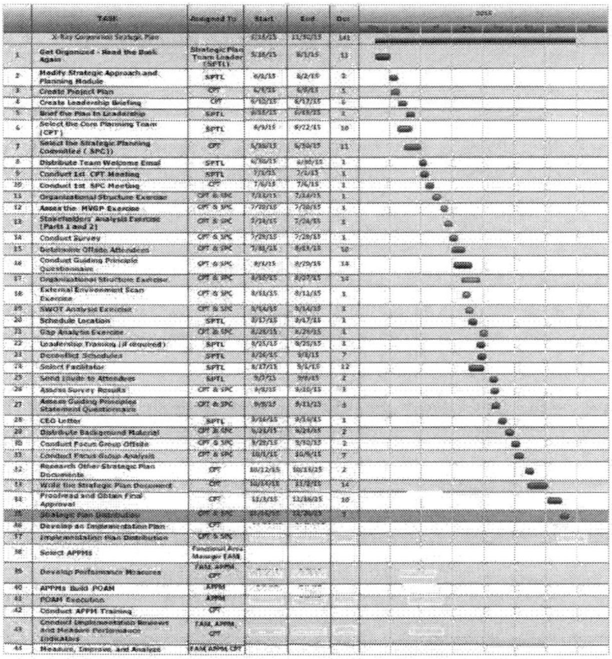

Figure 5. Project plan

Appendix C
First Brief to Leadership

The following is a sample of your first briefing to the leadership. The briefing is available in an editable format at www.allonscg.com.

Purpose

Provide our strategic planning methodology for 2016-2020 to enhance value added to X-Ray Corporation and the National Medical Enterprise.

Gain your approval to proceed as recommended.

What Is Strategic Planning?

- ✓ Deliberate, disciplined effort to produce a strategy that results in actions that shape what an organization is, what it does, why it does it, and what it will do in the future
- ✓ Future-focused
- ✓ Ensures the long-term relevance and survivability of our organization and the community in which it resides
- ✓ Determines and reveals the organization's *objectives, purposes,* or *goals*; produces the *principal policies* and plans for achieving those goals; and defines the range of business the organization is to pursue, the kind of economic and human organization it intends to be, and the nature of the economic and noneconomic contribution it intends to make to its shareholders, employees, customers, and communities.

Why a Strategic Plan?

- ✓ Increase effectiveness
- ✓ Increase efficiency
- ✓ Improve understanding of the organizational environment and growth
- ✓ Improve decision making
- ✓ Enhance organizational capabilities
- ✓ Improve communications and public relations
- ✓ Increase political, community, and consumer support
- ✓ Provide relevancy to the organization
- ✓ Build organizational and individual growth
- ✓ Enhance culture and improve employee morale
- ✓ Most important, keep the organization in step with environmental changes

Appendix C

What Drives the Strategic Plan?

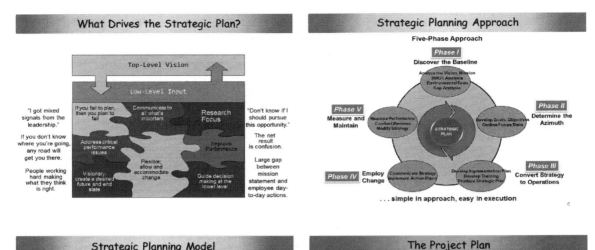

Top-Level Vision

Low-Level Input

If you fail to plan, then you plan to fail

Communicate to all what's important

Research Focus

Address critical performance issues

Improve Performance

Visionary; create a desired future and end state

Flexible; allow and accommodate change

Guide decision making at the lower level

"I got mixed signals from the leadership."

If you don't know where you're going, any road will get you there.

People working hard making what they think is right.

"Don't know if I should pursue this opportunity."

The net result is confusion.

Large gap between mission statement and employee day-to-day actions.

Strategic Planning Approach

Five-Phase Approach

Phase I Discover the Baseline
Analyze the Vision, Mission
SWOT Analysis
Environmental Scan
Gap Analysis

Phase II Determine the Azimuth
Develop Goals, Objectives
Outline Future State

Phase III Convert Strategy to Operations
Develop Implementation Plan
Develop Training
Produce Strategic Plan

Phase IV Employ Change
Communicate Strategy
Implement Action Plans

Phase V Measure and Maintain
Measure Performance
Conduct Reviews
Modify Strategy

STRATEGIC PLAN

... simple in approach, easy in execution

Strategic Planning Model

WHERE WE ARE NOW?	WHERE ARE WE GOING?	HOW ARE WE GOING TO GET THERE?		
WHAT IS OUR BASELINE?	WHAT IS OUR FUTURE STATE?	WHAT IS OUR PLAN TO GET THERE?	HOW WILL WE EMPLOY CHANGE?	HOW WILL WE MEASURE SUCCESS?
Environmental Scan	Conduct Focus Group	Develop Implementation Plan	Communicate Strategies and New Strategic Plan	Conduct Implementation Review and Measure Performance
Analyze Current Vision, Mission, and Guiding Principles (Internal Scan)	Develop restated Vision, Mission, Guiding Principles	Develop Plan of Action and Milestones (POAM)	Develop Performance Measures	Refine Goals, Strategies and Processes
Conduct SWOT Analysis (External Scan)	Outline the Future State	Develop Training	Apply Resources	Align Organization to Support Strategy
Conduct stakeholders Analysis	Develop Goals and Objectives	Link Objectives to Budget	Fix Responsibilities	
Assess Readiness	Prioritize Goals and Objectives		Execute Action Plans	Actualize Strategy
Conduct Gap Analysis	Link Goals and Objectives to Strategic Perspectives	Produce the Strategic Plan Document		
Develop Solution Set/Recommendations				
Conduct leadership Training				
Conduct Focus Group				
Phase I/Chapter 1	Phase II/Chapter 2	Phase III/Chapter 3	Phase IV/Chapter 4	Phase V/Chapter 5
Discover the Baseline	Determine the Azimuth	Convert Strategy to Operations	Employ Change	Measure and Maintain

The Project Plan

The First Step

Establish Our Teams

- ✓ Have fundamental skills to do the job
- ✓ Possess initiative, the drive that makes the difference
- ✓ Share knowledge and expertise and not withhold information
- ✓ Respect the opinions of others
- ✓ Show willingness to listen
- ✓ Be dependable; fulfill all tasks assigned
- ✓ Be action oriented
- ✓ Develop two basic teams:
    Core Planning Team (CPT)
    Strategic Planning Committee (SPC)

Mission Statement Analysis

- ✓ Captures the essence of why the organization exists – who we are and what we do
- ✓ Explains the basic needs that we fulfill
- ✓ Expresses the core values of the organization
- ✓ Is brief and to the point
- ✓ Focuses on one common purpose
- ✓ Conveys the unique nature of our organization and its role that differentiates it from others
- ✓ Includes fixed or directed mission

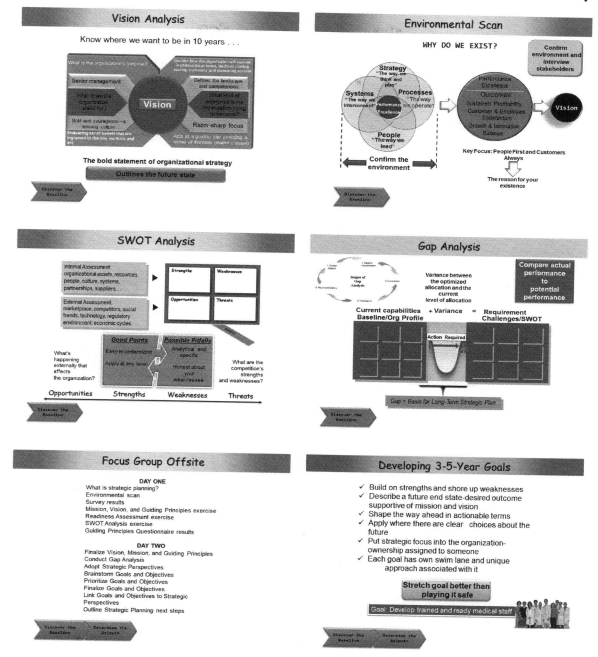

Appendix C

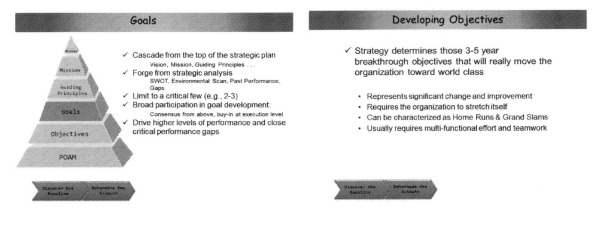

Goals

- ✓ Cascade from the top of the strategic plan
  Vision, Mission, Guiding Principles . . .
- ✓ Forge from strategic analysis
  SWOT, Environmental Scan, Past Performance, Gaps
- ✓ Limit to a critical few (e.g., 2-3)
- ✓ Broad participation in goal development:
  Consensus from above, buy-in at execution level
- ✓ Drive higher levels of performance and close critical performance gaps

Developing Objectives

- ✓ Strategy determines those 3-5 year breakthrough objectives that will really move the organization toward world class

- • Represents significant change and improvement
- • Requires the organization to stretch itself
- • Can be characterized as Home Runs & Grand Slams
- • Usually requires multi-functional effort and teamwork

Objectives

- ✓ Relevant – directly supports the goal
- ✓ Compelling – drives the organization into action
- ✓ Specific enough to quantify and measure the results
- ✓ Simple and easy to understand
- ✓ Realistic and attainable
- ✓ Clear as to responsibility and ownership
- ✓ Acceptable to who must execute
- ✓ Several objectives to meet a goal

Developing a Plan of Action and Milestones (POAM)

- ✓ Identify specific steps to achieve initiatives and strategic objectives – where the rubber meets road
- ✓ Ensure that each initiative has a supporting POAM(s) attached to it
- ✓ Gear toward operations, procedures, and processes
- ✓ Describe **who** does **what**, **where, when** it will be completed, and **how** the organization knows when steps are completed
- ✓ Monitor progress – measure as needed

Characteristics of a POAM

- ✓ Responsibility assigned for successful completion
- ✓ Required steps to achieve initiative detailed
- ✓ Established time frame for completion of each step spelled out
- ✓ Established resources required to complete steps detailed
- ✓ Specific actions (steps) that must be taken to implement initiative detailed
- ✓ Deliverables (in measurable terms) that should result from completion of individual steps determined
- ✓ Expected results and milestones of the plan of action and milestones (POAM) defined
- ✓ Status report on each step – completed or not

Cascading Linkage

Is everything linked and connected for a tight, end-to-end model for driving strategic execution?

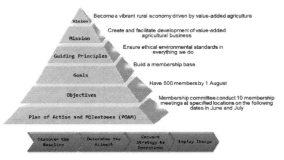

POAM Execution

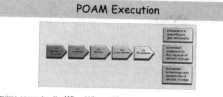

✓ Requires answering the **Who, What, Where, How**, and **When** questions related to initiative that drives strategic execution
✓ Coordinate with lower level sections, administrative and operating personnel: they execute the POAM
✓ Assign action responsibility and set timelines – develop working plans and schedules
✓ Resource the project or initiative and document in the form of detailed budgets
✓ Monitor progress against milestones and measurements
✓ Correct and revise action plans per comparison of actual results against original POAM

Measurements

✓ Measure your milestones – short-term outcomes at POAM
✓ Measure the outcomes of your objectives
✓ Keep your measures at one per objective, if possible
✓ Include lead and lag measures (as needed) to depict cause/effect relationships if you are uncertain about driving (leading) the desired outcome
✓ Establish measures using a template to capture critical data elements

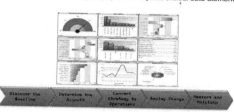

Example of Measures

✓ PPM improvement rate from 50% to 75% by 6/30
✓ Average lead time from 20 to 10 days by 9/1
✓ Cost reductions of $1M implemented by 10/31
✓ Thermography – approved business-case dollars from X to Y by Q3

Top-level priorities are measurable but not a measure!

Linking Budget to Strategic Planning

✓ The best strategic plan will fail when not adequately resourced through the budgeting process.
✓ Strategic plans cannot succeed without people, time, money, and other key resources.
✓ Aligning resources validates that initiatives and action plans comprising the strategic plan support the strategic objectives.

Establish a budget resource board. Are the resources available to meet the goal?

Appendix C

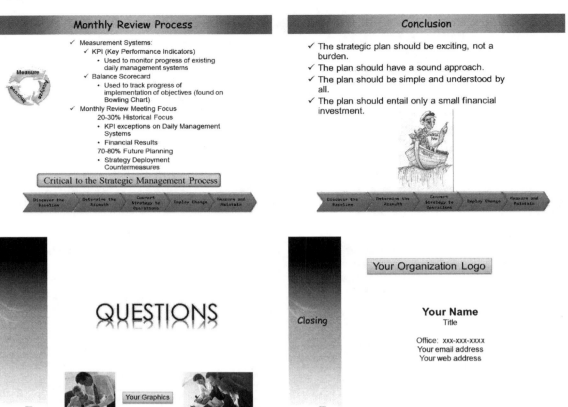

Monthly Review Process

- ✓ Measurement Systems:
  - ✓ KPI (Key Performance Indicators)
    - • Used to monitor progress of existing daily management systems
  - ✓ Balance Scorecard
    - • Used to track progress of implementation of objectives (found on Bowling Chart)
- ✓ Monthly Review Meeting Focus
  - 20-30% Historical Focus
    - • KPI exceptions on Daily Management Systems
    - • Financial Results
  - 70-80% Future Planning
    - • Strategy Deployment Countermeasures

Critical to the Strategic Management Process

Conclusion

- ✓ The strategic plan should be exciting, not a burden.
- ✓ The plan should have a sound approach.
- ✓ The plan should be simple and understood by all.
- ✓ The plan should entail only a small financial investment.

QUESTIONS

Your Graphics

Closing

Your Organization Logo

Your Name
Title

Office: xxx-xxx-xxxx
Your email address
Your web address

YOUR TAG LINE

Appendix D
Sample Team Welcome E-mail

Fellow team member:

Thank you for volunteering to serve on the core planning team (CPT) for this year's strategic plan development. You are playing a critical role that will prove to be both rewarding to you and highly beneficial to our organization, our customers, and our stakeholders. Our theme throughout the process is "Make It Possible." We will weave this theme into everything we do.

As a member of the CPT, you are vital to the success of the strategic plan development and overall future of our organization. Soon, you will receive planning information and materials and may be asked to participate in training designed to be minimally intrusive to your time while supplying you with the tools to make the strategic plan development a success. One of your first tasks is to review your schedule for the entire plan-development time frame, which I anticipate will encompass six months. We will need your availability for the duration of the entire six months. Our start date is June 1, 2015. Please provide your contact information and current position within the organization. We will use this information as the basis for all communication with you and ask that you e-mail it to Ms. Davis at ddavis@ xraycorp.com.

I would like to emphasize that from the beginning and throughout this process, your leadership, enthusiasm, and commitment to the strategic plan and to your fellow team members is critical for making the strategic plan development process a success. Success is not just reaching our goal, but providing everything within our power to ensure our organization's longevity and relevance in a fast-changing, competitive environment.

Our first meeting will take place on June 1, 2015, in Bldg. 51, Room 1215, at 10:00 a.m. I will distribute a meeting invitation with an informational packet when I have details on the agenda and other matters. Please plan to attend this initial meeting, a critical first step in our move forward. Future meetings will be held every Thursday from 10:00–11:00 a.m. I ask that you please schedule this recurring time now. If you should need assistance or have any questions, please contact me at any time at retter@xraycorp.com.

Again, thank you for your service. Your willingness to take on this most important responsibility is greatly appreciated.

Sincerely,
Randy Etter
Strategic plan team leader

Appendix E
Sample Core Planning Team Meeting Agenda

The following sample meeting agenda provides a concise layout for your first meeting with the core planning team (CPT). As for all meetings, you must arrive fully prepared. Have your administrative assistant help with the logistics of setting up the meeting (to include connectivity) and ensuring full attendance. Be prepared to provide requirements for each team member so that he or she is fully engaged from the beginning of the planning process. Ensure that all distributed documents are constructed and written in a professional manner that reflects positively on your leadership abilities. You may want to include the organizational logo on each document you distribute or create a unique logo for strategic plan briefing slides and documents. Use this template for all future meetings.

X-Ray Corporation CPT Meeting Agenda

June 10, 2015 (10:00–11:00 a.m.), Bldg. 51, Room 1215
Conference call tel.: 866-858-6765; code: 80889 (for remote members)

Introductions—Strategic plan leader

Opening remarks—Strategic plan champion (first meeting only)

Team introductions—include experience in strategic planning as team members introduce themselves and the functional area from which they originate (first meeting only)

Administrative Items—discuss at a minimum the following:

1. Meeting schedule—weekly (for example, every Thursday at 10:00 AM).
2. Team dynamics—some team concepts described in "Let's Get Started" and throughout this book.
3. Core team orientation briefing.
4. Key points of the CPT briefing. Obtain consensus on the strategic planning approach and the strategic planning model (SPM) and their roles and responsibilities in developing and executing the strategic plan. Conduct in "round-robin" manner to get verbal "buy-in" from each team member.
5. Any issues, including commitment issues, such as a team member scheduled to attend a three-week training module. Consider that the team member may have to be replaced.
6. Tasking—assign tasks so that members are prepared for next meeting. Remember to provide a "suspense" (due) date for all tasks and to hold members accountable to avoid "continuous catch-up loop."

Follow-on meeting: Feb. 22, 2015

Appendix F
Core Planning Team Orientation Brief

The following is a sample CPT orientation briefing. The briefing is available in an editable format at www.allonscg.com.

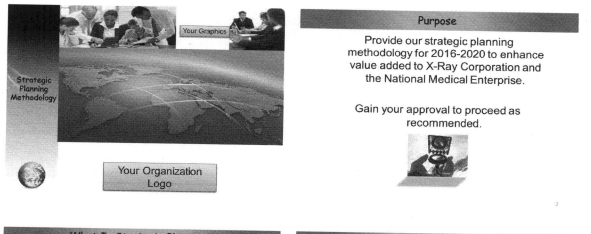

Purpose

Provide our strategic planning methodology for 2016-2020 to enhance value added to X-Ray Corporation and the National Medical Enterprise.

Gain your approval to proceed as recommended.

What Is Strategic Planning?

- ✓ Deliberate, disciplined effort to produce a strategy that results in actions that shape what an organization is, what it does, why it does it, and what it will do in the future
- ✓ Future-focused
- ✓ Ensures the long-term relevance and survivability of our organization and the community in which it resides
- ✓ Determines and reveals the organization's *objectives, purposes,* or *goals*; produces the *principal policies* and plans for achieving those goals; and defines the range of business the organization is to pursue, the kind of economic and human organization it intends to be, and the nature of the economic and noneconomic contribution it intends to make to its shareholders, employees, customers, and communities.

Why a Strategic Plan?

- ✓ Increase effectiveness
- ✓ Increase efficiency
- ✓ Improve understanding of the organizational environment and growth
- ✓ Improve decision-making
- ✓ Enhance organizational capabilities
- ✓ Improve communications and public relations
- ✓ Increase political, community, and consumer support
- ✓ Provide relevancy to the organization
- ✓ Build organizational and individual growth
- ✓ Enhance culture and improve employee–morale
- ✓ Most important, keeps the organization in step with environmental changes

Appendix F

What Drives the Strategic Plan?

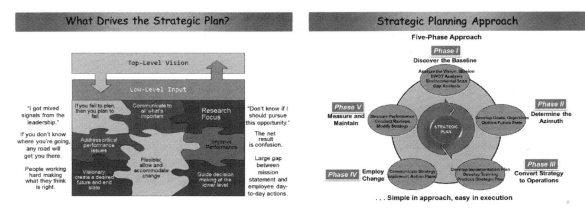

Top-Level Vision

Low-Level Input

Research Focus

"I got mixed signals from the leadership."

If you don't know where you're going, any road will get you there.

People working hard making what they think is right.

If you fail to plan, then you plan to fail

Communicate to all what's important

Address critical performance issues

Improve Performance

Flexible; allow and accommodate change

Visionary, create a desired future and end state

Guide decision making at the lower level

"Don't know if I should pursue this opportunity."

The net result is confusion.

Large gap between mission statement and employee day-to-day actions.

Strategic Planning Approach

Five-Phase Approach

Phase I — Discover the Baseline — Analyze the Vision, Mission, SWOT Analysis, Environmental Scan, Gap Analysis

Phase II — Determine the Azimuth — Develop Goals, Objectives, Outline Future State

Phase III — Convert Strategy to Operations — Develop Implementation Plan, Develop Training, Produce Strategic Plan

Phase IV — Employ Change — Communicate Strategy, Implement Action Plans

Phase V — Measure and Maintain — Measure Performance, Conduct Reviews, Modify Strategy

STRATEGIC PLAN

. . . Simple in approach, easy in execution

Strategic Planning Model

WHERE ARE WE NOW?	WHERE ARE WE GOING?	HOW ARE WE GOING TO GET THERE?	HOW WILL WE EMPLOY CHANGE?	HOW WILL WE MEASURE SUCCESS?
WHAT IS OUR BASELINE?	**WHAT IS OUR FUTURE STATE?**	**WHAT IS OUR PLAN TO GET THERE?**		
Environmental Scan	Conduct Focus Group	Develop Implementation Plan	Communicate Strategies and New Strategic Plan	Conduct Implementation Review and Measure Performance
Analyze Current Vision, Mission, and Guiding Principles (Internal Scan)	Develop restated Vision, Mission, Guiding Principles	Develop Plan of Action and Milestones (POAM)	Develop Performance Measures	Refine Goals, Strategies and Processes
Conduct SWOT Analysis (External Scan)	Outline the Future State	Develop Training	Apply Resources	Align Organization to Support Strategy
Conduct stakeholders Analysis	Develop Goals and Objectives	Link Objectives to Budget	Fix Responsibilities	Actualize Strategy
Assess Readiness	Prioritize Goals and Objectives	Produce the Strategic Plan Document	Execute Action Plans	Measure
Conduct Gap Analysis	Link Goals and Objectives to Strategic Perspectives			
Develop Solution Set/Recommendations				
Conduct leadership Training				
Conduct Focus Group				
Phase I/Chapter 1	**Phase II/Chapter 2**	**Phase III/Chapter 3**	**Phase IV/Chapter 4**	**Phase V/Chapter 5**
Discover the Baseline	Determine the Azimuth	Convert Strategy to Operations	Employ Change	Measure and Maintain

The First Step

Establish Our Teams

✓ Have fundamental skills to do the job
✓ Possess initiative, the drive that makes the difference
✓ Share knowledge and expertise and not withhold information
✓ Respect the opinions of others
✓ Show willingness to listen
✓ Be dependable; fulfill all tasks assigned
✓ Be action oriented
✓ Develop two basic teams:
    Core Planning Team (CPT)
    Strategic Planning Committee (SPC)

Core Planning Team

✓ Consists of strategic plan champion, strategic plan team leader, two strategic planners, and administrative assistant, with IT and graphics support
✓ Serves as the nucleus for the organization's strategic planning process
✓ Plans, guides, develops, executes, and monitors the full spectrum of the organization's strategic plan, from the concept to the execution and monitor phases
✓ Is the "easy button" for every aspect of the strategic plan, from its cradle to its rebirth in its new cradle.

The Core Planning Team

Organizational Chart

CEO — James Hodge

Strategic Plan Champion — Hannah Ellen

Strategic Plan Team Leader — Randy Etter

Strategic Planner — Tony Sparks

Strategic Planner — Robert Little

Graphic and IT Support — As Required

Administrative Assistant — Debbie Davis

Strategic Planning Committee

The Core Planning Team

Lead Strategic Planner

- ✓ Serves as the project manager responsible for executing entire strategic plan development and makes decisions that affect the development, execution, and monitoring of the strategic plan
- ✓ Should have experience with project management, planning, and strategic development
- ✓ Is responsible and accountable for everything that goes right and everything that goes wrong in developing the strategic plan and ensuring that all goals and objectives are met on time

The Core Planning Team

Strategic Planners

- ✓ Are responsible for assisting team leader with his or her responsibilities and for acting as team leader in team leader's absence.
- ✓ Have background, though not necessarily expertise, in strategic planning.
- ✓ Keep team and organization on course, keep track of progress, and pay attention to all details.
- ✓ Are skilled in the art of group dynamics and interpersonal relationships.
- ✓ Have expertise in facilitation and are able to keep strategic planning high on people's agendas.
- ✓ Are committed to a successful *process*, not to specific solutions to the strategic issues.
- ✓ Think about what has to come together, such as people, information, resources, and completed work.
- ✓ Rally participants to push the process along.
- ✓ Are sensitive to power differences and able to engage all implementers to find ways to share power to increase chances of planning success.

The Core Planning Team

Administrative Assistant

- ✓ Responsible for performing all administrative tasks associated with the planning and execution of the plan
- ✓ Skilled in graphic-design software such as Microsoft Office and Adobe Graphics
- ✓ Skilled in software such as Microsoft Project Manager
- ✓ Able to develop meeting agendas, take notes, maintain scheduling, document and archive materials, and carry out administrative tasks associated with project management protocols
- ✓ And more . . .

The Strategic Planning Committee

- ✓ Is larger than but subordinate to the CPT
- ✓ Has no more than 10-12 members
- ✓ Members represent functional areas such as personnel, finance, operations, marketing, logistics, and information technology
- ✓ Has direct influence on the course of the organization's day-to-day responsibilities
- ✓ Is capable of making decisions for moving the planning process forward
- ✓ Members have middle-to senior-level management experience, are knowledgeable about their functional area, and can make decisions that will affect the organization's future and move the planning process forward
- ✓ Provide information about their departments and contribute to every aspect of the strategic plan

The Strategic Planning Committee

Organizational Chart

The Project Plan

Appendix F

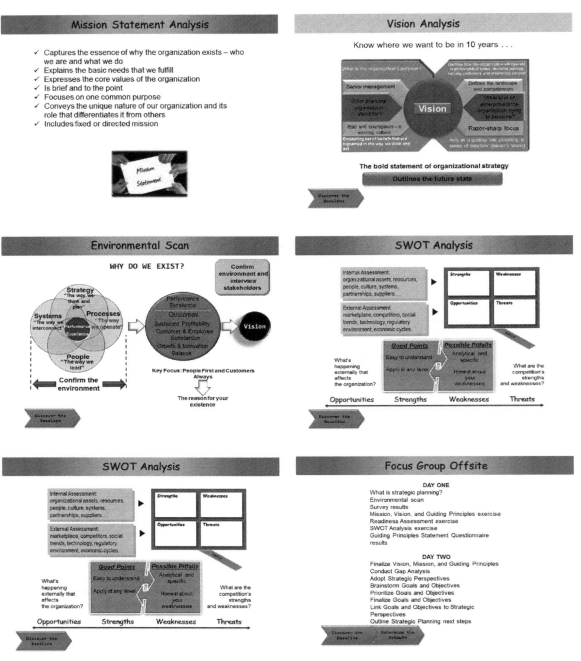

Mission Statement Analysis

- ✓ Captures the essence of why the organization exists – who we are and what we do
- ✓ Explains the basic needs that we fulfill
- ✓ Expresses the core values of the organization
- ✓ Is brief and to the point
- ✓ Focuses on one common purpose
- ✓ Conveys the unique nature of our organization and its role that differentiates it from others
- ✓ Includes fixed or directed mission

Vision Analysis

Know where we want to be in 10 years . . .

The bold statement of organizational strategy

Outlines the future state

Environmental Scan

WHY DO WE EXIST?

Key Focus: People First and Customers Always

The reason for your existence

SWOT Analysis

Internal Assessment: organizational assets, resources, people, culture, systems, partnerships, suppliers...

External Assessment: marketplace, competitors, social trends, technology, regulatory environment, economic cycles.

What's happening externally that affects the organization?

What are the competition's strengths and weaknesses?

Opportunities · Strengths · Weaknesses · Threats

SWOT Analysis

Internal Assessment: organizational assets, resources, people, culture, systems, partnerships, suppliers...

External Assessment: marketplace, competitors, social trends, technology, regulatory environment, economic cycles.

What's happening externally that affects the organization?

What are the competition's strengths and weaknesses?

Opportunities · Strengths · Weaknesses · Threats

Focus Group Offsite

DAY ONE
What is strategic planning?
Environmental scan
Survey results
Mission, Vision, and Guiding Principles exercise
Readiness Assessment exercise
SWOT Analysis exercise
Guiding Principles Statement Questionnaire results

DAY TWO
Finalize Vision, Mission, and Guiding Principles
Conduct Gap Analysis
Adopt Strategic Perspectives
Brainstorm Goals and Objectives
Prioritize Goals and Objectives
Finalize Goals and Objectives
Link Goals and Objectives to Strategic Perspectives
Outline Strategic Planning next steps

Core Planning Team Orientation Brief

Developing 3-5 Year Goals

- ✓ Build on strengths and shore up weaknesses
- ✓ Describe a future end state-desired outcome supportive of mission and vision
- ✓ Shape the way ahead in actionable terms
- ✓ Apply where there are clear choices about the future
- ✓ Put strategic focus into the organization; ownership assigned to someone
- ✓ Each goal has own swim lane and unique approach associated with it

Stretch goal better than playing it safe

Goal: Develop trained and ready medical staff

Goals

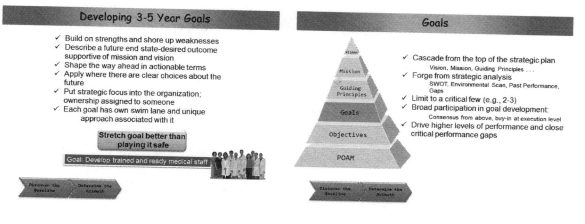

- ✓ Cascade from the top of the strategic plan
  Vision, Mission, Guiding Principles . . .
- ✓ Forge from strategic analysis
  SWOT, Environmental Scan, Past Performance, Gaps
- ✓ Limit to a critical few (e.g., 2-3)
- ✓ Broad participation in goal development:
  Consensus from above, buy-in at execution level
- ✓ Drive higher levels of performance and close critical performance gaps

Developing Objectives

- ✓ Strategy determines those 3-5 year breakthrough objectives that will really move the organization toward world class

  - ✓ Represents significant change and improvement
  - ✓ Requires the organization to stretch itself
  - ✓ Can be characterized as Home Runs & Grand Slams
  - ✓ Usually requires multi-functional effort and teamwork

Objectives

- ✓ Relevant – directly supports the goal
- ✓ Compelling – drives the organization into action
- ✓ Specific enough to quantify and measure the results
- ✓ Simple and easy to understand
- ✓ Realistic and attainable
- ✓ Clear as to responsibility and ownership
- ✓ Acceptable to who must execute
- ✓ Several objectives to meet a goal

Developing a Plan of Action and Milestones (POAM)

- ✓ Identify specific steps to achieve initiatives and strategic objectives – where the rubber meets road
- ✓ Ensure that each initiative has a supporting POAM(s) attached to it
- Gear toward operations, procedures, and processes
- Describe **who** does **what**, **where, when** it will be completed, and **how** the organization knows when steps are completed
- ✓ Monitor progress – measure as needed

Characteristics of a POAM

- ✓ Responsibility assigned for successful completion
- ✓ Required steps to achieve initiative detailed
- ✓ Established time frame for completion of each step spelled out
- ✓ Established resources required to complete steps detailed
- ✓ Specific actions (steps) that must be taken to implement initiative detailed
- ✓ Deliverables (in measurable terms) that should result from completion of individual steps determined
- ✓ Expected results and milestones of the plan of action and milestones (POAM) defined
- ✓ Status report on each step – completed or not

197

Appendix F

Cascading Linkage

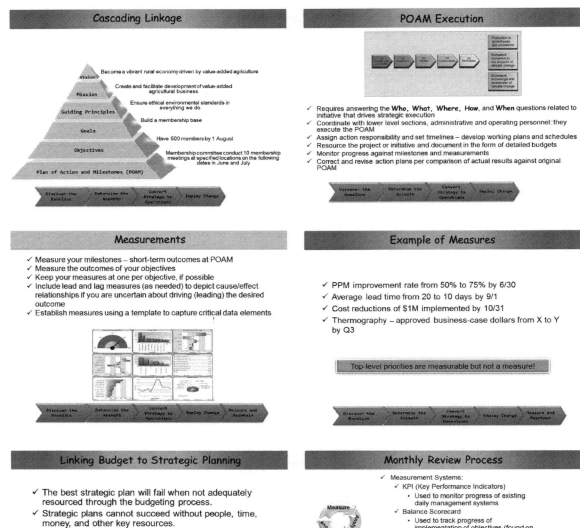

- Vision — Become a vibrant rural economy driven by value-added agriculture
- Mission — Create and facilitate development of value-added agricultural business
- Guiding Principles — Ensure ethical environmental standards in everything we do
- Goals — Build a membership base
- Objectives — Have 500 members by 1 August
- Plan of Action and Milestones (POAM) — Membership committee conduct 10 membership meetings at specified locations on the following dates in June and July

Discover the Baseline | Determine the Azimuth | Convert Strategy to Operations | Deploy Change

POAM Execution

- ✓ Requires answering the **Who, What, Where, How,** and **When** questions related to initiative that drives strategic execution
- ✓ Coordinate with lower level sections, administrative and operating personnel: they execute the POAM
- ✓ Assign action responsibility and set timelines – develop working plans and schedules
- ✓ Resource the project or initiative and document in the form of detailed budgets
- ✓ Monitor progress against milestones and measurements
- ✓ Correct and revise action plans per comparison of actual results against original POAM

Discover the Baseline | Determine the Azimuth | Convert Strategy to Operations | Deploy Change

Measurements

- ✓ Measure your milestones – short-term outcomes at POAM
- ✓ Measure the outcomes of your objectives
- ✓ Keep your measures at one per objective, if possible
- ✓ Include lead and lag measures (as needed) to depict cause/effect relationships if you are uncertain about driving (leading) the desired outcome
- ✓ Establish measures using a template to capture critical data elements

Discover the Baseline | Determine the Azimuth | Convert Strategy to Operations | Deploy Change | Measure and Maintain

Example of Measures

- ✓ PPM improvement rate from 50% to 75% by 6/30
- ✓ Average lead time from 20 to 10 days by 9/1
- ✓ Cost reductions of $1M implemented by 10/31
- ✓ Thermography – approved business-case dollars from X to Y by Q3

Top-level priorities are measurable but not a measure!

Discover the Baseline | Determine the Azimuth | Convert Strategy to Operations | Deploy Change | Measure and Maintain

Linking Budget to Strategic Planning

- ✓ The best strategic plan will fail when not adequately resourced through the budgeting process.
- ✓ Strategic plans cannot succeed without people, time, money, and other key resources.
- ✓ Aligning resources validates that initiatives and action plans comprising the strategic plan support the strategic objectives.

Establish a budget resource board: Are the resources available to meet the goal?

Discover the Baseline | Determine the Azimuth | Convert Strategy to Operations | Deploy Change | Measure and Maintain

Monthly Review Process

- ✓ Measurement Systems:
  - ✓ KPI (Key Performance Indicators)
    - Used to monitor progress of existing daily management systems
  - ✓ Balance Scorecard
    - Used to track progress of implementation of objectives (found on Bowling Chart)
- ✓ Monthly Review Meeting Focus
  - 20-30% Historical Focus
    - KPI exceptions on Daily Management Systems
    - Financial Results
  - 70-80% Future Planning
    - Strategy Deployment Countermeasures

Critical to the Strategic Management Process

Discover the Baseline | Determine the Azimuth | Convert Strategy to Operations | Deploy Change | Measure and Maintain

Conclusion

- ✓ The strategic plan should be exciting, not a burden.
- ✓ The plan should have a sound approach.
- ✓ The plan should be simple and understood by all.
- ✓ The plan should entail only a small financial investment.

Tasking

- ✓ Read the book, *Strategic Planning: As Simple as A, B, C*

Add additional tasks as you deem appropriate

Your Organization Logo

Your Name
Title

Office: xxx-xxx-xxxx
Your email address
Your web address

YOUR TAG LINE

Closing

QUESTIONS

Your Graphics

Appendix G
Sample Team Meeting Minutes

Note that these minutes are somewhat different from the agenda in appendix E. This appendix is geared toward providing greater detail on the preparation of meeting minutes. Use this template for all future meetings, adding your organization's logo or stationery, if applicable.

Core Planning Team Meeting
June 10, 2015
Bldg. 51, Room 1215

Participants: *List all participants in attendance as well as those not in attendance.*

Agenda: (1) (2) (3)

(1) Introductions

- Mr. Etter introduced the guest speakers from Sycore Health.
- Sycore Health formerly offered care solely to LGBT and HIV/AIDS patients. It now offers comprehensive primary health care, such as medical, mental health, and dental care, to the community.
- Sycore Health also offers the community pharmacy, legal assistance, estate planning, will assistance, and other services. Sycore will not turn anyone away regardless of his or her ability to pay.
- Sycore provided a briefing on its strategic plan for 2016.

(2) Updates since last meeting

- Strategic plan approach
  Mr. Little recommended some minor changes to the strategic plan approach. After discussion, his recommendations were accepted by the team.

- Mission and vision
  After discussion, a decision was made by the team leader to conduct a mission and vision analysis in the near future.

- Training
  To date, ten strategic planning committee (SPC) alternates are scheduled for training on strategic planning. Managers were asked to send the names of the employees who require training; a webinar will be considered for that training. Managers were provided with training sign-up sheets through June 28.

- Focus group offsite planning
  There was consensus among team members about conducting the offsite focus group toward the end of September 2015.

- Survey
  Mr. Little was given the responsibility of planning, conducting, and developing the analysis for the strategic plan survey.

- CEO all-hands e-mail
  Mr. Sparks was assigned the task of drafting an all-hands e-mail from the CEO announcing the beginning of the strategic planning process.

(3) Administrative Items

- Team meetings will be held every Thursday at 10:00 a.m. in this conference room.
- Mr. Little advised team members that he has extended an offer to meet with them one on one for the purpose of providing support and assistance. He requested that members provide him an e-mail with dates and times they will be available.
- Mr. Little advised team members to gain more insight on strategic planning so that they are better prepared to provide such to the

organization. He provided and recommended reading the book *Strategic Planning: As Simple as A, B, C.*, by David McClean.

Action Item	Due Date	Responsible Individual(s)
Provide the names of employees who require training to Mrs. Davis.	**ASAP**	**Managers**
Provide managers with training sign-up sheets.	**June 20, 2015**	**Ms. Davis**
Develop organizational survey.	**TBD**	**Mr. Little**
Provide draft of all-hands CEO e-mail.	**June 15, 2015**	**Mr. Sparks**
Establish team-meeting schedule and secure conference room for next six months.	**Ongoing**	**Ms. Davis**
Provide Ms. Davis an e-mail with dates and times of availability for one-on-one meetings, if needed.	**June 17, 2015**	**Managers**
Develop greater insight into strategic planning.	**Ongoing**	**All team members**

NEXT MEETING:
June 17, 2015, 10:00 – 11:00 a.m., Bldg. 51, Room 1215

Appendix H
Brainstorming

As I discussed in chapter 1, it can be very productive for the strategic planning teams to hold brainstorming sessions to develop the MVGP and numerous other steps and requirements for planning development.

Brainstorming with a group is a powerful technique. It creates new ideas, solves problems, motivates members, and develops teams through the different stages of group dynamics discussed in chapter 1. Brainstorming motivates because it involves members of a team in strategic issues, and it gets a team working together to generate ideas on the future vision of the organization. However, brainstorming is not simply a random activity. It must be structured and follows certain principles and rules.

Brainstorming should take place in a comfortable, relaxing setting that encourages creativity and problem solving. It is meant to encourage groups to come up with thoughts and ideas that can contribute to the overall purpose of resolving issues and solving problems. Some of these thoughts and ideas can be crafted into original, creative solutions to a problem, while others can spark even more ideas. This helps to get your teams unstuck by pushing you out of your normal ways of thinking. Therefore, I recommend you find a location away from the organization's day-to-day activities to conduct your brainstorming sessions. For example, I've often conducted brainstorming sessions at small pizza parlors and restaurants.

Advertising pioneer Alex Osborn developed the idea of brainstorming in his 1942 book *How to "Think Up."* He indicated that brainstorming was intended to:

✓ Reduce social inhibitions among group members

✓ Stimulate idea generation
✓ Increase overall creativity of the group

When holding brainstorming sessions with your teams, keep Osborn's general rules in mind but also be aware that since his time, researchers have made many improvements to the original technique, coming up with other methods for generating and collecting ideas. I recommend using two of these newer techniques (discussed below) with your teams as well as when you're prioritizing goals and objectives at the focus group offsite.

Nominal group technique

This technique enhances brainstorming by adding a voting step that is used to rank the most useful ideas for further brainstorming or for prioritizing. In other words, the technique allows ideas to be brainstormed by small groups and then reviewed by a larger group.

The Delphi technique

The Delphi technique is a method used to arrive at a consensus among experts. A selected panel answers questions and provides feedback regarding the responses from each round of requirement-gathering from a group of experts. Responses are only available to the facilitator so as to maintain anonymity. The facilitator uses questions to solicit ideas important to the planning process. Responses are summarized and recirculated to the expert panel for further comment. Consensus may be reached within a few rounds. The technique helps reduce bias in the data and keeps any one person from having undue influence on the outcome.

During brainstorming sessions, you should avoid criticizing or rewarding ideas. You're trying to open up possibilities and break down incorrect assumptions about the problem's limits. Judgment and analysis at this stage stunts idea generation  and limits creativity. Some brainstorming guidelines follow:

ADVICE:
Supporting an idea
is encouraging
an idea.

✓ Include subject-matter experts and key stakeholders on your teams.
✓ Don't disregard ideas—just annotate them on a flip chart or dry-erase board.
✓ Don't hold back on suggestions.

✓ Don't evaluate others' ideas.
✓ There's no wrong, right, good, or bad idea in a brainstorming session.

The brainstorming process

In the brainstorming process, you will:

✓ Define and agree on the objective
✓ Brainstorm ideas and suggestions with a set time limit and categorize the topic—for example, "Develop the vision statement")
✓ Assess and analyze the effects or results
✓ Prioritize the results
✓ Agree on the final results—for example, "The new vision statement is ..."
✓ Follow up

Plan and agree on the brainstorming aim

Ensure that everyone participating in the brainstorming sessions understands and agrees with the aim of the sessions. When conducting brainstorming sessions, I always begin with the theme statement—for example, to formulate a new vision statement, to formulate a robust distribution process, to solve a software malfunction, to identify cost-saving opportunities, etc. Keep the brainstorming objective simple. And allocate a time limit, which will enable you to keep the random brainstorming activity under control and on track.

The content of the agenda depends on new groups' working relationships, how long the members have been with the organization, and how much each member knows about the findings, conclusions, and recommendations arrived at and the analysis of these.

Manage the actual brainstorming activity

Brainstorming gives people the opportunity to suggest ideas at random. Your job or that of the facilitator is to encourage everyone to participate, to dismiss nothing, and to prevent others from raining contempt on the more peculiar suggestions (some of the best ideas are initially the most bizarre ones; in addition, team members won't participate if their suggestions are ridiculed). During the collection of ideas you must record every suggestion on the flip chart. At the end of the time limit, or when ideas have been exhausted, use different-colored pens to categorize, group, connect, and link the random ideas. Condense and refine the ideas by making new headings or lists. You can diplomatically combine or include the weaker ideas within other ideas to avoid dismissing or rejecting contributions (remember, brainstorming is about team building and motivation; you don't want it to have the reverse effect on some of your team members in this or later sessions). With your team, assess, evaluate, and analyze the effects and validity of the ideas on the lists. Develop and prioritize the ideas into a more finished list or set of actions or options.

Implement the actions agreed on in the brainstorming

Come to an agreement on a timetable and on the group's next actions and who is to take responsibility for them. After the session, circulate notes and give feedback. It's crucial to develop a clear and positive outcome so that team members feel their efforts and contributions were worthwhile. When they see that their efforts have resulted in action and change, they will be motivated and eager to help again. Utilize techniques discussed earlier to arrive at a consensus before ending the brainstorming process.

Appendix I
Stakeholder Analysis

One element of the environmental scan is the analysis of the stakeholders' guiding principles. By stakeholders, we mean those individuals, groups, and organizations that will be affected by or who are likely to be interested in the organization's strategic plan and the planning process. Included are all those who believe that, rightly or wrongly, they have a stake in the organization's future and not merely a selected few such as the planning team. Stakeholders may have control or influence over the strategic plan development with varying levels of responsibilities and authority, which can change over the course of the planning life cycle. Stakeholders can have an adverse impact on the plan objectives. Thus, identifying stakeholders and understanding their relative degree of control or influence on the plan is critical. Failure to do so can extend the planning timeline and delay the plan's implementation. It can even derail the entire planning process. Some stakeholders benefit from a successful process, while others perceive negative outcomes as success. For example, business leaders from the community who will benefit from a commercial hotel project by positive economic benefits to the community will support a strategic plan that advocates a commercial hotel project. In this case, the stakeholders with positive expectations of the project will be best served by helping the project succeed. If you overlook stakeholders in opposition (negative stakeholders), it can result in increased likelihood of failure of the strategic planning and implementation.

As stated in chapter 1, the stakeholder analysis identifies the interests, expectations, and influence of the stakeholders and relates them to the purpose of the plan. It also helps identify stakeholder relationships that can be leveraged to build coalitions and potential partnerships to enhance the plan's chance of success. The stakeholder analysis follows the two steps described below:

Step one. Identify all potential stakeholders and collect relevant information about them, such as their roles, departments, interests, knowledge levels, expectations, and influence levels. Key stakeholders are usually easy to identify. They include anyone in a decision-making or management role who is affected by the project outcome, such as a sponsor, project manager, or primary customer.

Step two. Identify the potential impacts supporting stakeholders can generate, and classify them so as to define an approach strategy. There are multiple classification models available including, but not limited to:

- ✓ Power/interest grid: moving the stakeholders based on their level of authority (power) and their level of concern (interest) regarding the strategic planning outcome.
- ✓ Power/influence grid: grouping the stakeholders based on their level of authority (power) and their active involvement (influence) in the planning process.
- ✓ Influence/impact grid: grouping the stakeholders based on their active involvement (influence) in the project and their ability to affect changes to the project's planning or execution (impact).
- ✓ Salient model: describing classes of stakeholders based on their power (ability to impose their will), urgency (need for immediate attention), and legitimacy (appropriateness of their development).

Figure I-1, Power/Interest Grid, is an example of a power/interest grid, with each letter within the grid representing the placement of generic stakeholders. Some theories call for creating a separate internal as well as a separate external stakeholder analysis. You will conduct the analysis as a combined effort. By using Figure I-1 you can map your internal and external stakeholders on one graphic depiction. This will give you an overall picture of both the internal and the external environments.

Exercise #3: Stakeholder Analysis, Part 1

Using our discussion in chapter 1 with reference to stakeholders as well as the preceding paragraphs, make a list of internal and external stakeholders. Then, using a power/interest grid (Figure I-1), conduct the stakeholders exercise.

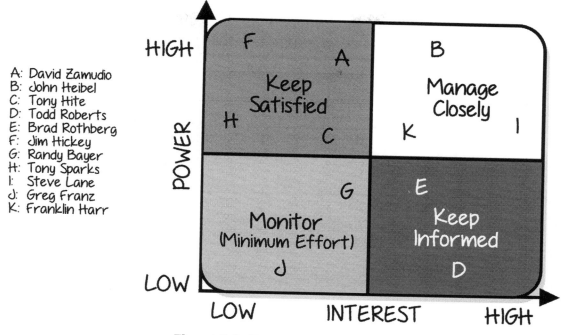

A: David Zamudio
B: John Heibel
C: Tony Hite
D: Todd Roberts
E: Brad Rothberg
F: Jim Hickey
G: Randy Bayer
H: Tony Sparks
I: Steve Lane
J: Greg Franz
K: Franklin Harr

Figure I-1. Power/Interest Grid

First, create a list with your teams of all your internal and external stakeholders. Then carefully work your way down the list of internal stakeholders and place them in the applicable quadrant. Some internal stakeholders could be policy-board members, members of management, support employees, technical employees, or unions.

Using another (or the same) graphic, repeat the steps for your external stakeholders. Some examples of external stakeholders are the public, the community, nonprofit organizations, clients, decision makers, legislators, regulators, competing organizations, federal agencies, service partners, the press, and state and local agencies. You may distinguish internal and external stakeholders by using an "i" and "x," respectively. For example, internal stakeholder A equates to Ai and external stakeholder A equates to Ax. In the event that you have numerous internal and external stakeholders, or you believe that the model is too "busy," create two separate grids—one for internal and one for external stakeholders.

Take a close look at the personnel you've placed in each quadrant. Now, with your teams, discuss the obstacles or the benefits of those personnel in the Keep Satisfied quadrant, the Manage Closely quadrant, the Monitor quadrant, and the Keep Informed quadrant. Will the stakeholders help you achieve success? Will they be a hindrance to your success? Let's work our way through the second exercise.

Stakeholder-management strategy

The stakeholder-management strategy defines an approach to increase the support and minimize the negative impacts of stakeholders throughout the entire strategic planning process. It includes such elements as:

- ✓ Key stakeholders significantly affecting the planning process
- ✓ Desired level of participation for each identified stakeholder
- ✓ Stakeholder groups and their management affecting the planning process

A common way to represent stakeholder-management strategies is by means of a stakeholder analysis matrix. (An example with column headers is provided in Table I-1, Stakeholder Analysis Matrix.)

Exercise #3: Stakeholder Analysis, Part 2

Using the graphic in Table I-1, Stakeholder Analysis Matrix, along with your teams, list your stakeholders in the stakeholders (i.e., first) column. In the second column, indicate their interest in the strategic plan. In the third column, make an assessment of their impact. Finally, in the fourth and fifth columns, make some notes on potential strategies for gaining support or reducing obstacles.

Stakeholders	Stakeholders Interest in the Plan	Assessment of Impact	Strategy for gaining support	Strategy for Reducing Obstacles
Jim Barnes	X		provide planning process brief	
John Heibel		requires leadership intervention		
Tony Hite		supportive to the plan		
Todd Roberts			,	great stake in the process
Brad Rothberg	fully support the plan			
Jim Hickey	X		inclusion in planning process	
Randy Bayer	agreed to provide resources			

Table I-1. Stakeholder Analysis Matrix

You may believe there is no need to conduct these exercises. You may think, "I already know all this." However, I urge you to take the time with your teams and work through these two exercises. They will help you understand the thinking of your team members about stakeholders within your internal and external environments. I guarantee you that stakeholders you did not think of will materialize. In completing the exercises, you will also gain consensus among your team members on who is important for success (on the high end of your power/interest grid), who needs to be "in the loop" during the plan development process (on the low end of the power/interest grid), and who needs to be managed closely. Finally, I want you to discuss the results of these exercises with the strategic plan champion. Gain some feedback and insight that may prove advantageous. Since you're not really sure if you and the teams got it right, get a second opinion.

Also important is that you will discuss the results of this stakeholder analysis at the offsite.

Appendix J
Survey Information

Surveys are tools for research and data gathering. In any bona fide survey, the sample pool is not selected haphazardly. It is selected among persons who volunteered to participate, scientifically chosen so that each person in the survey population will have a measurable chance of selection. In this way, the results can be reliably projected from the sample to the larger population. Information is collected by means of standardized procedures such that every individual is asked the same questions in more or less the same way. A survey's intent is not to describe the particular individuals who, by chance, are part of the sample but to obtain a composite profile of the population the survey represents.

The suggested sample size should be based on survey population in order to realize reasonable error rates. The greater your survey population, the larger your participation pool. Keep the pool small but ensure that the target population and the questions are "on point." If you have a large and diverse customer base, you may consider a sample size greater than one hundred. The last survey I completed had a sample size of fifty. The previous one was 1,480.

It is important to clearly articulate the goals of your survey. Why are you conducting the survey? What, specifically, will you do with the survey results? How will the information help you improve your strategic plan development? Make sure that each question will give you the right kind of feedback to reach the survey's goals. When in doubt, contact a statistician or survey expert for help with survey and question design.

> *ADVICE:*
> *I recommend using SurveyMonkey to conduct your survey. I've gotten good results with it and usually find it's well within my or my client's budget. There is a data-integrity issue about SurveyMonkey for government surveys. Surveys holding data must meet government security requirements. Most contracted companies conducting surveys for the government include a security and compliance disclaimer on their surveys.*

You should introduce the survey, explaining who is collecting the survey feedback data and why. You should also include some reasons for participants to take part and share the details about the confidentiality of the information you're collecting. The introduction should also set expectations about the survey length and estimate the time it will take someone to complete it. Remember, I stated in chapter 1 that the average estimated time for a survey is fifteen minutes (noting that a shorter survey will deliver a higher response rate). The opening questions should be easy to answer, to increase participants' trust and to encourage them to continue answering questions. Questions should be relevant to the participants to reduce abandonment of the survey. In addition, to minimize confusion, questions should follow a logical flow, with similar questions grouped together.

The target population for your survey is the key stakeholders (both internally and externally) who can help shape the organization's future. I want you to develop the objectives for the survey, the survey questions, and the administration protocols. The survey should address measures of customer satisfaction, areas to drive improvement, and other "nuggets" from the customer about various aspects of the organization. Include some policy-related questions if you deem them necessary. To limit the burden on respondents, I recommend the use of closed-ended questions and that you work to ensure that the survey takes an average of fifteen minutes to complete. Sample survey questions can be found in appendix J, TAB 1, Sample Survey Questions.

I have always used Theresa Cruz's, four-phase approach to conduct surveys. As Figure J-1, Four-phase approach, depicts, the approach begins with planning and ends with a final assessment, typically a report. Ms. Cruz is highly experienced in conducting program and policy-based research with extensive knowledge of quantitative and qualitative methods, including six sigma analytical tools, government accounting and economic analysis, sampling, survey design and conduct, statistical analyses, and focus group management. Additional survey graphics are available at my website.

In phase 1 (Figure J-1), you will work with the strategic planning teams to finalize the list of respondents within your target population as well as obtain their input to develop approval for the proposed survey questions.

PHASE 1: PLANNING

- Build survey instrument communications
- Circulate survey instruments and communications to assure alignment to study objectives
- Finalize surveys
- Build mailing lists and sampling strategy
- Program surveys to web platform and test functionality

PHASE 2: CONDUCT

- Establish help-desk function
- Survey alert message
- Correct bad email addresses (ongoing)
- Second communication with link
- Monitor response rates (ongoing)
- Reminder to non-responders (up to 3 as necessary)
- Close surveys

PHASE 3: ANALYSIS

- Download survey data for analysis
- Identify response distributions
- Perform stastical analysis (chi-square tests) on responses
- Prepare graphical and tabular presentations
- Perform comment analysis

PHASE 4: REPORTING

- Identify improvement areas/strategic initiatives based on survey scores and comment analysis
- Provide guidance for selection of strategic initiatives
- Develop briefings of survey results

Figure J-1. Four-phase survey approach

You may choose to edit, increase, or decrease the sample questions in appendix J, TAB 1, Sample Survey Questions. Designing the right type and number of questions is critical to getting the responses you require and ensuring ease in conducting the analysis. Some common types of survey questions are listed below.

✓ Multiple-choice questions:
  • Questions that present more than one answer option.

- Useful for all types of feedback, including collecting demographic information.
- Answers can be stated as yes/no (although not desirable) or a choice of multiple answers.
- Should not leave out answer options or use questions that are not mutually exclusive. Example: Do you work in this organization? (Yes/No)

✓ Rank-order-scale questions:
  - Questions that require the rank of potential answer choices by specific characteristics. These questions can provide insight into how important something is to a customer.
  - Good for online or paper surveys, but not for phone surveys.
  - Example: Please rank the following customer-service factors, from most to least important to you, when interacting with our organization (1 equals most important, 5 equals least important).

  - Likert-scale questions:
    - "Agree/disagree" with a statement. Responses often range from "strongly disagree" to "strongly agree," with five answer options.
    - Each option ascribed a score (1 equals strongly disagree to 5 equals strongly agree); scores can be used in survey-response analysis.
    - Should include a "neutral" category ("neither agree nor disagree").
    - Example: The customer service representative was knowledgeable (1 strongly disagree, 2 disagree, 3 neither agree nor disagree, 4 agree, 5 strongly agree).

✓ Open-ended questions:
  - Questions with no specific answer choices.
  - Particularly helpful for collecting feedback from participants about their attitudes or opinions. May require extra time or can be challenging to answer, so participants may skip and/or abandon the survey.
  - Analysis can be difficult to automate; may require extra time or resources to review and conduct analysis.

In phase 2, you will be required to craft a message from the leadership to all respondents encouraging them to participate in the survey. Appendix J, TAB 2, provides a sample survey leadership letter. Prior to releasing the survey, conduct a pilot test to ensure validity and reliability. Administer the survey using the Internet or a web-based survey portal. The Internet facilitates the greatest involvement across the participant groups, while the web survey portal provides the desired security, authenticating participants through encrypted identifications, passwords, and user-specific uniform resource locators (URLs). We recommend that all communications include the name, e-mail address, and phone number of a planning team member to provide "help desk" assistance to survey participants.

> *INSTRUCTION:*
> *Thank your participants after they've completed the survey.*

In phase 3, you will perform the survey analysis. The survey analysis should be a simple matter, depending on the survey tool utilized to administer the survey. Here again, I recommend SurveyMonkey, an automated tool I have used on numerous occasions that's affordable and extremely easy to navigate. The analysis provided by this tool suits the requirements for developing strategic plans. Survey feedback usually is provided in the form of descriptive statistics such as numbers that summarize how items were answered on the questionnaire. Here are typical descriptive statistics for surveys:

- ✓ Frequency, or how many responses there are for each item. For example, 6 of 24 responses for answer A, 4 of 20 responses for B, 10 of 20 for C.
- ✓ Percentage, which converts frequency to a proportion by dividing the number of assist-specific responses by the total number of responses and multiplying by 100. For example, 25 percent response for answer A, 20 percent for B, and 50 percent for C.
- ✓ Cumulative frequency, which identifies how many respondents selected a specific number such as on a Likert scale. For example, twenty-one hundred gave a ranking of three.
- ✓ Cumulative percentage, which converts cumulative frequency to a proportion. For example, 20 percent gave a ranking of 3 on a scale of 1 to 5 for the frequency of a twenty-four-hour help desk response.
- ✓ Values, expressed as a single number.

- *Mean* is most commonly thought of as an average, and it represents all data values added together and divided by the number of items in the list.
- *Median* is the middle or middle point of a group list of numbers put in value order.
- *Mode* is the most repeated value in a group list.

Phase 4 provides the survey results. Here, you focus on the key points from the survey that will drive the strategic plan development, such as vision, mission, guiding principles, goals, and objectives. For example, if 50 percent of your customers responded saying the operations department does not return phone calls, you will certainly want to include that in your gap analysis and use it in crafting goals and objectives.

> **ADVICE:**
> Always apply consistency in analyzing data.

Appendix J
Survey Information
TAB 1: Sample Survey Questions

1. Overall, to what extent are you satisfied or dissatisfied with the support you received from the X-Ray Corporation?
    a. Satisfied
    b. Very satisfied
    c. Sometimes satisfied, sometimes dissatisfied
    d. Dissatisfied
    e. Very dissatisfied

2. To what extent do you agree or disagree with the following statements concerning the general performance of X-Ray Corporation
    a. Employees deal with me in a courteous, businesslike manner.
    b. The corporation provides the services and solutions I need.
    c. The corporation's employees try their best to meet my requirements.
    d. The corporation's employees meet my requirements in a timely manner.
    e. The corporation's resource management department responds to billing inquiries in a timely manner.
    f. I find it easy to contact the right X-Ray department to meet my needs.

3. To what extent do you agree or disagree with the following statements concerning X-Ray Corporation and its stakeholders?
    a. X-Ray effectively collaborates with stakeholders/customers to meet its mission objectives.

    b. X-Ray collaborates with me during execution of medical services.

    c. X-Ray collaborates with me on medical services early in the planning process.

    d. X-Ray collaborates with me after medical services are carried out.

4. To what extent do you agree or disagree with the following statements concerning X-Ray Corporation's communication with stakeholders/ customers?

    a. The corporation communicates general information about medical services in a timely manner.

    b. The corporation communicates information about organizational policy changes in a timely manner.

5. To what extent do you agree or disagree with the following statements regarding communication with X-Ray Corporation representatives?

    a. Representatives deal with me in a courteous, businesslike manner.

    b. Representatives help me to solve problems effectively.

    c. Representatives understand the needs of my organization.

    d. Representatives return calls in a timely manner.

    e. Specific representatives are usually available to talk to.

    f. Representatives are knowledgeable in their subject area.

6. When you contact X-Ray Corporation representatives, about how long does it take to get an answer to your questions?

    a. Less than one business day.

    b. One to three business days.

    c. Four to five business days.

    d. More than five business days.

    e. They do not get back to me.

7. To what extent do you agree or disagree with the following statements about X-Ray Corporation's Intranet website?

    a. Overall, I'm satisfied with the website.

    b. Information on the website is up to date.

    c. The website is easy to navigate.

8. To what extent do you agree or disagree with the following statements concerning X-Ray Corporation's policies and procedures?
    a. The company is committed to providing reliable medical services.
    b. The company conducts its operations with a high degree of integrity.
    c. The company works closely with me to ensure that medical equipment is delivered by the agreed date.
    d. The company uses the appropriate tools to make my job easier.
    e. The company works closely with me to monitor performance.
    f. The company's policies and procedures are clear and easy to understand.

9. To what extent do you agree or disagree with the following statements concerning X-Ray Corporation's financial resources?
    a. The resource-management invoice department works well for processing payments.
    b. Invoices are processed within thirty to forty-five days.
    c. Resource management responds to billing inquiries within one business day.

10. Rate each of the following statements on a 0-to-5 scale using the guidelines given:
    a. I understand the corporate mission (purpose for existence).
    (0 = no idea what the corporate mission is to 5 = I understand the corporate mission and how my job contributes to it.)

    b. I understand the vision of what the organization is working to become.
    (0 = no idea what the organization vision is to 5 = I understand the vision and how my job contributes to realizing it.)

    c. I see clearly defined strategies in place that support the mission and vision.
    (0 = strategies are not clear and what I see doesn't seem to link together to 5 = strategies are clear and everything works toward what needs to be done).

d. Performance measurements are in place for tracking progress. (0 = there are no performance measurements to 5 = well-defined measurements are in place and are used to take corrective action).

e. I know how my work contributes value to the organization. (0 = a little, but mostly I just concentrate on getting the work done to 5 = I understand how my job fits together with other jobs to build organization value and how my work helps others do their job).

f. I have a career plan that fits within a larger, personal life plan. (0 = I haven't really thought much about it to 5 = I am actively developing myself with career objectives and life goals in mind).

g. I have thought about the future I would like to have for me and my family. (0 = I haven't really thought much about it to 5 = I'm working toward this personal vision with specific plans).

Appendix J
Survey Information
TAB 2: Sample Survey Leadership Letter

The following is a sample letter from the CEO or senior leadership.

Dear colleagues,

Our organization provides mobile medical command-and-control and distribution services to meet our customers' and community's needs. I require your help to measure our performance and make improvements in our planning, execution, and processes so that we can provide greater service to our customers, employees, and community.

This survey is intended for our key stakeholders and employees, including customers and community agents. We need your input to strengthen our company's strategic relationships and, thereby, to provide the best possible service within our organizational environment.

Your responses to this survey will have no impact on your service or employment. Please answer all applicable questions based on your personal experience with the company over the past twelve months.

The survey is anonymous and all answers will be kept confidential. We will share only the combined survey results with our partners. As noted, not all sections of the survey will be applicable to you. Please answer only those questions related to the programs you provide with services. If you wish to offer suggestions for improvement in any other aspect of support or would like to qualify an answer to any question, please use the comments section at the end of the survey for this purpose.

The survey should take approximately fifteen minutes to complete. Please return it to the web address on the survey by Feb. 25, 2015.

Thank you again for your hard work and support for the X-Ray Corporation. Your efforts are very much appreciated.

Very cordially yours,

JH
Jim Hodge

Appendix K
Guiding Principles Questionnaire

As mentioned in chapter 1, the guiding principles questionnaire provides additional data for your internal environmental scan. Follow the instructions in chapter 1 and your project plan to ensure that this questionnaire is completed and analysis is conducted prior to the focus group offsite. In order to improve the analysis and conduct of this questionnaire, I recommend transcribing the questions and the respondents' data fields with a survey program such as SurveyMonkey (discussed in appendix J). You may add or delete questions as you deem them applicable to your organization.

Dedication

We are in a place where people love to come to work, where stakeholders, customers, and suppliers love to work with us because of our drive, determination, and commitment.												
Never or not at all true			**Seldom true**			**Often true**			**Always true**			**Comment, Suggestion, or Alternative Statement**
1	2	3	4	5	6	7	8	9	10	11	12	**X** here if you don't understand what the statement means in practice.

We encourage, recognize, and reward the commitment, hard work, and achievements of individuals and teams and celebrate success.												
Never or not at all true			**Seldom true**			**Often true**			**Always true**			**Comment, Suggestion, or Alternative Statement**
1	2	3	4	5	6	7	8	9	10	11	12	**X** here if you don't understand what the statement means in practice.

We serve and delight our stakeholders through the quality of our programs and services and the way we operate.												
Never or not at all true			**Seldom true**			**Often true**			**Always true**			**Comment, Suggestion, or Alternative Statement**
1	2	3	4	5	6	7	8	9	10	11	12	**X** here if you don't understand what the statement means in practice.

Passion

We show pride, enthusiasm, and dedication in everything we do.												
Never or not at all true			**Seldom true**			**Often true**			**Always true**			**Comment, Suggestion, or Alternative Statement**
1	2	3	4	5	6	7	8	9	10	11	12	**X** here if you don't understand what the statement means in practice.

We are committed to developing and delivering high-quality programs and services.													
Never or not at all true			Seldom true			Often true			Always true				Comment, Suggestion, or Alternative Statement
1	2	3	4	5	6	7	8	9	10	11	12		X here if you don't understand what the statement means in practice.

Integrity

We build trust in all interactions by displaying consistently high standards of ethical and professional business practices.													
Never or not at all true			Seldom true			Often true			Always true				Comment, Suggestion, or Alternative Statement
1	2	3	4	5	6	7	8	9	10	11	12		X here if you don't understand what the statement means in practice.

We show respect for and value all individuals for their diverse backgrounds, experience, styles, approaches, and ideas.													
Never or not at all true			Seldom true			Often true			Always true				Comment, Suggestion, or Alternative Statement
1	2	3	4	5	6	7	8	9	10	11	12		X here if you don't understand what the statement means in practice.

We speak positively and supportively of team members when we're not together.				
Never or not at all true	**Seldom true**	**Often true**	**Always true**	**Comment, Suggestion, or Alternative Statement**
1 2 3	4 5 6	7 8 9	10 11 12	**X** here if you don't understand what the statement means in practice.

We always try to listen to others with understanding.				
Never or not at all true	**Seldom true**	**Often true**	**Always true**	**Comment, Suggestion, or Alternative Statement**
1 2 3	4 5 6	7 8 9	10 11 12	**X** here if you don't understand what the statement means in practice.

Innovation and Creativity

We thrive on creativity and resourcefulness.				
Never or not at all true	**Seldom true**	**Often true**	**Always true**	**Comment, Suggestion, or Alternative Statement**
1 2 3	4 5 6	7 8 9	10 11 12	**X** here if you don't understand what the statement means in practice.

We encourage everyone to come up with new, creative ideas that have the potential to improve our processes.													
Never or not at all true			Seldom true			Often true			Always true			Comment, Suggestion, or Alternative Statement	
1	2	3	4	5	6	7	8	9	10	11	12		X here if you don't understand what the statement means in practice.

We promote and implement creative and innovative ideas and solutions.													
Never or not at all true			Seldom true			Often true			Always true			Comment, Suggestion, or Alternative Statement	
1	2	3	4	5	6	7	8	9	10	11	12		X here if you don't understand what the statement means in practice.

Reliability and Accountability

We accept personal accountability for our own actions and results.													
Never or not at all true			Seldom true			Often true			Always true			Comment, Suggestion, or Alternative Statement	
1	2	3	4	5	6	7	8	9	10	11	12		X here if you don't understand what the statement means in practice.

We focus on finding solutions and achieving results, rather than on making excuses or placing blame.

Never or not at all true			Seldom true			Often true			Always true			Comment, Suggestion, or Alternative Statement
1	2	3	4	5	6	7	8	9	10	11	12	X here if you don't understand what the statement means in practice.

We keep our promises and commitments.

Never or not at all true			Seldom true			Often true			Always true			Comment, Suggestion, or Alternative Statement
1	2	3	4	5	6	7	8	9	10	11	12	X here if you don't understand what the statement means in practice.

We take responsibility for our actions that influence the lives of our clients and fellow workers.

Never or not at all true			Seldom true			Often true			Always true			Comment, Suggestion, or Alternative Statement
1	2	3	4	5	6	7	8	9	10	11	12	X here if you don't understand what the statement means in practice.

Financial Responsibility

We are committed to practices that keep our organization financially strong.												
Never or not at all true			**Seldom true**			**Often true**			**Always true**			**Comment, Suggestion, or Alternative Statement**
1	2	3	4	5	6	7	8	9	10	11	12	**X** here if you don't understand what the statement means in practice.

We keep accurate account of our financial resources for tax and audit purposes.												
Never or not at all true			**Seldom true**			**Often true**			**Always true**			**Comment, Suggestion, or Alternative Statement**
1	2	3	4	5	6	7	8	9	10	11	12	**X** here if you don't understand what the statement means in practice.

Excellence

We deliver excellence, strive for continuous process improvement, and respond enthusiastically to change.												
Never or not at all true			**Seldom true**			**Often true**			**Always true**			**Comment, Suggestion, or Alternative Statement**
1	2	3	4	5	6	7	8	9	10	11	12	**X** here if you don't understand what the statement means in practice.

We don't take shortcuts or make the fewest possible assumptions—we do our "research."											
Never or not at all true			Seldom true			Often true			Always true			Comment, Suggestion, or Alternative Statement
1	2	3	4	5	6	7	8	9	10	11	12	**X** here if you don't understand what the statement means in practice.

We value and master the technology that produces a more accurate and useful product or service.											
Never or not at all true			Seldom true			Often true			Always true			Comment, Suggestion, or Alternative Statement
1	2	3	4	5	6	7	8	9	10	11	12	**X** here if you don't understand what the statement means in practice.

Empowerment

We support employees through policy, training, involvement, and collaboration to take the initiative and give their best.											
Never or not at all true			Seldom true			Often true			Always true			Comment, Suggestion, or Alternative Statement
1	2	3	4	5	6	7	8	9	10	11	12	**X** here if you don't understand what the statement means in practice.

We are committed to openness and trust in all relationships to help people realize their full potential.													
Never or not at all true			Seldom true			Often true			Always true			Comment, Suggestion, or Alternative Statement
1	2	3	4	5	6	7	8	9	10	11	12		**X** here if you don't understand what the statement means in practice.

Customer Service

We believe in respecting our customers, listening to their requests, and understanding their expectations.													
Never or not at all true			Seldom true			Often true			Always true			Comment, Suggestion, or Alternative Statement
1	2	3	4	5	6	7	8	9	10	11	12		**X** here if you don't understand what the statement means in practice.

We strive to exceed our customers' expectations in affordability, quality, and on-time delivery.													
Never or not at all true			Seldom true			Often true			Always true			Comment, Suggestion, or Alternative Statement
1	2	3	4	5	6	7	8	9	10	11	12		**X** here if you don't understand what the statement means in practice.

We owe and show our suppliers the same type of respect that we show our clients. Our suppliers deserve fair and equitable treatment, clear agreements, and honest feedback on performance.

Never or not at all true			Seldom true			Often true			Always true			Comment, Suggestion, or Alternative Statement
1	2	3	4	5	6	7	8	9	10	11	12	**X** here if you don't understand what the statement means in practice.

We give each project the technical attention it deserves without engaging in excess.

Never or not at all true			Seldom true			Often true			Always true			Comment, Suggestion, or Alternative Statement
1	2	3	4	5	6	7	8	9	10	11	12	**X** here if you don't understand what the statement means in practice.

We respond to every reasonable request, even when it might cost us.

Never or not at all true			Seldom true			Often true			Always true			Comment, Suggestion, or Alternative Statement
1	2	3	4	5	6	7	8	9	10	11	12	**X** here if you don't understand what the statement means in practice.

233

We represent our customers' best interests.												
Never or not at all true			**Seldom true**			**Often true**			**Always true**			**Comment, Suggestion, or Alternative Statement**
1	2	3	4	5	6	7	8	9	10	11	12	**X** here if you don't understand what the statement means in practice.

When necessary, we educate our clients about the technical or ethical consequences of our work.												
Never or not at all true			**Seldom true**			**Often true**			**Always true**			**Comment, Suggestion, or Alternative Statement**
1	2	3	4	5	6	7	8	9	10	11	12	**X** here if you don't understand what the statement means in practice.

Appendix L
SWOT Analysis

A Strengths, Weaknesses, Opportunities, and Threats (SWOT) analysis is a structured planning method that can be applied across diverse functions and activities, but it is particularly appropriate to the early stages of conducting an environmental scan. Performing a SWOT analysis involves the generation and recording of the strengths, weaknesses, opportunities, and threats in relation to a particular task, discussion, or environment. It is customary for the analysis to consider internal resources and capabilities (strengths and weakness) and factors external to the organization (opportunities and threats). A SWOT analysis provides:

✓ A framework for identifying and analyzing strengths, weaknesses, opportunities, and threats
✓ An impetus to analyze a situation and develop suitable strategies and tactics
✓ A basis for assessing core capabilities and competences
✓ Evidence for, and cultural keys to, change
✓ Stimuli for participation in a focus group experience

The internal organization scan looks at identifying the strengths and weaknesses of your organization. By breaking down your internal environment into capabilities, resources, and processes, you then begin to assess your organization.

You, as team leader, must understand group dynamics before working through the SWOT analysis, gap analysis, or any other collective gathering so that each session or meeting can have a positive outcome that provides definitive and concrete results that will contribute to the strategic planning process. Refer to the discussion in "Let's Get Started" and appendix H on group and team brainstorming.

Undertaking a SWOT analysis

The following checklist is for carrying out a SWOT analysis. SWOT is a simple, much-used method that can help to prepare or amend plans in problem solving and decision making.

- ✓ Establish the objectives—what is it you want to analyze?
- ✓ Select appropriate contributors.
- ✓ Allocate research and information-gathering tasks.
- ✓ Create a workshop environment.
- ✓ List strengths.
- ✓ List weaknesses.
- ✓ List opportunities.
- ✓ List threats.
- ✓ Evaluate listed possibilities against the objectives.
- ✓ Carry findings forward.

When developing a SWOT analysis:

- ✓ Make assumptions about the environment and global impact affecting your organization.
- ✓ Establish the objectives. The first key step in any project is to be clear on what you are doing and why. The purpose of conducting a SWOT analysis may be wide or narrow, general or specific. Determine the gaps and provide solutions to the organization's current state.
- ✓ Make assumptions about threats and opportunities.
- ✓ Take everything into account; do not dismiss gaps, suggestions, or recommendations.
- ✓ Look backward to move forward. Analyze historical data and trend analysis to help determine the organization's current state.
- ✓ Analyze why the customer wants your services.
- ✓ Determine customers' core needs and then develop the strategy to satisfy those needs.
- ✓ Be realistic—don't make outrageous assumptions, such as that your competition will perish in six months.
- ✓ Don't over think or overanalyze; just say what first comes to mind.

✓ Think about your current state and where the organization should be tomorrow.

✓ Recognize that SWOT is subjective and that you may need additional data to support your findings.

✓ Select appropriate contributors, an important consideration if the outcome is to result from consultation and discussion, not just personal views.

✓ Allocate research and information-gathering tasks. Background preparation is vital in order for the analysis to be effective and should be divided among members of your team. This preparation can be carried out in two stages: *exploratory* (i.e., data collection) and *detailed* (i.e., focused analysis). Gathering information on strengths and weaknesses should focus on the internal factors of skills, resources, and assets, or lack of them. Gathering information on opportunities and threats should focus on the external factors over which you have little or no control, such as social or economic factors. Remember, you've already collected some data from previously conducted exercises.

✓ Create a workshop environment. Encourage an atmosphere conducive to the free flow of information and to participants' saying what they feel to be appropriate, free from censure. The team leader/facilitator has a key role and should allow time for the free flow of thought, but not too much. An hour is more than enough time to spend, for example, on strengths, before moving on. It is important to be specific, evaluative, and analytical at the stage of compiling and recording the SWOT lists—mere description is not enough. Some recommended areas to analyze:

- Customer satisfaction
- Marketing performance
- Capital resources
- Innovation
- Niche
- Organizational design
- Internal systems
- Management
- Human resources
- Organizational culture

Internal and external environmental scan

It is something of an overstatement to say that "everyone is familiar with SWOT." But it isn't much of one. Indeed, most managers know that SWOT stands for strengths, weaknesses, opportunities, and threats. Yet, most do nothing with it. Looking both internally and externally at the SWOT analysis, you and your planning teams will itemize both the good and the bad. Your list may look like this: internal good news (strength), internal bad (weaknesses), external good (opportunities), and external bad (threats). A suggested internal weakness must pass yet one more test, for, very often, managers identify not fundamental weaknesses but rather *symptoms* of weaknesses. Solving the symptoms is a classic mistake during a SWOT analysis.

A SWOT analysis identifies the organizational strengths or competencies (for example, competitive advantage, strong brand, good locations, strong training programs for new managers), weaknesses (such as poor employee morale, startup cash drain, cash-flow problems, public reputation), opportunities (a new product line, technology, research, communication structure, employee-benefit structure), and threats (competition, the economy, weather or natural disasters, legislative regulations). You will have to recognize any symptoms as such, dig down beneath the symptoms and find the fundamental weaknesses which caused the symptoms. You do this by asking, "Why?" Until you've uncovered the fundamental weaknesses hidden beneath the symptoms, you're not moving forward—you're just running in place. Competencies, also known as success factors, are abilities, sets of actions, or strategies at which the organization is particularly good and that can be used to improve its performance in relation to these factors.

Planners tend to parachute right into strategic issues without understanding the issues' context. As a result, such issues are often not clearly identified or are misidentified, which in turn means that the strategies developed do not address the real issues. A SWOT analysis can help the organization identify its success factors. These are actions the organization must take or criteria it must meet in order to be successful in the eyes of its key stakeholders, especially those in its external environment.

Take a look at Figure L-1, SWOT Matrix. Keep the visual in mind when reading the explanation of strengths, weaknesses, opportunities, and threats. For your SWOT exercise, mentally determine what you would put in each quadrant. Two key pieces of data to determine the SWOT are your survey and the guiding principles questionnaire. What did "the voice of the customer," stakeholders, and employees say?

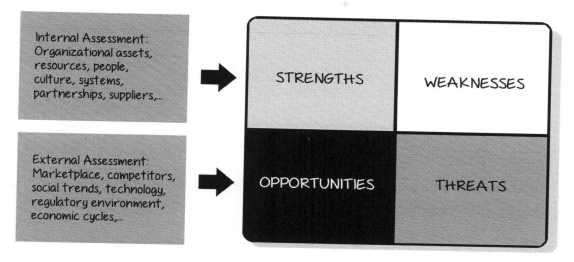

Figure L-1. SWOT Matrix

Strengths

Every organization—even successful ones—will have strengths and weaknesses. Unless an organization is absolutely perfect (remember your Plato: he claims there are no

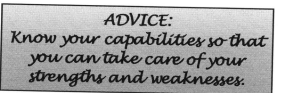

ADVICE:
Know your capabilities so that you can take care of your strengths and weaknesses.

absolutes), it will have some weaknesses, and in some cases its weaknesses are created by its strengths (recall our Kodak vignette—their weakness was that they believed their strength was invincible). This belief in invincibility is almost a natural law (I call it "an imagined reality.") One of the things I have found is that a lot of organizations think they are good at certain things that, in fact, they are not really very good at. It is often easy to convince yourself that you are good at something, but it's hard to convince yourself that you *not* good at something. Most interestingly, I have found this is more prevalent in governmental organizations than in nongovernmental ones.

Conversely, a weakness can become or be seen as a strength. The battle of Thermopylae is a good example of the former. Thermopylae, a narrow pass that was wide enough for, maybe, five hundred men at a time, was the site twenty-five hundred years ago of a standoff between a greatly outnumbered force of Greeks and an invading army of tens of thousands of Persians. For three days, the Greeks were able to defend the pass against the invaders because they had geared the battle to their strengths. In business terms, painting and drawing are not the strong suits of a cow. Milk is its strength. If you have a cow, you may already have value. You don't need to teach it to paint and draw—even if the inability to create art for sale is a noticeable weakness of the cow. Just as the Greeks and the cow focused on their strengths, so must your organization. However, don't just focus on the strengths; look at the weaknesses as well.

Count only those strengths that you can apply to support the strategic level of the organization. There is a tendency, at this point, to go organization-wide and list strengths that are not particularly related to the issue at hand. For example, if your vision is about effectiveness and efficiency, it really doesn't matter that you offer great medical products; it *does* matter that your intellectual capital is people with PhD-level solutions in process improvement. It is a good idea to start with what you identified as your organization's guiding principles. What specifically is it that you can call on in your company's culture to reinforce the vision's attainment? What attitudes and behaviors will accelerate the vision's implementation? For example, if the strategic issue is "new-product development," can you count on a supportive culture of innovation and risk taking? Use some findings from your organizational culture exercise in your SWOT analysis to assist in determining strengths and weaknesses.

Areas to consider when identifying strengths and weaknesses include competitive advantages, customer satisfaction, marketing, and sales performance, capital resources, cost and pricing, innovation, organizational design, internal systems, management, human resources, and corporate culture. For example, consider the strength "We have a sales force in place in the market area where that opportunity exists." Or "We have additional capacity in research and development to develop a new product." See the relationship? You're aligning the particular opportunity with the corresponding internal strength. Examine your internal business processes and analyze them to determine those that require work—that is, those that need to be fixed. Table L-1, Processes, depicts some processes you may choose to examine and discuss.

Processes	
Review internal processes	Organizational process
Examine information systems	Customer management process
Evaluate facilities and equipment	Relationship managment process
Assess the skills and experience of the team	Innovation and technology process
Coordinate internal capabilities	Communication process
Determine areas for improvement	Productivity process

Table L-1. Processes

Internal strengths

Strengths can relate to a group, to the environment, to perceptions, and to people. "People" elements include skills, capabilities, and knowledge, where people are:

- ✓ Motivated, cooperative and supportive
- ✓ Involved through delegation and trust
- ✓ Focused on what they do best

Answer these questions to determine your internal strengths:

- ✓ What employee skills are available to apply to the vision's execution?
- ✓ Is there sophisticated technological know-how? Can you count on tapping into these skill sets in your available personnel?
- ✓ What assets that you'll need to implement the vision are readily available?
- ✓ What financial resources are available and for how long?
- ✓ Is there a productive organizational culture on which you can depend?

Capabilities revolve around the strengths and weaknesses of an organization. Those can be strengths or weaknesses in any area—for example, sources of competitive advantage and innovation, any functional areas such as sales or marketing, cost structure, capital resources, or, more commonly, management. Before you can craft a strategy, you need to know your capabilities so that you can take advantage of your strengths and overcome your weaknesses.

Financial strengths

Any honest evaluation requires a close look at the current financial health of the organization. A sound strategic process will have you laying out your existing financial resources in a simple, easy-to-understand format, such as an income statement. These numbers will give you a good basis for evaluating your organization.

The income statement looks at the last five years of your organization's operating performance. It starts with showing revenue as it streams into the organization, and applies costs against it—both fixed and variable. Is your income statement's operating performance a strength?

It is important to understand which areas of your business generate strong profits and which do not. Slice your "business lines" along some dimension that gives insight: by product, by distribution channel, by customer type, or, most important, by market segment. Are your finances a strength? Once you've gathered this financial-strength information, discuss it with your team and at the offsite, the idea being to let participants know the financial data so they can decide if the organization has the resources to implement the plan.

Like any commander, you must inventory your human and physical resources before setting out to meet the objective; otherwise, you may find yourself attacking the objective only to discover that you have no follow-on forces and are out of ammunition. This is not a good thing. Likewise, before you approach the objective, it is a good idea to do an inventory—an analysis—of your strengths, weaknesses, opportunities, and threats. This is why a key military tenet is to perform pre-execution checks before departing on every mission—it ensures that you have everything you need before committing to an objective. You need to analyze:

- ✓ What you have to work with (strengths to build on)
- ✓ What you don't have to work with (weaknesses to correct or finesse)
- ✓ Immediate opportunities that can be exploited in order to triumph
- ✓ What you perceive as threats

By itself, a SWOT analysis isn't actionable. By matching up factors from one quadrant with factors from another quadrant in the SWOT matrix, you identify potential actions based on the analysis. The purpose of matching internal factors with external factors is to identify a fit between organizational strengths and market opportunities. In other words, what opportunities can you take advantage of, based on what you already have to work with? Also, in matching weaknesses with opportunities or threats, you may see some compelling ventures that are worth pursuing. In exercise #8 below, get creative! Put all your ideas down, even if they seem ridiculous. Allow yourself and your team to brainstorm not just out of the box but into the stratosphere. You can pull things back down to earth at the end of the exercise.

Exercise #8: SWOT Analysis, Part 1

Before you begin the exercise, draw a large SWOT matrix on a dry erase board or wallpaper. Set up a parking lot for ideas that do not fall neatly into one of the SWOT matrix quadrants. Ensure that your administrative assistant is taking copious notes on all discussion items.

List internal strengths

- ✓ List as many internal strengths as necessary to derive a complete list in the *strengths* quadrant in Figure L–1, SWOT Matrix. Then discuss each to determine those that are high priority.
- ✓ Put an asterisk next to five to eight strengths, in order, beginning with the most important. Identify the strategic issues that may be associated with the list.
- ✓ Look at the list and determine actions for preserving or enhancing the strengths. Note any that might be pursued immediately without unnecessarily or unwisely foreclosing future choices and then discuss.

Internal weaknesses

This topic should not constitute an opportunity to focus on the negative but be an honest appraisal of the way things are. Key questions include:

- ✓ What obstacles may prevent progress?
- ✓ Which elements need strengthening?
- ✓ Are there any weak links in the organization?

✓ Are the capabilities current with today's technology?

It is not unusual for people problems—poor communication, inadequate leadership, lack of motivation, too little delegation, no trust, etc.—to turn up among the internal weaknesses.

Now turn your strengths upside down to determine if any weaknesses need to be addressed or corrected to implement your vision. What may be lacking in, or a hindrance to, your organization's

> *IDEA:*
> *In some cases weaknesses are caused by organizational strengths; that is, the tortoise lacks speed due to its protection.*

culture, attitudes, and behavior to support your vision (such as an attitude of risk averseness)? What specific employee skills do you require that may not be present (such as technological skills)? What equipment may be missing? Will a budget be established, or do you have to work on a "shoestring," and even if a budget is set, will it be realistic as to how much and how long you'll need to fund it? An internal weakness may read: "We have obsolete software, making our customers' costs high." Yes, that weakness does correspond to the low-cost competitive threat. Another internal weakness may be your poor balance sheet. If so, then it, too, relates to a specific threat, for a poor balance sheet would prohibit the capital investment required to upgrade the obsolete software. In one organization, I actually saw 80-column Hollerith computer punch cards. This was in 2010. These cards were outdated in the 1980s. Yet this organization thought it best to keep them on hand. When asked why, the project manager said, "They're a backup." Really? This sort of organizational thinking is a weakness.

Exercise #8: SWOT Analysis, Part 2

List internal weaknesses

Internal weaknesses are deficiencies in resources or capabilities that hinder an organization's ability to meet its mandates, fulfill its mission, realize its vision, and create public value. In this exercise, you will:

✓ List as many internal weaknesses as necessary to derive a complete list in the *weaknesses* quadrant in Figure L-1, SWOT Matrix. Then discuss each to determine those that are high priority.

✓ Put an asterisk next to five to eight weaknesses, in order, beginning with the most important. Identify the strategic issues that may be associated with the list.

✓ Look at the list and determine actions for mitigating the weaknesses. Note any that might be pursued immediately without unnecessarily or unwisely foreclosing future choices and then discuss.

Identify opportunities and threats

When responding to opportunities and threats in your environment, you need to react proactively. Being ready for the "what ifs" can help you determine your strategic position. You need to take a quick pulse of your organization's opportunities and threats to exit from, act on, and assess your external environment.

Opportunities and threats are external factors, forces that you can't control but can take advantage of if appropriate. For example, an opportunity may be that a rising number of Asian consumers could lead to an increased demand for your product if your company is positioned correctly. A threat might be that the proliferation of technology is making a current product obsolete. Remember, the purpose of a SWOT analysis is to help produce a good fit between your organization's resources and capabilities and its external environment.

Your SWOT analysis is a balance sheet of your strategic position right now; in it, you bring together all your internal factors—strengths and weaknesses— and your external factors—opportunities and threats. Strengths and weaknesses are factors that you control and affect. Opportunities and threats are external factors that you can't control or influence. You must either try to take advantage of them or try to minimize them.

Opportunities

If you have a major assignment, start off with the easy stuff. Even though you know it's an artificial maneuver, there is nevertheless a confidence boost when you successfully accomplish these early steps of the strategic plan. When I took the project management professional (PMP) exam, I answered the easy questions first to build my confidence before I tackled the more difficult ones. Think of it as a form of triage, with the easiest questions/assignments being tackled first. What opportunities, or external conditions, do you see that can give you some quick wins (i.e., what are the low-hanging fruit)? In other words, where are the opportunities facing your organization? You might ask, "Where should we look for opportunities and threats?" First, look at your macroenvironment. Remember that concentric circles graphic (Figure 1–6) that identified external forces affecting your organization that we discussed earlier? Use it to gauge your environment. I also recommend using the SPEELT (societal, political, economic, environmental, legal, technological) method of looking at the macroenvironment. Then look at your microenvironment. Review each of the SPEELT factors (in the macroenvironment) below and determine how they affect your organization's opportunities.

- ✓ Societal—diversified market and changing demographics
- ✓ Political—different political views concerning your market niche
- ✓ Economic—rising cost of goods and services
- ✓ Environmental—restrictions on producing your product or services
- ✓ Legal—local, state, or federal laws and regulations
- ✓ Technological—availability of new technology

Issues in this macroenvironment may not be specific to your organization. They may not even be specific to your industry. But you care about them because they affect your organization. They include economic conditions, for example. Economic conditions are not specific to

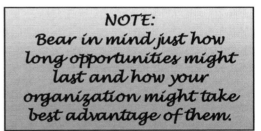

NOTE:
Bear in mind just how long opportunities might last and how your organization might take best advantage of them.

any one industry. Rather, economic conditions affect all organizations. The economy, then, is a macroenvironmental issue that includes such matters as government regulations, politics, and customer attitudes. The microenvironment includes the segment of the marketplace to which your customers belong. It includes the reasons why customers buy your products or services. The reasons why some of your prospective customers *don't* buy your products and/or services may be found in such areas as relationships with suppliers or your labor market-microenvironmental factors, all specific to your industry. Always look at the macro before drilling into the micro. But "stay out of the weeds."

Exercise #8: SWOT Analysis, Part 3

List opportunities

- ✓ List as many opportunities as necessary to derive a complete list in the *opportunities* quadrant in Figure L-1, SWOT Matrix. Then discuss each to determine those that are high priority.
- ✓ Put an asterisk next to five to eight opportunities, in order, beginning with the most important. Identify the strategic issues that may be associated with the list.
- ✓ Look at the list and determine actions for preserving or enhancing the opportunities. Note any that might be pursued immediately without unnecessarily or unwisely foreclosing future choices and discuss.

Threats

Threats can be perceived as the opposite of opportunities. Weighing threats against opportunities is not a reason to indulge in negativity; it is, rather, a question of considering how possible negative experiences may be limited or eliminated. The same factor may be seen as both a threat and an opportunity; for example, information technology may be a great opportunity to develop new software, yet it could be a threat to your existing software if another organization develops and markets something better. Most external factors are challenges, and whether you perceive them as opportunities or threats is often a valuable indicator of morale. Some examples of threats include:

- ✓ New market entrants
- ✓ Changes in customers' needs
- ✓ An economic downturn
- ✓ A rise in cost of production
- ✓ Competitive price pressure
- ✓ Better products by competitors

Exercise #8: SWOT Analysis, Part 4

List threats

External challenges are factors or situations that can affect your organization in a negative way—make it harder to fulfill its mission, mediate its mandates (difficult and often impossible), or maintain its public value.

- ✓ List as many threats as necessary to derive a complete list in the *threats* quadrant in Figure L–1, SWOT Matrix. Then discuss each to determine those that are high priority.
- ✓ Put an asterisk next to five to eight threats, in order, beginning with the most important. Identify the strategic issues that may be associated with the list.
- ✓ Look at the list and determine actions for avoiding or eliminating the threats. Note any that might be pursued immediately without unnecessarily or unwisely foreclosing future choices and discuss.

Dos and don'ts for SWOT analysis

Do:

- ✓ Be analytical and specific.
- ✓ Record all thoughts and ideas in the appropriate SWOT quadrant.
- ✓ Be selective in the final evaluation.
- ✓ Choose the right people for the exercise.
- ✓ Choose a suitable SWOT leader or facilitator.

Don't:

- ✓ Try to disguise weaknesses.
- ✓ Merely list errors and mistakes.
- ✓ Lose sight of external influences and trends.
- ✓ Allow the analysis to become a blame-laying exercise.
- ✓ Ignore the outcomes at later stages of the planning process.

Exercise #8: SWOT Analysis, Part 5

Once the lists of strengths, weaknesses, opportunities, and threats are compiled, sort and group them. Then list your priorities in each SWOT quadrant. If the lists are lengthy, you may want to sculpt them down to between five and eight items per quadrant. Clarity is vital to this process, as evaluation and elimination will be necessary to weed out the irrelevant topics. Although some aspects may require further information or research, a clear picture should, at this stage, start to emerge in response to the objective. The end state of this exercise is to develop a SWOT matrix that illustrates strengths, weaknesses, opportunities, and threats that will help shape the strategic plan to realize its vision.

Beyond the SWOT matrix

Clearly there are some issues that will not fall neatly into any of the quadrants we've discussed (your parking-lot issues), while others will instead fall into one or more of the quadrants or outside the model entirely. Allow me to give you an example of an experience I had with a client. It involved an issue that fell into the threats category (the lower right corner of the SWOT matrix). Some years ago, the management team for the client (a Department of Defense organization) was absolutely paranoid about the "reduction in force" levied at their organization. The number-one threat that came up during the organization's "leadership survey" was: "How will the organization manage the personnel cuts." We therefore put that threat (reduction in force) first on the list—with very little discussion. But if you were to look around the organization, you would find no evidence whatsoever that the organization was vulnerable to such cuts. Their mission was critical to the Department of Defense, working conditions were excellent, and the cuts were minimal. Actually, the reductions were properly called for and when instituted improved readiness, performance, and efficiency. Nonetheless, you could not go to a planning session with this management team without the reduction threat emerging early in the discussion. The hand-wringing never stopped. They just could not come to terms with how to make their perceived threat into an opportunity for the organization. If you were to place this issue on the SWOT matrix, it would go in the lower right quadrant—the alignment of internal weaknesses and external threats. If the matter had been properly analyzed, the management team would have realized that all the concern was for naught. As Socrates would doubtless agree, a SWOT analysis would have infused logic and reason into this issue and quelled any perceived threats to the organization.

Appendix L

Slaying a bad idea

There are times you find yourself asking, "What in the world are we going to do with this opportunity?" Or, "Which of our strengths would support our going after this opportunity?" On one occasion, I was on a team discussing opportunities for an organization. We looked at the list of internal strengths and did not find a single internal strength to support the organization's pursuing a specific opportunity. The organization was a high-quality, low-quantity, high-priced operation, yet the opportunity called for high-quantity and low price. All in all, it was the opposite of the organization's market sector, an entirely different business. After about twenty minutes of discussion the team was still floundering in indecision. So I went to the dry-erase board (where opportunities were listed) and drew a red X over the opportunity. In effect, I eliminated the opportunity. The opportunity was for someone else, not for this particular organization. We then proceeded to discuss the next opportunity. Do not "get on the bus to Abilene." Kill bad ideas and move on. Do rock the boat (or bus).

Please notice one thing about the SWOT analysis. If you create long lists of strengths, weaknesses, opportunities, and threats, you'll develop too many strategies. You will lose focus, and a long list of bewildering "tactical" strategies will result. The solution is simple. Develop a short, prioritized list of strengths, weaknesses, opportunities, and threats. Remember, in the entire strategic plan development process, stay on track with one of our key themes: least is best.

Appendix M
Gap Analysis

There are several ways to conduct a gap analysis. Using the approach in my book, you can quickly discover where significant gaps exist and close them as needed. Let's focus on the key themes to guide our gap analysis moving forward. The gap- analysis strategy should include specific recommendations for building organizational capability and driving commitment to the strategic planning effort.

The gap analysis provides answers to the questions of whether the skills and resources on hand are sufficient to bridge or close the gap. If the analysis suggests that the gap is not closable with on-hand resources, then the planning team must create new ways to close the gap. The gap analysis seeks answers to the following questions:

- ✓ How does the desired state compare with the current one?
- ✓ How do the planned goals, objectives, and strategic perspectives fit with the existing ones and the resources, both current and planned, to make them operational?
- ✓ Where do current success indicators stand, and what does that signify about the capacity to meet new ones?
- ✓ What are the current strategies, and what do they tell us about the capacity to execute new ones?
- ✓ What are the differences between the existing culture and the desired culture?

Analyzing the collected data

Analysis of processes, information systems, resources, and team skills allows for planning within your capabilities. Two primary methods are used

251

to analyze data when developing a strategic plan: thematic analysis and quantitative analysis. In thematic analysis, data groups are classified by specific content areas related to the strategic plan. This method helps you identify trends and validate similarities across the data. Data gathered through interviews and background research is typically analyzed using thematic analysis. In quantitative analysis, data are assigned numbers and viewed statistically. Percentages, counts, comparisons, and mathematical calculations are performed and compiled to create findings. Although this type of analysis is most often used with surveys, it can also be used with data gleaned from interviews, focus groups, and other forms of information (data) gathering. Data analysis is an examination of the elements of, and relationships among, pieces of information to arrive at a finding or breakthrough.

> *ADVICE:*
> *Be careful not to ignore what the planning process reveals.*

Your first step in data analysis is to identify how the data relate to the strategic plan and its corresponding outcomes, goals, and objectives. Coding your data, as you would do with interviews or research, lets you build a data audit trail so that, as findings, conclusions, and recommendations are developed, you can trace them back to the original data on which you based them.

> *INSTRUCTION:*
> *Get all relevant information before drawing a conclusion. Know when to move on, as overanalysis can lead to paralysis. A good artist knows when to stop painting.*

Coding can be completed in two ways: by strategy-related outcome or by specific topic(s). Survey responses and notes from interviews, focus groups, and background research all can be coded. The common categories of background research are:

- ✓ *Mission.* The organization's fundamental purpose or reason for existence.
- ✓ *Key challenges and business drivers*. The significant trials and barriers (key challenges) that meet the internal and external forces (business drivers) that in turn affect the organization as a whole.
- ✓ *Strategic outcomes*. What you hope will happen as a result of your goals and objectives.

- ✓ *Risk and risk mitigation.* The potential undesired consequences of implementing the strength of your tactics, products, and services, and how best to avoid these consequences.
- ✓ *Tools and techniques.* The detailed information on tasks, time frames, resource requirements, and budget requirements for the method and approach used to achieve the mission.
- ✓ *Metrics.* Measurements that guide the strategic performance and track progress of its goals and objectives.
- ✓ *Resources.* The human, financial, and other assets needed to support the strategy and meet (or exceed) desired outcome(s).

Outcome of gap analysis

The expected outcome of the gap analysis is a strategic plan that has a reasonable probability of success. Priorities must be based on the limits of available resources. In any organization, the equipment, people, funding, and other resources are finite. As a result of the gap analysis, these resources should be properly committed to actions determined to have the highest organizational payoff. There are multiple options to close the gap between an organization's current state and its future state. Generally, these options fall into either a growth or a retrenchment category, depending on the relationship of the current organization to its desired future. In chapter 3, I discussed implementation plans to close gaps.

If it appears unlikely that the gap can be closed, the planning team must return to the strategic plan development and reexamine the desired goals and objectives it wants to achieve. Re-cycling between gap analyses and working tasks in the strategic plan should continue until solutions emerge that clearly lend themselves to successful accomplishment. After this happens, two things must occur:

- ✓ A POAM must be developed to carry the carefully crafted strategic plan to the operational level. The POAM (discussed in chapter 3) must be achievable.
- ✓ A contingency plan must be developed to prepare the organization to adjust to potentially significant changes in the internal or external environment.

Exercise #9: Gap Analysis

The resources required for this exercise will be all the materials, outcomes, and analyses of all exercises completed thus far and, obviously, the CPT and SPC input. Procure a large room with significant wall space so that you can hang paper sheets for capturing key discussion points. Large dry-erase boards will work as well. Review Table M-1, Gap Analysis Matrix.

Organizational Factors	Current State	Future State	Gap	Bridge Requirement
Organizational Structure				
Mission				
Vision				
Guiding Principles				
Organizational Culture				
Stakeholders				
Internal Environment Scan (Survey)				
Guiding Principles Statement Questionnaire				
External Environmental Scan				
SWOT Analysis				

Table M-1. Gap Analysis Matrix

You will note that at the top of the *x*-axis are the headings Organizational Factors, Current State, Future State, Gap, and Bridge Requirement. Along the *y*-axis are the organizational factors. You may, of course, add factors as they pertain to your organization. However, the ones in Table M-1 form the basis of every organizational requirement. These factors have already been determined, debated, and developed by you and your teams. What I mean by this is simply that you and your teams have already worked on an exercise for each one of those organizational factors. In essence you've completed the first step: *Develop a concise understanding of the current state.* (Note: You may add to the organizational factors as you deem necessary.)

Now create the matrix on your wall sheet or board and then walk through the steps below.

1. *Develop a concise understanding of the current state.* On your wall rendition of the gap-analysis matrix have team members note key points within each cell of the current state. Once this is complete, have a discussion and list priorities so that only the essential current-state data are noted. Remember, you've conducted significant research already. Therefore, everything noted as being current state should be a refresher.

2. *Define the desired future state.* The next step is to outline the future state. As you did before, have the team members go to the matrix and list their perspective on the future state for each organizational factor. Again, have a discussion and list the future state inputs by priority.

3. *Identify any significant shortcomings in the current and the desired end states.* Step three examines the differences between the current state and the future state. That is your gap. Discuss with the teams the gaps between the current and future state of each organizational factor and note the gaps in the appropriate columns. As you've done before, list the gaps by priority. Remember the least-is-best principle I outlined early on. I would recommend no more than five gaps for each organizational factor. Ensure that all relevant information is used before drawing a conclusion. Include some of the following topics in your discussion:

   ✓ Customer satisfaction—why the customer wants your services
   ✓ Marketing performance
   ✓ Capital resources
   ✓ Innovation
   ✓ Niche
   ✓ Organizational design
   ✓ Internal systems (IT) and processes
   ✓ Management
   ✓ Human and financial resources

4. *List your priorities from the gap analysis.* Use my recommended methods of prioritization (see chapter 2) to trim your list of gaps. Remember not to get trapped in the "weeds" by discussing microdetails of the gaps. Balance yourself somewhere between the macro and

micro level. Otherwise, this exercise can last for hours—and you do not want that.

5. *List recommended solutions.* Finally, list possible solutions in the Bridge Requirement column. Caution: do not spend a significant amount of time finding solutions. This exercise will be conducted in another forum. Your end state now is to determine the gaps in each of the organizational factors.

Finally, digest the work you just completed with your teams. Review and discuss the gaps and the recommendations to bridge those gaps. Ask the "so what" questions to determine the relevance of the gaps and recommendations. Some questions to discuss with your teams:

> ADVICE:
> In data analysis,
> always ask
> "so what?"

- ✓ Which gaps have the most impact on the organization?
- ✓ How detrimental is that impact?
- ✓ Does the gap need to be fixed now, or can it wait for the strategic plan implementation?

Appendix N
Strategic Planning Focus Group Offsite

Conducting focus groups

As I discussed in chapter 2, a focus group is an excellent technique because it requires a relatively small portion of time from a smaller number of people than is the case with many other social-science methods.

The focus group is a data-collection technique widely used to drive market research. The typical objective of a focus group is not to generate consensus or debate but rather to generate ideas, make decisions, and provide opportunities for stakeholders to express feelings and expertise about a particular topic. Formal focus groups have been around since the 1940s, and during this time they have been used for an array of purposes. For example, Höijer (2008) suggests they can help:

- ✓ Stimulate new ideas and concepts for both the researcher and the participants
- ✓ Inform organizations about impressions of product and service effectiveness or management issues
- ✓ Inform participants/organizations about general information regarding a specific topic
- ✓ Generate new hypotheses for future research opportunities
- ✓ Develop sound qualitative and quantitative research approaches
- ✓ Reveal how respondents communicate about topics of interest (what words they use, what concepts they understand, etc.)
- ✓ Enhance the utility of survey content and delivery mechanisms

✓ Determine what additional research tools may be useful for follow-up information collection

✓ Better interpret previously obtained quantitative information.

Tabs 1 through 6 provide more information about conducting the FGOS. The tabs are as follows:

✓ TAB 1: Offsite Agenda
✓ TAB 2: Survey Results Briefing (PowerPoint presentation)
✓ TAB 3: CEO Letter
✓ TAB 4: Opening Briefing (PowerPoint presentation)
✓ TAB 5: Required Resources and Conference Room Checklist
✓ TAB 6: Focus Group Data Analysis

Appendix N
Strategic Planning
Focus Group Offsite
TAB 1: Offsite Agenda

DAY ONE

8:00–9:00 a.m.	Registration
9:00–9:15 a.m.	CEO opening remarks Introductions
9:15–11:15 a.m.	What is strategic planning? Survey results Guiding principles questionnaire results Environmental scan
11:15–11:30 a.m.	Break
11:30–12:30 p.m.	Mission, vision, and guiding principles exercise
12:30–1:30 p.m.	Lunch
1:30–3:30 p.m.	SWOT analysis exercise Finalize mission, vision, and guiding principles
3:30–3:45 p.m.	Break

3:45–4:15 p.m.	Next-day agenda

DAY TWO

9:00–9:15 a.m.	CEO opening remarks Recap of day one activities
9:15–10:15 a.m.	Conduct gap analysis
10:15–12:15 p.m.	Develop strategic perspectives Brainstorm goals and objectives Prioritize goals and objectives
12:15–1:00 p.m.	Lunch (or working lunch based on remaining time)
1:00–3:00 p.m.	Finalize goals and objectives Link goals and objectives to strategic perspectives
3:00–4:00 p.m.	Outline next strategic planning steps
4:00–5:00 p.m.	Debriefing and closing remarks

Strategic Planning Focus Group Offsite
TAB 2: Survey Results Briefing

The following is a sample survey results briefing. The briefing is available in an editable format at www.allonscg.com.

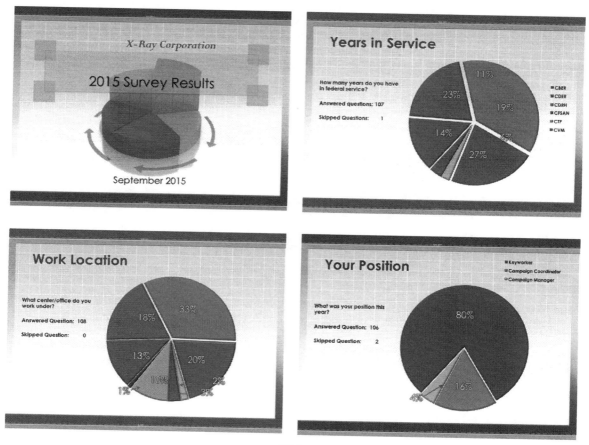

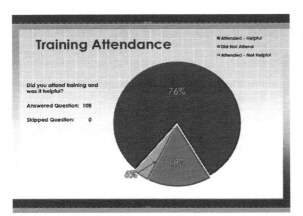

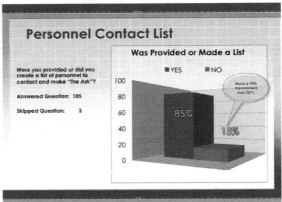

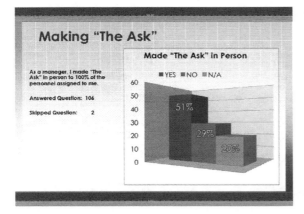

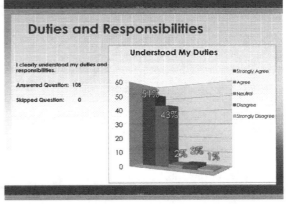

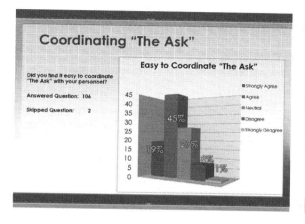

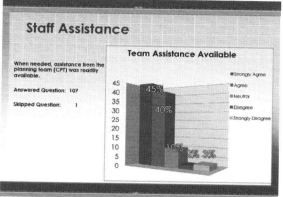

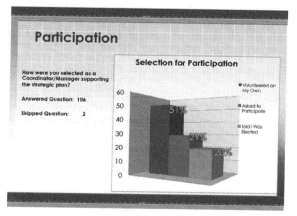

Appendix N
Strategic Planning Focus Group Offsite
TAB 3: CEO Letter

The following is a sample letter from the CEO or senior leadership.

Dear colleagues,

Over the last few months we have accomplished much due to your hard work in executing our mission. In an ever-changing environment, our organization is poised to move forward to improve our processes and provide services to meet our employees', customers', and communities' needs.

I now need your help to develop our strategy for the future.

In order to accomplish this, we will hold a two-day strategic planning focus group offsite to share ideas and determine our path forward. The goal of the offsite is to obtain your feedback and make decisions for developing a strategic plan for the next three to five years. In the coming days you will receive materials to better prepare you to participate. Please study the materials and formulate discussion points well in advance of the offsite. We will have a lot to accomplish in just two days. Therefore, I urge you to prepare to the fullest extent possible so that our time is well spent.

I want to thank you again for all your hard work and support for the X-Ray Corporation. Your efforts are not taken lightly and are very much appreciated.

Please contact Mr. Randy Etter at retter@xray.com if you should have any questions.

Thank you for all your great work, and I look forward to seeing you at the offsite.

Very cordially yours,

JH
Jim Hodge

Appendix N
Strategic Planning
Focus Group Offsite
TAB 4: Opening Briefing

The following is a sample opening briefing at the FGOS. The briefing is available in an editable format at www.allonscg.com.

Purpose

✓ Provide our strategic planning methodology for 2016-2020 to enhance value added to X-Ray Corporation and the National Medical Enterprise.

✓ Conduct a focus group offsite where participants contribute their insight and recommendation to develop our strategic plan.

✓ Make committments key facets to drive the strategic plan forward.

Agenda

DAY ONE
What is strategic planning?
Environmental scan
Survey results
Mission, Vision, and Guiding Principles exercise
Readiness Assessment exercise
SWOT Analysis exercise
Guiding Principles Questionnaire results

DAY TWO
Finalize Vision, Mission, and Guiding Principles
Conduct Gap Analysis
Adopt Strategic Perspectives
Brainstorm Goals and Objectives
Prioritize Goals and Objectives
Finalize Goals and Objectives
Link Goals and Objectives to Strategic
Perspectives
Outline Strategic Planning next steps

Administrative Remarks

Turn off all cell phones and media devices.
Restrooms are located . . .
Lunch: cafeteria on 1st floor, 3 local restaurants, etc.
Can order food in.
Be on time after breaks.
Add additional items as required...

The Project Plan

The Core Planning Team

Organizational Chart

The Strategic Planning Committee

Organizational Chart

What Is Strategic Planning?

✓ Deliberate, disciplined effort to produce a strategy that results in actions that shape what an organization is, what it does, why it does it, and what it will do in the future
✓ Future-focused
✓ Ensures the long-term relevance and survivability of our organization and the community in which it resides
✓ Determines and reveals the organization's *objectives, purposes*, or *goals*; produces the *principal policies* and plans for achieving those goals; and defines the range of business the organization is to pursue, the kind of economic and human organization it intends to be, and the nature of the economic and noneconomic contribution it intends to make to its shareholders, employees, customers, and communities.

Appendix N

Why a Strategic Plan?

- ✓ Increase effectiveness
- ✓ Increase efficiency
- ✓ Improve understanding of the organizational environment and growth
- ✓ Improve decision-making
- ✓ Enhance organizational capabilities
- ✓ Improve communications and public relations
- ✓ Increase political, community, and consumer support
- ✓ Provide relevancy to the organization
- ✓ Build organizational and individual growth
- ✓ Enhance culture and improve employee–morale
- ✓ Most important, keeps the organization in step with environmental changes

What Drives the Strategic Plan?

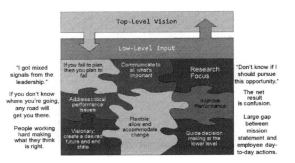

The Strategic Bridge

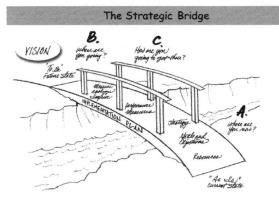

Strategic Planning Approach

Strategic Planning Model

Goals

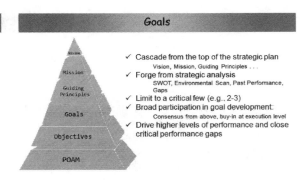

- ✓ Cascade from the top of the strategic plan
  Vision, Mission, Guiding Principles . . .
- ✓ Forge from strategic analysis
  SWOT, Environmental Scan, Past Performance, Gaps
- ✓ Limit to a critical few (e.g., 2-3)
- ✓ Broad participation in goal development:
  Consensus from above, buy-in at execution level
- ✓ Drive higher levels of performance and close critical performance gaps

Objectives

✓ Relevant – directly supports the goal
✓ Compelling – drives the organization into action
✓ Specific enough to quantify and measure the results
✓ Simple and easy to understand
✓ Realistic and attainable
✓ Clear as to responsibility and ownership
✓ Acceptable to who must execute
✓ Several objectives to meet a goal

Cascading Linkage

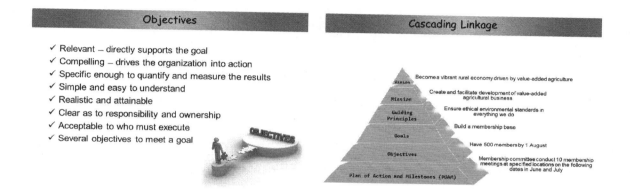

QUESTIONS

Before we begin with our first exercise:
Environmental Scan

Your Graphics

Appendix N
Strategic Planning Focus Group Offsite
TAB 5: Required Resources and Conference Room Checklist

Preparing for the focus group

Your goal is to provide a familiar, safe, comfortable setting that will allow for lively discussion. Endeavor to select a location that is accessible (consider transportation issues) to your participants. Above all, the location should be quiet enough to allow your recording devices (if used) to pick up all of the conversations and should not be located where you may be subject to disturbances such as nonparticipants entering and exiting or loudspeaker announcements interrupting your discussion.

Focus group logistics

The following are recommended requirements for the offsite:

- ✓ Prepare room and all equipment and supplies.
    - Arrange chairs and tables as needed—normally, key participants, such as the CEO, sit at the front, with senior leaders followed by the other participants in subsequent rows.
    - Set up flip charts to capture notes.
    - Tack large sheets of paper to the wall to conduct exercises.
    - Set up tape recorder.
    - Set up laptop for presentations and note taking.

- Arrange chairs so that participants can see each other; provide name tags.
- Arrange all office supplies; along with materials such as those you distributed in the read-ahead packet, place a pen and a small notebook on each participant's seat.
- Utilize facility staff to assist in audiovisual setup, seating arrangements, refreshments, etc.
- Decorate room as you deem appropriate (i.e., American flag, company logo, unit symbols etc.)

✓ Welcome participants as they enter the room.
- Have attendees sign in.
- Provide name tags. Some facilities may require security badges. If so, process entry as required.
- Distribute any relevant handouts.
- Escort senior leadership to their seats.
- Direct participants to refreshments.
- Invite participants to be seated.

Your assistant in charge of the FGOS's operational and logistical requirements must ensure that the following are completed and provided:

✓ Effective lighting in the conference room (know where the lighting controls are located)
✓ Small, portable tables for supplies
✓ Comfortable chairs and tables for participants
✓ Water and coffee at CEO's place
✓ Several breakout areas for discussion groups
✓ Wall space for taping charts, "butcher" paper, or illustrations
✓ Adequate number of extension cords and power strips
✓ High-speed Internet connection
✓ Video teleconferencing connection (if used)
✓ Ample food and drink such as bread, fresh fruit, cheese tray, coffee, tea, water, soft drinks, etc. (coordinate with facility staff to replenish as required)
✓ Special-needs requirements, such as accessibility
✓ Information-technology devices, including primary and backup microphones, projection systems, and call button to reach support, if needed, checked
✓ Visible clock for speaker(s) to tailor presentation to allotted time

- ✓ Backup batteries
- ✓ Proper room temperature for comfort
- ✓ Seating arrangements (get attendee list and protocol assistance, if necessary)
- ✓ Accessible, clean restrooms
- ✓ Rehearsal at the location with team
- ✓ Full assortment of office supplies (tape, pens, paper, paper clips, staplers, etc.)
- ✓ Accessible, working phones
- ✓ Laser pointers for senior leadership

Depending on the legal rules and policies within your organization, and the facility, a fee to cover the cost of the offsite may be required. It is important to ensure that the fee is not excessively high—$25 per person is a reasonable amount.

Audio recording

If fiscally possible, audio record your focus groups. You will need to inform the participants that they are being recorded. This may require a consent form. The CPT administrative assistant should still take notes, especially to record nonverbal information, but the recording and resulting transcripts are your more reliable data.

Appendix N
Strategic Planning Focus Group Offsite
TAB 6: Focus Group Data Analysis

Once the FGOS data have been collected, it's time to think about how the results will be interpreted so that they can produce decisions and action. The following is a systematic approach to analysis and data interpretation (adapted from Taylor-Powell & Renner, 2003; and Krueger, 2002).

✓ **Get to know the data.** In this preliminary step, the objective is for the facilitator to become as familiar as possible with the data. This may take a considerable amount of time, depending on the volume of information available. If the focus group sessions have been recorded (which is recommended), it is useful to transcribe the recordings. Listen to the recordings several times, noting the tone (pauses, enthusiasm, and reluctance) projected by the respondent. (Krueger, 2002).

It is important to transcribe these impressions as soon as possible so that critical information will not be lost or forgotten. At the same time, also consider the usefulness of all data points, since a high volume of data does not guarantee a high volume of useful information. Potential biases of the facilitator should also be considered. This is the main reason I recommend a neutral facilitator, such as an outside contractor, to facilitate the FGOS and assist with the analysis. I would also offer the reminder that the facilitator does not have to be an expert on your organization or your market niche. It is important that you ascertain all possible data limitations up front to provide a realistic account of what the limitations may explain (or not explain). If you neglect data limitations, the strength of the findings could be tarnished.

- ✓ **Focus on the analysis.** Revisit the FGOS goals and objectives. Write down key information needs. How should the analysis be focused—by question or topic? Or by case or group?
- ✓ **Categorize information**. The purpose here is to give meaning to words and phrases. Identify trends, general themes, and patterns, including ideas, concepts, behaviors, terminology and jargon, and phrases used. Organize data into topic areas (from the two-day agenda, such as the SWOT analysis) that summarize and bring meaning to the text. This is the crux of qualitative analysis. Try to read between the lines/comments.
- ✓ **Identify patterns.** When the analysis is under way, connections within the text will begin to appear. It is important to take note of the various themes and pay close attention to any subtleties that may be crucial to the analysis, such as those that are:

  - **Within a single topic**. All the data that pertain to a particular topic should be assembled. What are the key ideas being expressed? What are the similarities in the way people responded, including subtle variations? Writing a summary that answers these questions for each topic is helpful.

    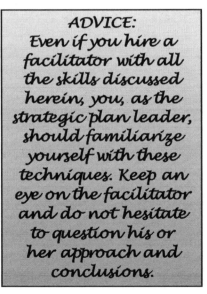

    ADVICE: Even if you hire a facilitator with all the skills discussed herein, you, as the strategic plan leader, should familiarize yourself with these techniques. Keep an eye on the facilitator and do not hesitate to question his or her approach and conclusions.

  - **Within larger or combined topics**. You may wish to combine topics to form larger topics. Doing this usually means working up from the more specific topics to larger ideas and concepts. This approach helps you see how the parts relate to the whole.
  - **Of relative importance**. To determine importance, the facilitator may want to count the number of times a theme comes up, or the number of times a unique respondent refers to certain themes. These counts can provide a rough estimate of relative importance. Though not statistically rigorous, they can reveal general patterns in the data.

- **In relationship**. Two or more themes may occur together consistently in the data. An example would be "supply" and "transportation." From this relationship it might be concluded that transportation is primarily perceived as a function of supply. Relationships can help explain why something occurs. Be careful not to assume relationships are cause and effect, since this is rarely the case. Seldom is human behavior so simple! At the same time, pay attention to statements that do not fit into specific themes. This information can often be valuable.

Offer interpretation. Here, the facilitator should articulate clearly what has been learned. This will provide a richness and meaning to the analysis. Some general questions to guide the interpretation include the following:

- What does all this information mean?
- What are the information's most important aspects?
- What information has been learned for the first time?
- What are the main points with which the reader should be made familiar?
- What are the users of this information most interested in learning?

It is also sometimes helpful to include examples to illustrate key points and display the data in a practical context. Finally, consider the use of graphics with arrows and boxes to display how multiple pieces fit together and where gaps exist and greater engagement may be required. Above all, avoid the use of generalization. Qualitative data are not intended to be generalized across populations. Rather, they are meant to provide subjective insight into the perspectives within a particular population of interest. To avoid generalization, select direct quotes carefully if using them in the report. Direct quotes are often effective in providing context and meaning, but they can be easily misused to exaggerate success or to oversell a particular point, which can lead to bias. Be up front about paying attention to a specific quote and heed its message. Below is a summary checklist.

Summary qualitative data analysis checklist

✓ Get to know the data:

- Read and familiarize yourself with the information.

- Write down impressions.
- Describe the integrity and quality of the information.
- Explain the limitations.

✓ Focus on the analysis:

- Write down key information needs that are based on goals.
- Decide how to focus the analysis (by question? by group? by topic?).

✓ Categorize information:

- Identify and write down any trends or themes that present themselves.
- Organize your data into these categories.

✓ Identify connections:

- Consider combining similar categories to strengthen data groupings.
- Consider the relative importance level of each category, based on goals.
- Identify any connections or relationships between categories.

✓ Interpret the data:

- Describe, in depth, what has been learned.
- Draw attention to the main points.
- Consider what information is most useful for the end user.

Analysis of focus group data

The following six questions by Berkowitz (1997) offer some good tips for analyzing focus group data. I have used these questions when coding and analyzing qualitative data and found them very helpful in focus group analysis.

✓ What common themes emerge in response to specific topics? How do these themes/patterns (or lack thereof) help to illuminate the broader central question(s)?

✓ Are there deviations from these patterns? If so, are there any factors that might explain these deviations?

✓ How are participants' environments or past experiences related to their behaviors and attitudes?

✓ What interesting stories emerge from the responses? How do they help illuminate the central question(s)?

✓ Do any of these patterns suggest that additional data may be needed? Do any of the central questions need to be revised?

✓ Are the patterns that emerge similar to the findings of other studies on the same topic? If not, what might explain these discrepancies?

Coding focus group data—What is coding?

Coding is simply parsing speech into categories that enable you to organize large amounts of text and to discover patterns that would be difficult to detect by just listening to a tape recording or reading a transcript. If you decide to code your data, Bogdan and Biklen (1998) provide the following common types of coding categories but emphasize that your central questions should shape your coding scheme.

✓ **Setting/Context** codes provide background information on the setting, topic, or subjects.

✓ **Defining the situation** codes categorize the worldview of respondents and how they see themselves in relation to a setting or your topic.

✓ **Respondent perspective** codes capture how respondents define a particular aspect of a setting. These perspectives may be summed up in phrases they use, such as, "Say what you mean, but don't say it mean."

✓ **Respondents' ways of thinking about people and objects** codes capture how respondents categorize and view each other, outsiders, and objects. For example, a dean at a private school may categorize students as, "There are crackerjack kids and there are slow kids."

✓ **Process** codes categorize sequences of events and change over time.

✓ **Activity** codes identify recurring informal and formal types of behavior.

✓ **Event codes** are directed at infrequent or unique happenings in the settings or lives of respondents.

✓ **Strategy** codes relate to ways people accomplish things, such as how instructors maintain students' attention during lectures.

✓ **Relationship and social structure** codes tell you about alliances, friendships, and adversaries as well as about more formally defined relations such as social roles.

✓ **Method** codes identify your research approaches, procedures, dilemmas, and breakthroughs.

Conduct your initial coding by generating codes for each organizational factor as you read responses and label data that are related without worrying about the variety of factors. Then write notes listing ideas or diagramming relationships you notice and watch for special vocabulary that respondents use because it often indicates an important topic. Because codes are not always mutually exclusive, a piece of text might be assigned several codes. Last, use focused coding to eliminate, combine, or subdivide coding categories and look for repeating ideas and larger themes that connect codes. Repeating ideas are the same ideas expressed by different respondents or across focus groups, while a theme is a larger topic that organizes or connects a group of repeating ideas.

A great proliferation of software packages to aid analysis of qualitative data has been developed in recent years. Most of these packages have been reviewed by Weitzman and Miles, who grouped them into six types: word processors, word retrievers, text-based managers, code-and-retrieve programs, code-based theory builders, and conceptual-network builders. All have strengths and weaknesses. Since this review, software has significantly improved and provides "user-friendly" processes to analyze data. If you choose to use software, use what is most helpful to you and your organization. A web search for focus group-data analytical software will get you headed in the right direction.

> *ADVICE:*
> *Be selective when using computer software packages in qualitative analysis— find one that meets your needs.*

Two caveats are in order. First, computer software packages for qualitative data analysis can aid in the manipulation of relevant segments of text. But while helpful in marking, coding, and moving data segments more quickly and efficiently than can be done manually, the software cannot determine meaningful categories for coding and analysis or define salient themes or factors. In qualitative analysis, as seen above, concepts must take precedence over mechanics: the analytic underpinnings of the procedures must still be supplied by the analyst. Software packages cannot and should not be used to evade the hard intellectual labor of qualitative analysis. Second, since it takes time and resources to become adept at utilizing a given software package and learning its peculiarities, you may want to consider whether the scope of the project or the ongoing needs truly warrant the investment (Berkowitz, 1997).

Other useful tools when analyzing your focus group data

Use visual devices to organize and guide your study. Matrices, concept maps, mind mapping, flow charts, and/or diagrams to illustrate relationships or themes may be helpful. Visual devices can aid critical thinking, confirmation of themes, or consideration of new relationships or explanations.

Have more than one person review your transcripts for coding and themes. These can be your CPT members or a person familiar with your research. Fresh eyes may identify new codes and themes. Even a third person can be helpful, but more than that and analysis becomes too tortuous.

Appendix O
Plan of Action and Milestones (POAM)

Action planning is a process that can help you focus your resources on realizing your organization's goals and objectives. The product of this planning focus is called a plan of action and milestones, or POAM. Your POAM should include at least the following components:

- ✓ Recommendations: how the POAM links to or supports the strategic plan.
- ✓ Actions: the actions that will be implemented to support the recommendations.
- ✓ A timeline: a schedule of milestones for implementing the plan—a project plan.
- ✓ Metrics: the measures that will be used to determine the success of the actions.
- ✓ Resources: the resources required to complete the plan.
- ✓ Assigned responsibility: the person responsible and accountable for the plan.

As we discussed in chapter 3, each objective will fall under a functional area or department for planning and execution. Consequently, that department or functional area manager will have overall responsibility for providing the resources and commitment to develop and execute the POAM. Remember, the POAM supports the objectives, which

> *SUGGESTION:*
> *In most organizations, resources are scarce. Therefore, you may have to expend time and effort making a strong case to justify resource needs and explain how they relate to the overall strategic plan.*

support the strategic goals, which ensure vision attainment. Therefore, ensure that your plan ultimately results in meeting the strategic goals.

What is a POAM?

The POAM is a plan of action that sets milestones for accomplishing specific tasks. It is a simple roadmap that leads to a competent execution of an objective. Each objective will have an associated POAM. Obviously, in some cases, an objective may have more than one POAM. However, if this is the case, I recommend you take a hard look at how you are determining the execution of the objective. A POAM is usually only several pages long. At the top of each page is a header that contains critical reference information such as the date of the last revision, the objective written out in full, the author's name, and the priority of the objective. The body of the action plan is divided into several columns, as shown in figure O-1, Sample plan of action and milestones (POAM).

Strategic Perspective	Learning and Growth						
Goal:	High Caliber Employees			Administrative Notes			
Objective:	Develop Knowledge and Information Sharing Environme						
Priority:	2						
APPM:	Franklyn Harricharan						

Task Number	Description	Resources	Funds	Responsibility	Days	Start Date	Completion Date
Provide a reference number for each task	Provide a clear description of activities required to complete the task. For example, Create Functional Area Planning Team	Provide the required resources and funding stream	Amount of funds required to complete the task	Name of those responsible to complete the task	Include days required to complete the task	Date task started	Date task started

Figure O-1. Sample Plan of Action and Milestones (POAM)

The body of the POAM is the same as the body of the project plan. As you will recall from chapter 1, you created a project plan for developing the overall strategic plan. In the same vein, the action plan project managers (APPMs) are replicating that process when building the milestones of a POAM. A good POAM:

- ✓ Identifies and understands the objective
- ✓ Creates and involves an action planning group of three to five people for the planning and execution of the POAM

- ✓ Includes an outline for the action planning team to review
- ✓ Demonstrates achievability and measurability (performance measures)
- ✓ Defines steps in a clear sequence; that is, creates a viable project plan
- ✓ Uses all elements of the project-management process
- ✓ Identifies specific action steps to achieve the strategic objectives
- ✓ Ensures that each objective has a supporting POAM geared toward operations, procedures, and processes
- ✓ Describes who does what, when it is to be completed, and how the organization knows when it is completed
- ✓ Exhibits simplicity, clarity, and conciseness
- ✓ Assigns responsibility for successful completion—procuring AAPMs with the intellectual capital to plan and execute the POAM
- ✓ Details all required steps to achieve the initiative and determines all tasks and subtasks required to meet the objective
- ✓ Establishes a time frame for the completion of each step (i.e., milestones)
- ✓ Establishes the resources required to complete each task
- ✓ Defines the specific actions (tasks) that must be developed to implement the objective
- ✓ Determines the deliverables (in measurable terms) that result from completion of individual tasks

> *SUGGESTION:*
> *Ensure your POAM makes "cents."*

- ✓ Defines the expected results of each milestone
- ✓ Provides a status report on each step, whether completed or not
- ✓ Details the financial requirements to realize the objective

Who is responsible for planning and executing the POAM?

You are the strategic plan leader, but you are *not* the person responsible for executing the POAM. You are, however, accountable for ensuring that it gets completed. The responsible individual for planning and executing the POAM, as mentioned earlier, is appointed by a department head or functional area manager tasked to execute a specific

> *NOTE:*
> *You may want to review your stakeholder analysis to see if the senior manager or director of a functional area tasked with executing an objective is one of your key stakeholders. If so, in which quadrant was he or she placed?*

objective. Once a goal and objective are noted in the strategic plan and responsibility is fixed for executing them, it is incumbent upon that functional manager to carry out all components of the POAM to support the goals and objectives. Certainly, you do not just Xerox the portions of this book on the POAM and hand them to the APPM. Your role in this is to measure and track the POAM to ensure that it is meeting the overall timeline of the strategic plan. You are the program manager; the assigned functional manager is the accountable and responsible project manager. Note that I said that you are the *program* manager, not the *project* manager.

Developing a POAM

In reviewing the cascading linkages that got us to the POAM (shown in Figure O-2, POAM linkage), you will see that you started with the strategic alignment (Learning and Growth) and waterfall into the POAM with the goal to "develop high-caliber employees" and an objective to "develop a knowledge- and information-sharing environment."

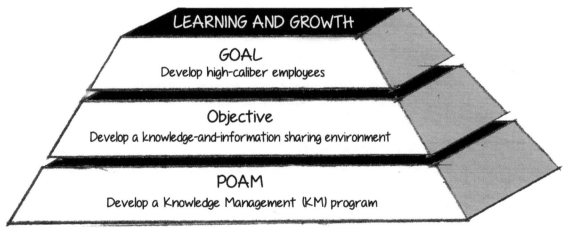

Figure O-2. POAM Linkage

From this objective, the implementation action team (with the APPM as lead) will develop a POAM to outline the required actions and milestones. To summarize, first go once again to Figure 2–5, Strategic alignments linkage. As you can see, the Learning and Growth strategic perspective has several objectives, one of which is "Develop knowledge- and information-sharing environment." The POAM task to execute the objective follows: "Develop

283

a knowledge management (KM) program." In an actual case, the following steps were taken to realize that objective:

1. Fix responsibility—select the APPM

This objective was given to the director of information technology (IT) for planning and execution. The first step was designating the APPM. The IT director selected one of his brightest project managers with technical, knowledge management, and project management expertise. Given the importance of gaining full support from senior management of the area from which the APPM was chosen, the IT director ensured that the selected individual had the time and resources to finish the objective implementation in accordance with the project requirements and the strategic plan timeline.

2. Analyze the goal and objective

The next step undertaken by the APPM was to develop an implementation planning team (IPT). The team consisted of five individuals, including the APPM. The team held a brainstorming session to identify all the necessary tasks to execute the requirement. This was accomplished by analyzing the goal and then the objective. The team agreed that the main task was to "develop a KM program within the organization."

3. Arrange tasks in chronological order

The first question was, "What are the specified and implied tasks in the objective?" The IPT then listed the tasks and subtasks required to accomplish the objective and, after discussion, prioritized each task. The prioritized tasks were then allocated an estimated time to complete, ranked in chronological order, and noted on a Gantt chart using Microsoft Project. It was in this step that the team created the milestones and, thus, a project plan. For example, for one task they developed, "create a standard operating procedure (SOP) for KM," the IPT allocated forty-five days and specified a start date, end date, resource requirements, lead and lag times, and responsibility with a named team member. The project plan was similar to the one discussed in appendix B, Project Plan. The project plan included all the key aspects of a POAM discussed earlier. It provided:

✓ A level of priority for each task
✓ A description of the task

- ✓ Human resource requirements
- ✓ Financial requirements
- ✓ A timeline (milestones) for executing each task
- ✓ The information as to who was responsible for leading each task
- ✓ Start and end dates
- ✓ The percentage of the project completed

Based on the overall milestones, the project plan required twelve months for completion. For individuals working on the plan, that represented a lengthy commitment of time while still working on their day-to-day operational responsibilities. Realizing the significant requirement of time, the IPT decided to request external support. Depending on your objectives and plan requirements, outside contractor support may be a wise choice. As I stated before, it may take from six months to several years to achieve some goals.

4. Allocate resources

A meeting was held with resource management (RM) and acquisition to provide project funding for software and hardware needs and contractor support. RM allocated funds for a limited amount of contractor support and full funding for IT needs. An additional team (IPT support team) was developed to support the IPT. It was comprised of individuals from each functional area within the organization. For the overall KM implementation to be successful, it was required that each functional area implement a KM structure within its organizational structure; thus, the IPT required additional resources to implement those specific tasks.

5. Execute the POAM

Numerous meetings (with the IPT and IPT support team) were held to design the KM IT system as well as to develop procedures, processes, tools, and techniques for operational implementation. Once consensus was achieved, the project plan was revised to accommodate changes in the timeline and tasks to be performed. Tasks were then assigned to each functional area, and implementation of the organization's KM capability was thus begun. The IPT used the POAM as the basic structure to guide it in completing each task. The result was a successful KM capability achieved within twelve months. The APPM implemented the objective, and the goal was realized.

6. Review progress

The IPT conducted weekly reviews of its progress. Monthly in-progress reviews (IPR) were also conducted in which the APPM briefed the IT director as well as the implementation planning sponsor. As I mentioned in an earlier case, these IPRs served as an impetus to ensure that the APPM's "feet were held to the fire" and the goal was achieved. The main reason for the organization's success was that leadership involved itself in the process from beginning to end.

> *FACT:*
> *Skills + processes + knowledge = action.*

Metrics

Metrics were developed for each task and served as the nucleus of the IPR. The main question the metrics should answer—Is the plan on track?—discussed in greater detail in chapter 5.

Glossary

action plan project manager (APPM) An individual appointed by a functional area to plan and execute objectives. The APPM must possess the technical and project management skills, initiative, and drive to execute the objective.

Balanced Scorecard A strategic planning and management system that is used extensively in business and industry, government, and nonprofit organizations to align business activities to the vision and strategy of the organization, improve internal and external communications, and monitor organization performance against strategic goals.

brainstorming A powerful group technique that creates new ideas, solves problems, motivates members, and develops teams through the different stages of group dynamics. It involves members of a team in discussing strategic issues and gets them working together to generate ideas on the vision of the organization.

branding The marketing practice of creating a name, symbol, or design that identifies and differentiates a product from other products. Brand identity is an essential component of the strategic plan and vision of an organization. Customers recognize products and services by a brand, and vital to a successful organization is building that brand identity.

budget resource board (BRB) The purpose of the BRB is to prioritize and allocate financial resources to meet the strategic plan goals.

CARVER method	The military method of target selection: criticality, accessibility, recuperability, vulnerability, effect, and recognizability. A value of 1 (lowest) to 5 (highest) is assigned for each CARVER factor, thereby creating a CARVER matrix. The sum of the six CARVER values gives a score for each target. The higher the score, the more "important" the target becomes.
coding	Placing speech into categories that enable you to organize large amounts of text and to discover patterns that would be difficult to detect by just listening to a taped recording or reading a transcript.
communications management	The systematic planning, implementing, monitoring, and revising of all the channels of communication within an organization and between organizations; also includes the organization and dissemination of new communication directives connected with an organization, network, or communications technology. It is the primary method for gaining and sustaining stakeholder commitment and is therefore a key to attaining goals.
competencies	Abilities, sets of actions, or strategies at which the organization is particularly good and which can be used to improve its performance in relation to such "success factors."
composite organization	An organization type that, in essence, combines elements of functional and matrix organizations.
contingency planning	Involves planning for potentially high-impact events that do not have the highest probability of success.
core planning team (CPT)	The CPT is responsible for planning, guiding, developing, executing, and monitoring the full spectrum of the organization's strategic plan, from concept to execution to monitoring. It sets the rhythm for the planning and execution of the strategic plan.

dashboard	A graphic display that provides an overview of how you're performing by displaying summaries of different reports as consoles on a single page. With a dashboard, you can display many metrics at once, so you can quickly check the health of your accounts or see correlations among different reports.
Deal and Kennedy's 2 x 2 Matrix and Cultural Model	Deal and Kennedy propose that one of the key drivers for the success or failure of an organization is corporate culture. By examining cultural elements across organizations, they demonstrate that the risk involved in making a poor decision and the time it takes to find out whether the decision is the right one is reflective of an organization's culture.
Decision Matrix	Uses a measured criteria technique in which ratings are given for each criterion. The decision matrix is a variation of the L-shaped matrix that utilizes points (usually from 0 to 10) that are predefined per criterion (criterion A=5) and may vary among criteria depending on the criterion's relative importance in the final decision.
Delphi technique	The Delphi technique is a means for arriving at a consensus among experts during a brainstorming session. A selected group of experts answers questions and provides feedback regarding the responses to each round of questions.
environmental scan	A type of "radar" for scanning the environment that seeks to identify forces that positively and negatively affect an organization.
envisioning	The process by which a vision or dream of a future state is developed for your organization that is both sufficiently clear and powerfully evident as to stimulate and sustain the actions necessary for that vision to become reality.

facilitator

Someone who helps a group of people understand their common objectives and assists them in achieving those objectives without taking a particular position in the process. A facilitator will try to assist the group in reaching a consensus on any disagreements that preexist or emerge during the process so that the consensus has a strong basis for future action.

focus group offsite

A group formed (at a location away from the organization) to conduct qualitative research where a designated number of people is asked about their perceptions, opinions, beliefs, and attitudes toward a product, service, concept, advertisement, idea, or packaging. Questions are asked in an interactive group setting where participants are free to talk with other group members. Focus groups employ a committee-style approach so that key members and stakeholders of the organization can have direct input into the construction of the strategic plan.

functional organization

An organization that consists of a hierarchical structure where each employee has one clearly designated supervisor. In such a structure, staff members are grouped by specialties such as operations, marketing, human resources, resource management, and the like.

gap analysis

A technique that organizations use to determine what steps need to be taken in order to move from the organization's current state to its desired, future state. Also called need-gap analysis, needs analysis, and needs assessment.

goal

A broad statement of what will be accomplished. Goals are general, intangible, and abstract. They are concerned with the final impact or outcome that you wish to bring about.

goal setting	A process of determining what the organization's goals are, working toward them, and measuring progress in accordance with a plan. A generally accepted paradigm for setting goals is one that is specific, measurable, achievable, realistic, and time related (the SMART criteria).
guiding principles	Rules or "laws" that are universal in nature. Such principles concern the overall behavior of an organization and how the organization interacts within its community and within the organizational environment.
human resource (HR) plan	A process that identifies current and future human resource needs for an organization to achieve its goals. Human resource planning should serve as a link between human resource management and the overall strategic plan of an organization. It is a process that ensures that HR requirements are identified and plans are made for satisfying those requirements.
identifying stakeholders	A process of identifying all the people within and outside of the organization who are affected by the strategic plan and documenting the relevant information regarding their interest, involvement, and impact on the strategic planning success.
implementation action team (IAT)	A group of individuals led by an action plan project manager (APPM) who are designated by their functional area supervisors, department heads, or anyone with supervisory authority over them to review strategic alignments, goals, and objectives and create a list of actions required to realize the objectives.
implementation plan	Consists of actionable tasks to realize an organization's goals and objectives and ultimately its mission and vision.

interim progress report (IPR)	A comprehensive report formatted into sections correlating to each strategic alignment and the administration/execution of such. The report provides the current status of each goal, objective, and milestone required to implement the strategy plan.
Lean Six Sigma (LSS)	A rigorous, focused, and highly effective managerial concept of proven principles and techniques, LSS incorporates elements from the work of many original thinkers, especially at Motorola. Six Sigma aims for virtually error-free business performance and focuses on helping an organization improve customer value and efficiency.
Likert scale	A scale commonly involved in research that employs questionnaires. It is the most widely used approach to scaling responses in survey research. A Likert scale measures attitudes and behaviors using answer choices that range from one extreme to the other (for example, not at all likely to extremely likely). Unlike a simple yes/no question, a Likert scale allows researchers to uncover degrees of opinion such as agree/disagree with a statement.
matrix organization	An organization that is a blend of functional and project-oriented characteristics. Weak-matrix organizations retain many of the characteristics of a functional organization, where the project manager is more of a coordinator or expediter than a true project manager.
mission statement	A declaration of the purpose of an organization, the mission statement is a concise and direct assertion of the reasons for the organization's existence. The mission statement should guide the actions of the organization, spell out its overall goal, stake out a path, and guide decision making. It gives the organization a framework for devising the services, products, and programs it will offer its customers in fulfillment of its mission.

monthly status report (MSR)	A monthly report that provides the current status of the strategic plan. It outlines the past month's accomplishments and the next month's priorities. Included in the report are status-of-performance measures, issues, risks, plans to mitigate risk, and next steps.
nominal group technique	A technique for enhancing brainstorming by adding a voting step that is used to rank the most useful ideas for further brainstorming or for prioritizing. The technique allows ideas to be brainstormed by small groups and then reviewed by a larger group.
objective	A specific result that a person or system aims to achieve within an established time frame and with available resources. In general, objectives are more specific and easier to measure than goals. Objectives are basic tools that underlie all planning and strategic activities. Objectives are narrow, precise, tangible, concrete, and measurable.
operational level	The level of war at which campaigns and major operations are planned, conducted, and sustained to accomplish strategic objectives within theaters or areas of operation. Activities at this level link tactics and strategy by establishing operational objectives needed to accomplish the strategic objectives, sequencing events to achieve the operational objectives, initiating actions, and applying resources to bring about and sustain the sequenced events.
operational planning	A plan prepared by a unit of an organization that clearly defines actions it will take to support the strategic objectives and plans of upper management. Operational planning is the day-by-day and month-by-month planning for what an organization is and will be doing.

order of merit list (OML)	A technique used to prioritize or sequence items in order from the most to the least important. It employs a number ranking such as OML 1, OML 2, OML 3, and so on. It is a basic method for ranking elements in a list.
organization	A social unit of people that is structured and managed to meet a need or to pursue collective goals. All organizations have a management structure that determines relationships between the different activities and the members and subdivides and assigns roles, responsibilities, and authority to carry out different tasks. An organization can be private (i.e., for profit) or governmental (not for profit) or similar.
organizational culture	One of the most important building blocks for a highly successful organization and an extraordinary workplace, organizational culture is a set of shared beliefs, truths, assumptions, and guiding principles that operates in organizations. Essentially, it is how people behave when no one is looking.
organizational structure	The typically hierarchical arrangement of lines of authority, communications, rights, and duties of an organization. Organizational structure determines how roles, power, and responsibilities are assigned, controlled, and coordinated and how information flows between and among the different levels of management.
performance cycle	The strategic plan is always in a continuous cycle of measurement, analysis, and improvement. This cycle is called the performance cycle and allows for measuring the performance of the strategic plan and developing methodologies to infuse continuous improvements.

performance indicators (PI)	A type of performance measurement that helps an organization define and measure progress toward organizational goals. An organization may use PIs to evaluate its success or that of a particular activity in which it is engaged. Success is defined in terms of making progress toward strategic goals, but often success is simply the repeated, periodic achievement of some levels of an operational goal (zero defects, 100 percent customer satisfaction, etc.).
performance measures	The process of collecting, analyzing, and/or reporting information regarding the performance of an individual, group, organization, system or component and usually tied to a goal or an objective (the target). Performance measures can be represented by single-dimensional units (hours, meters, nanoseconds, dollars, number of reports, etc.).
performance standard	A way of measuring an organization's progress and how effective and efficient it is at running its business. It is a good way to gauge how well a business and its workers are doing. For example, a performance standard may define what an employee must know and/or be able to do to reach a certain level, such as attain a particular rank of certification or score at a certain level of proficiency on a measurement scale.
plan of action and milestones (POAM)	A tool that identifies actions and milestones to be accomplished in order to realize an objective. The POAM document identifies the tasks needing to be accomplished, resources required to accomplish the elements of the plan, any milestones in meeting the tasks, and scheduled completion dates for the milestones.

processes	A series of actions that produces something or that leads to a particular result; a sequence of interdependent and linked procedures that, at every stage, consume one or more resources (employee time, energy, machines, money) to convert inputs (data, material, parts, etc.) into outputs.
project plan	According to *A Guide to the Project Management Body of Knowledge Guide,* "a formal, approved document used to guide both project execution and project control. The primary uses of the project plan are to document planning assumptions and decisions, facilitate communication among stakeholders, and document approved scope, cost, and schedule baselines." A project plan may be summarized or detailed.
qualitative analysis	The use of nonquantifiable methods to evaluate opportunities and make decisions. This type of analysis technique is different than quantitative analysis, which focuses on numbers. The two techniques, however, will often be used together. Qualitative research and qualitative data analysis are often used for policy and program evaluation research since it can answer certain important questions more efficiently and effectively than quantitative approaches. Qualitative approaches have the advantage of allowing for more diversity in responses as well as the capacity to adapt to new developments or issues during the research process itself.
quantitative analysis	An analysis technique that seeks to understand behavior by using complex mathematical and statistical modeling, measurement, and research. By assigning a numerical value to variables, quantitative analysts try to replicate reality mathematically.

SMART	A generally accepted paradigm for developing goals and objectives is one that is specific, measurable, attainable, realistic, and time related (the SMART criteria).
staffing management plan	Defines the required human resources needed to deliver the desired objective (POAM) deliverables. It involves the selection and assignment of teams such as the IAT and CPT. The staffing plan must provide the appropriate skill sets to manage the project and to perform the tasks that produce the specified deliverables.
stakeholder	Any person, group, or organization that can place a claim on the organization's resources, production of output, or their effect on internal structuring.
stakeholder analysis	A technique of systematically gathering and analyzing quantitative and qualitative data and information to determine whose interests should be taken into account throughout the strategic planning process.
Stephen Covey Time Management Matrix	A template designed to maximize productivity and eliminate unnecessary or irrelevant activities through a four-quadrant system. Every activity can be put in one of the four quadrants, with the whole used for prioritizing tasks. After analysis, activities can be assigned to the appropriate quadrant before evaluating where changes are required.
strategic alignments	Special focal points—stakeholders, internal processes, learning and growth, resources, etc.—toward which an organization directs its efforts.

strategic level

Military strategy is a set of ideas implemented by military organizations to pursue desired strategic goals. Activities at this level establish national and multinational military objectives, sequence initiatives, define limits and assess risks for the use of military and other instruments of national power, develop global plans or theater war plans to achieve these objectives, and provide military forces and other capabilities in accordance with strategic plans.

strategic plan

A document used to communicate organizational goals along with actions needed to achieve those goals. A strategic plan is an organization's process of defining its strategy, or direction, and making decisions on allocating its resources to pursue this strategy. It is executed by strategic planners or strategists who involve many parties and research resources in their analysis of the organization and its relationship to the environment to which it belongs and in which it competes.

strategic plan approach

An approach in five phases that is used to develop a strategic plan. The strategic plan approach is geared to ensure that an organization's strategic plan focuses on top-level vision while garnering input from the organization's lower levels as well as its internal and external environment.

strategic plan champion

An individual with the primary responsibility to ensure that the strategic plan is developed and executed in accordance with leadership's vision and the organizational mission, values, and budgetary constraints. He or she must have enough status, power, and authority to commit the organization's resources to strategic planning and to hold people accountable for doing the planning well.

strategic plan team leader	Serves as the project manager responsible for all the operational decisions that affect the development, execution, and monitoring of the strategic plan. The team leader should have experience with project management, operational planning, and strategic development. He or she is responsible for everything that goes right (and everything that goes wrong) in developing the strategic plan and for ensuring that all goals and objectives are met and met on time.
strategic planner	Responsible for assisting the team leader with his or her responsibilities and for filling in for the team leader in the leader's absence. He or she must have a background in strategic planning. The strategic planner's primary responsibility is to keep the CPT and the organization on course, keep track of progress, and pay attention to all the details that pertain to the strategic planning and execution process.
strategic planning	A deliberate, disciplined effort to produce a strategy that results in actions that shape what an organization is, what it does, why it does it, and what it will do in the future.
strategic planning committee (SPC)	A group of individuals representing various functional areas within the organization. The SPC is responsible for providing functional area support and input in the planning, developing, executing, and monitoring of the organization's strategic plan.
strategic planning Model (SPM)	A model designed to walk you step by step through the strategic planning process. It answers the *A*, *B*, *C* questions (*A*: Where are you now? *B*: Where you going? *C*: How are you going to get there?) and outlines all major tasks required to develop the strategic plan.

strategy	Strategy is the pattern of decisions in an organization that determines and reveals its objectives, purposes, or goals; produces the principal policies and plans for achieving those goals; and defines the range of business the organization is to pursue, the kind of economic and human organization it intends to be, and the nature of the economic and noneconomic contribution it intends to make to its shareholders, employees, customers, and communities.

surveys	An essential tool for research and data collection. Surveys define and measure the quality of a product or service; identify the gaps between minimum, desired, and perceived levels of the product or service; and serve as a data point for conducting an environmental scan.

SWOT Analysis	A SWOT analysis is a structured planning method that can be applied across diverse functions and activities and is particularly appropriate to the early stages of conducting an environmental scan. Performing a SWOT analysis involves the generation and recording of an organization's strengths, weaknesses, opportunities, and threats (SWOT) in relation to a particular task, discussion, or environment.

SWOT Matrix	A way of determining strengths, weaknesses, opportunities, and threats, the matrix is the fundamental idea behind the SWOT framework and was developed to present the concept in a more understandable, graphic form. SWOT matrix templates are part of the SWOT analysis solution.

tactical level	At the tactical level are the small units from brigades to squads (that is, from about one thousand to nine people). These are the organizations where the focus is on the tactics of an engagement or operation. The tactical level is where the execution of the operation occurs.

theory	A contemplative and rational type of abstract or generalized thinking or the results of such thinking. A theory provides an explanatory framework for certain observations, and from the assumptions of the explanation follows a number of possible hypotheses that can be tested in order to provide support for, or challenge, the theory.
Tuckman Ladder	The forming, storming, norming, performing, and adjourning model of group development was first proposed by Bruce Tuckman in 1965. Tuckman maintained that these phases are all necessary and inevitable in order for an organizational team to grow, face up to challenges, tackle problems, find solutions, plan work, and deliver results.
values	Important and lasting beliefs or ideals shared by the members of a culture about what is good or bad and desirable or undesirable. Values have a major influence on an organization's behavior and attitude and serve as broad guidelines in all situations.
virtual teams	Teams whose members interact primarily via electronic communication. Members of a virtual team may be within the same building or across continents.
vision	The ability to think about or plan the future with imagination, wisdom, or a mental image of what the future will or could be like. Vision provides guidance about what core to preserve and what future toward which to make progress.
vision statement	A statement that describes where the organization is going or may go, a vision statement tends to be idealistic and inspirational. It is a declaration of an organization's goals for its long-term future. Ranging from one line to several paragraphs, a vision statement identifies what the organization would like to achieve or accomplish.

Index

207, 213, 217–218, 221, 236, 242,
   249, 251–253, 257, 260, 273–274,
   280–287, 290–293, 295, 297–300
Offsite Agenda 83, 85, 96, 98, 258–259
operational level 2–3, 253, 293
Organizational change management 163
organizational culture xxi, 44, 58, 64–
   65, 67–69, 77, 84, 138, 140–141,
   238, 240–241, 294
organizational structure 46, 49, 64,
   141–143, 165, 285, 294

P

performance indicators 103, 168–170,
   172, 180, 295
Performance measurement 149–150,
   170, 172, 221, 295
performance-measurement system 150
performance measures 16, 105, 109,
   125, 148–149, 151–157, 167–168,
   170, 174, 177, 282, 293, 295
performance standard 149, 295
Performing 27, 29, 35, 66, 73, 150, 165,
   235, 289, 300–301
Plan failure 9
planning team xix, 13, 20, 23, 25–26,
   28, 30–32, 40, 44, 49, 59, 75,
   93, 111, 189, 191, 193, 200, 203,
   207, 214, 216, 238, 251, 253, 282,
   284, 288
Plan of Action and Milestones 7, 15, 80,
   128, 143, 147–148, 280–281, 295
POAM 7, 15–16, 80, 84, 109, 120, 124–
   125, 128, 142–143, 145, 147–148,
   155–167, 169, 172–175, 177–178,
   253, 280–285, 295, 297
Power/Interest Grid 208–209, 211
prioritizing goals 112–113, 122, 204
problem statement 116–117
project plan 11, 16, 20–25, 31, 37–40,
   42, 64, 78, 80, 88, 94, 96, 98,
   127, 136, 145–147, 158–159, 162,
   167, 180, 182, 224, 280–282, 284–
   285, 296

Q

qualitative 61, 80, 85, 126, 148, 214,
   257, 274–276, 278–279, 290,
   296–297
qualitative analysis 274, 278–279, 296
quantitative analysis 126, 252, 296

R

resource constraints 164

S

Six Sigma 167, 214, 292, 307
SMARTER objectives 121
SMART principles 108–109, 122
staffing management plan 28–29, 297
stakeholder analysis 42, 61–62, 64, 75,
   87, 102–104, 129, 207–208, 210–
   211, 282, 297
stakeholder-management strategy 210
stakeholders xix, xx, 14–15, 19, 23,
   26, 28, 42–43, 51, 58, 60–64, 72,
   75–76, 80, 86–87, 90, 94, 102–104,
   109–110, 123, 126, 129, 132–134,
   136–139, 142, 149, 153–154, 156,
   162–163, 166, 175, 189, 204, 207–
   211, 213, 218–219, 222, 224–225,
   238–239, 257, 282, 288, 290–291,
   296–297
Stephen Covey Time Management Matrix
   117–118, 297
Storming 27, 301
strategic alignments 79, 86, 96,
   103–105, 110–111, 119, 123–125,
   133–135, 140, 143, 145, 150, 152,
   155, 166, 173–174, 177, 283, 291–
   292, 297
strategic issues 87, 91, 142, 203, 238,
   240, 243, 245, 247–248, 287
strategic level 1, 3–4, 240, 298
Strategic management 162–163, 173
strategic plan xvi–xxii, 1–13, 15–17,
   19–26, 28–34, 36, 38–39, 41, 43,
   49, 57–58, 60, 62, 68, 75–77, 80,
   85–88, 90–91, 93–94, 96–97,

306

About the Author

Colonel David R. McClean (USA, Ret.) is president of Allons Consulting Group LLC. Widely recognized in the military as a leader who served with distinction in both combat and peacetime settings, David regularly utilized calm thinking, selflessness, and the ability to work through difficult situations in an expedited and efficient manner to ensure mission success.

David has held tactical and strategic managerial and directorial positions throughout both his military and business careers, and with over thirty years' experience and a professional background in strategic planning, training and education, process improvement, and organizational development, brings particular expertise to strategic and operational planning at Allons Consulting.

Over the course of his career, David has created and executed innumerable strategic plans with unprecedented success in building successful organizations. He has developed many initiatives to refocus deficiencies and turn them into opportunities to improve business processes and set long-term strategic goals into motion to provide new and lasting benefits for organizations.

In addition to his numerous awards and decorations, David holds master's and bachelor's degrees and is a certified Lean Six Sigma black belt.

Made in the USA
San Bernardino, CA
08 April 2016